Musashino in Tuscany

Michigan Monograph Series in Japanese Studies
Number 50

Center for Japanese Studies
The University of Michigan

Musashino in Tuscany

❧

JAPANESE
OVERSEAS TRAVEL LITERATURE,
1860–1912

Susanna Fessler

Center for Japanese Studies
The University of Michigan
Ann Arbor, 2004

*Open access edition funded by the National Endowment for the Humanities/
Andrew W. Mellon Foundation Humanities Open Book Program.*

Copyright © 2004 The Regents of the University of Michigan

Published by
Center for Japanese Studies, The University of Michigan

Library of Congress Cataloging-in-Publication Data

Fessler, Susanna.
  Musashino in Tuscany : Japanese overseas travel literature, 1860–1912 /
Susanna Fessler.
    p. cm. — (Michigan monograph series in Japanese studies ; 50)
  Citations translated into English.
  Includes bibliographical references and index.
  ISBN 978-1-929280-29-2
  1. Authors, Japanese—19th century—Travel—Europe.   2. Authors,
Japanese—19th century—Travel—United States.   3. Europe—Description
and travel.   4. United States—Description and travel.   I. Title.   II. Series.

PL721.T75F47 2004
895.6'8420809491404—dc22

2004051705

Book design by City Desktop Productions

This book was set in Minister.

This publication meets the ANSI/NISO Standards for Permanence of Paper
for Publications and Documents in Libraries and Archives (Z39.48–1992).

Printed and bound by CPI Group (UK) Ltd, Croydon, CR0 4YY

ISBN 978-1-929280-29-2 (hardcover)
ISBN 978-0-472-03830-5 (paper)
ISBN 978-0-472-12801-3 (ebook)
ISBN 978-0-472-90197-5 (open access)

The light green leaves
of the birch tree
in Tuscany
I liken
to the spring in Musashino

Anezaki Chōfū, *Hanatsumi nikki*

Contents

Illustrations

Preface

It was my aim in writing this book to provide information that would both be informative for the scholar and entertaining for the layperson. Consequently, there are copious footnotes that are of primary interest to the researcher, but there is also a gentle reiteration of Japanese history—old hat for the Japanologist—in the text to help the non-expert place the context of the travelogues discussed. To avoid misconceptions and awkward terminology, I have left many Japanese terms untranslated, but I have also appended a glossary for those in need of it. Words that appear in italics in the main text are included in this glossary.

In the main text, titles of Japanese works are translated into English; if a work appears only in a footnote, then the title is given in romanization. Proper Japanese names appear with the surname followed by the given name, as is standard in Japan, except in the case of a citation of a work written in English by a Japanese, in which case the format is given name first, surname name second. Chinese characters (*kanji*) have all been converted to postwar simplified form. Chinese names and terms are represented in Pinyin romanization. Unless otherwise indicated, all translations are my own.

I have purposely chosen to use the masculine pronoun "he" as the generic marker for human beings where "one" is awkward. I know that feminists will be offended by this and wryly remark that I am bowing to the patriarchy. In my defense, I will say that in English "he" is acceptable for this use, and to use "she" when the sex of the subject is indeterminate calls attention to a nugatory aspect of the text.

Chapter one is a revised version of "Early Overseas Travel and Travel Writing in Japanese," in *The Journal of Intercultural Studies*, no. 26 (1999), pp. 20–44.

Many people have provided assistance in the production of this work. The University at Albany presented me with a Faculty Research Assistance Program grant, which helped procure many of the primary sources. The interlibrary loan staff at the University at Albany was also extremely helpful in their untiring efforts towards tracking down obscure manuscripts. My colleagues in the East Asian Studies Department—Charles Hartman, Jim Hargett, Tony DeBlasi, Shirley Chang, Mark Blum, Sachiko Funaba, and Michiyo Kaya Wojnovich—have been tremendously supportive of this project, and have provided many valuable comments and suggestions on the work-in-progress. Mike Rich and Pat Caddeau generously read an earlier draft of the manuscript and gave many helpful suggestions. Will Thomas patiently proofread draft after draft, providing yet more suggestions. Without all these people, the work would be a much lesser product, but the errors and omissions that are undoubtedly still buried within it are fully my responsibility.

Introduction

To address any topic, one must define the concept. Many literary critics have attempted to delineate what constitutes a travelogue, but there is no universal agreement on the issue. Some writers, in discussing travelogues, quickly diverge onto the idea of a mental journey, and equate that with a physical journey. An author, it is proposed, makes a journey in the process of relating a narrative (and the reader, likewise, makes a journey in reading the text), but this definition would then make almost any text a travelogue, and one is left with little in the way of useful defining characteristics. Likewise, many writers chose to describe their own evaluation and perusal of literature as a "journey" through texts, as is revealed by such titles as *A Journey in Search of the Self: Reading Children's Literature,*[1] *A Journey to the Literature of Sakhalin,*[2] and *A Mud Hen's Journey of Collected Literary Criticisms: Solzhenitsin, Yasuda Yojūrō, Shimao Toshio, and Others.*[3]

These figurative uses of the term "journey" aside, I propose that the unifying factor and defining characteristic of all travelogues is that they record a physical journey from one point to another. This journey can be short or long, domestic or abroad, solitary or accompanied, new or repeated, and for one or more of any number of purposes, such as work, leisure, or study. A travelogue is not necessarily a factual

1. *Jibun sagashi no tabi : jidō bungaku o yomu* (Kyōto: Kamogawa shuppan, 1993).
2. *Saharin bungaku no tabi* (Sapporo: Kyōdō bunkasha, 1994).
3. *Sakka ronshū kuina no tabi : Sorujenitsuin, Yasuda Yojūrō, Shimao Toshio hoka* (Tokyo: Yumani shobō, 1994).

account of a journey—in many cases, authors fictionalize some of their specific experiences while adhering to the general truths of the journey. The line between travelogues and travel fiction, then, is drawn between the records of journeys actually taken and those only conceived of in the comfort of one's home. This necessarily eliminates works such as Jonathan Swift's (1667–1745) *Gulliver's Travels* and Alexander Pope's (1688–1744) *The Dunciad*, but does not eliminate Richard Halliburton's (1900–39) *The Flying Carpet* or Matsuo Bashō's (1644–94) *Narrow Road to the Deep North*. Given this broad definition, it is not surprising that the resulting travelogues vary widely, but each and every one is an account of a physical journey.

In Japanese literature, the broadest term for travelogues is *kikōbungaku*, a genre that overlaps diary literature (*nikki bungaku*) but is not a concentric subset; there are diaries that do not narrate a journey, and there are journeys that are not recorded in diary form. A "travel diary" is a travelogue that is necessarily narrated in the first person, and often follows the events of a journey in a chronological fashion. The style of the travel diary is often one of daily, dated installments. In Japanese literary studies, these two genres of *kikōbungaku* and diary literature are often mentioned in the same breath, and placed together in volumes of collected works.[4] It is virtually impossible to study one without touching on the other, as many of the canonical masterpieces of Japanese literature, such as *The Diary of the Waning Moon* (c. 1280) and *A Record of Travel on the Coast Road* (c. 1223), fall into both genres. Although those works categorized as diary literature and/or travel literature date as far back as the tenth century, the term "diary literature" (*nikki bungaku*) itself is a relative newcomer to the literary scene: first mention of diary literature as a genre dates to the twentieth century.[5] Likewise, *kikōbungaku* (or *kikōbun*) is a relatively new term, but its referent is as old as the earliest Japanese literature.

4. Four examples of such studies are: *Nikki, kikōbungaku, Kenkyū shiryō Nihon koten bungaku*, vol. 9, Ōsone Shōsuke et al., ed. (Tokyo: Meiji shoin,1984); Donald Keene, *Travelers of a Hundred Ages: The Japanese as Revealed through 1,000 Years of Diaries* (New York: Henry Holt & Co., 1989); Donald Keene, *Modern Japanese Diaries: The Japanese at Home and Abroad as Revealed Through Their Diaries* (New York: Henry Holt & Co., 1995); and *Kindai Nihon no nikki*, Odagiri Susumu, ed. (Tokyo: Kōdansha, 1984).
5. The editors of *Nikki, kikōbungaku* place first mention of the term *nikki bungaku* in the Taishō period, in Doi Kōchi's work, *Bungaku josetsu* (An Introduction to Literature, 1922). *Nikki, kikōbungaku, Kenkyū shiryō Nihon koten bungaku*, vol. 9, Ōsone Shōsuke et al., ed. (Tokyo: Meiji shoin, 1984), 4.

The vast nature of the genre of travel literature, both Japanese and Western, leaves the scholar with a logistical problem of organization. When discussing and compiling travel literature, some scholars choose to divide their studies along lines of occupation of the traveler, such as Herbert Plutschow does in his study of medieval Japanese travel diaries, or Joshua Fogel does in his study of modern Japanese travelogues of China.[6] This division is not unlike the division made along the lines of purpose of the journey, purposes that range from religious to exploratory to educational, as motive closely correlates to occupation. Others choose to divide according to the theme of the travelogue, as Paul Fussell does in his anthology, *The Norton Book of Travel*. Travelogues may be compiled according to the traveler's destination, as in the Japanese anthology *A Compendium of Overseas Travel Writing*, which contains a different volume for each geographic region in the world (outside of Japan).[7] And finally, travelogues may be categorized in chronological order.

Needless to say, one study cannot do all of these things, and like other authors of works on travelogues, I have found it necessary to choose a specific tack. Although my overall intent has been to write a book that can be read straight through from beginning to end, by dividing the works as I have, I hope also to have created a work that can be treated as a reader. I examine, more or less in chronological order, travelogues written by Japanese of many occupations who traveled to the West during the period 1860–1912.[8] Japanologists will immediately recognize this time, which covers the *bakumatsu* and subsequent Meiji period (1868–1912), as one of dynamic change in the country. For the nonexpert, let it suffice to say that this fifty-two year period saw a remarkably rapid modernization of Japan, a country that had been, for all intents and purposes, closed to outside contacts for over 250 years. In the midnineteenth century, Japan opened her doors to the outside world, and in essence opened the flood gates

---

6. Herbert Plutschow, *Four Japanese Travel Diaries of the Middle Ages* (Ithaca: Cornell University, 1981) and Joshua A. Fogel, *The Literature of Travel in the Japanese Rediscovery of China: 1862–1945* (Stanford: Stanford University Press, 1996).
7. *Sekai kikō bungaku zenshū* (Tokyo: Horupu shuppan, 1979).
8. Even a chronological order is problematical, because in some cases the travelogue was published many years after the journey was taken. The best example is Mori Ōgai's trip to Germany, which lasted from 1884 to 1888, and the diary of which, *German Diary*, appeared in 1938.

to Western technology, philosophy, arts, government, medicine, education, and more. Many studies have examined the changes in Japan during this time; this study does not, at least not in a direct manner. Rather, this is an examination of two things: first, the evolution of Japanese travel writing during this period, and second, how the West was portrayed, and how that portrayal changed over the decades.

Some may criticize me for playing fast and loose with the term "the West," as if it were some monolithic entity. Others may complain that my choice to capitalize "Western" suggests a kind of Orientalism. Of course the West is not monolithic, and I would be the first to admit that. Even the earliest overseas Japanese recognized the qualitative differences between different Western countries and cultures. France was distinct from England, the United States was distinct from Germany, and so on. However, the Japanese did view these Western powers as similar in a fashion: they were industrially advanced, they maintained colonies or territories beyond their traditional boundaries, and they displayed a political domination that was enviable to an emerging nation. Hence, when I refer to "the West," I conspicuously leave out Spain, Portugal, Denmark, the Netherlands, Sweden, Norway, etc. Some of these countries had their heyday—certainly the Netherlands figured prominently to the Japanese from the sixteenth to the early nineteenth centuries—but by the Meiji Period they were not the destinations of overseas travelers. My focus is primarily on the United States, England, France, Germany, Italy, and Russia, where the majority of the Japanese headed. My choice to capitalize "West" and "Western" is grammatical, to distinguish them from the common noun and adjective they also represent.

In the early Meiji period, travel abroad was prohibitively expensive, and only the lucky few who were either independently wealthy or sponsored by the government had the opportunity to leave their native shores. Westerners had more opportunity to travel to Japan, but there were still relatively few of them, and their movements were limited within the country, thus minimizing their contact with the average Japanese.[9] Exposure to the outside world, for the average Japanese,

9. There is the notable exception of Isabella Bird, who travelled the "unbeaten tracks" of Japan in 1878 and whose travelogue of the journey comprises the letters she wrote to her sister. In urban areas, however, such as Tokyo, there was a foreign legation established to keep the foreign community at a safe distance from the native population. [Isabella Bird,

came thus not through personal experience but through others' personal experiences, whether it be (a translation of) a Western text, or an account of the West by a fellow Japanese.[10] This was a period that saw a flurry of translations of Western literature as the Japanese literary world tried to redefine its own literature vis-à-vis that of the West. Certainly many Japanese learned of the outside world by reading those (often hastily done and therefore flawed) translations.[11]

However, translations, no matter how skillfully executed, do not provide a cultural outsider with interpretive commentary, the sort of commentary often needed to fully comprehend the actual content behind the text. In other words, translators could convey the literal meaning of the text but could not also provide the complex details necessary to understand the cultural context of the narrative. For a narrative that provided such things, one needed an intermediary, a kind of cultural translator, who understood both the reader's context (early modern Japan) and the subject's context (the West). Enter the traveler. Of those who ventured to the West during the *bakumatsu* and

---

Unbeaten Tracks in Japan (New York: G.P. Putnam's Sons, 1880; reprint, Rutland, Vt.: Charles E. Tuttle Co., 1973), and Edward Seidensticker, *Low City, High City: Tokyo from Edo to the Earthquake* (New York: A.A. Knopf, 1983; reprint, Cambridge, Mass.: Harvard University Press, 1991), pp. 232–33.]

10. For a list of works on the West, including travelogues, published between 1696 and 1887, see *Meiji bunka zenshū*, vol. 16, Yoshino Sakuzō, ed. (Tokyo: Nihon hyōronsha, 1928), pp. 558–77.

11. Translations of Western works even found themselves on the Japanese best seller lists: Samuel Smile's *Self Help*, translated by Nakamura Masanao in 1871, John Stuart Mill's *On Liberty*, translated by Nakamura Keitarō in 1872, Jules Verne's *Around the World in Eighty Days*, translated by Kawashima Chūnosuke in 1878–80 (published in two parts), Daniel Defoe's *The Life and Strange Surprising Adventures of Robinson Crusoe of York, Mariner*, translated by Inoue Tsutomu in 1883, Edward George Bulwer-Lytton's *Ernest Maltravers*, translated by Oda Jun'ichirō in 1884, Jules Verne's *Twenty Thousand Leagues Under the Sea*, translated by Inoue Tsutomu in 1884, William Shakespeare's *Merchant of Venice*, translated by Inoue Tsutomu in 1886, and Johann Wolfgang von Goethe's *Reynard the Fox*, translated by Inoue Tsutomu in 1886, were all best sellers.

Translations of various nonfiction works from the *bakumatsu* and early Meiji period were also instrumental in introducing the West to the Japanese. These works included Yanagawa Shunsan's annotation of the Chinese translation of *Circle of Knowledge* (1866–68), a multiauthored translation of Peter Parley's *Universal History* (1870), Kawazu Magoshirō's translation of William Francis Collier's *The Great Events of History* (1870), a multiauthored translation of the National Society's *English History* (1870), Gotō Tatsuzō's translation of Friedrich Kohlrausch's *History of Germany* (1871), Atsu Sukeyuki's translation of Françoise Mignet's *Histoire de la Révolution Française* (1876), Nagamine Hideki's translation of François Guizot's *General history of civilization in Europe* (1877), and Takahashi Jirō's Chinese translation of Victor Duruy's *Histoire de France* (1878). (Source: *Meiji bunka zenshū*, vol. 16, pp. 558–77.) There were many other books available on the West, as well as periodicals, such as the journal published by the Meiji Six Society, the *Meiroku zasshi*, published between 1873 and 1875.

early Meiji periods, some wrote commentaries on the state of the
West, and others wrote firsthand accounts of their experiences.[12]
Both types of works helped disseminate information about the West
to compatriots at home, but for the purposes of this study, only the
latter will be examined.

During this period in Japan, the authors of travelogues of abroad
had varied motives, and varied literary talents; their travelogues served
different purposes, depending on the vocation of the writer and the
intended audience. These travelogues reflect a changing view of the
West, and changing artistic sensibilities in regard to the longstanding
Japanese literary tradition of travel writing. They not only bring a new
perspective of the Japanese view of the West, they also indirectly bring
a new perspective of how Westerners view themselves, in that the
Western reader may come to appreciate an aspect of his own culture
that heretofore he had never noticed. At least one Western author
believed that the Japanese travelogue was the best medium for commenting on Western society: Commander Hastings Berkeley wrote a
work entitled *Japanese Letters: Eastern Impressions of Western Men and
Manners*, in which are included the supposed letters from a young
Japanese who travels about the European continent. The correspondent writes home to his friend, commenting on Western culture, politics, and religion. Berkeley writes in the preface:

> In the past few years much has been written by Europeans,
> especially by Englishmen, concerning Japan and the Japan-
> ese. Moreover, that which has been written has been eagerly
> read. There is in this nothing surprising. The originality
> and excellence of Japanese art—particularly of Japanese
> decorative design—copied, disseminated, and, as usual in
> parallel cases, now vulgarised among us, have stimulated the
> slow curiosity of the public concerning this people,—a
> curiosity which, in inquiring minds, has grown the more
> lively on account of the remarkable experiment which the

12. In the *bakumatsu* and early Meiji period, commentaries on the West that were influential
included Yanagawa Shunsan's *Bankoku shinwa* (pub. 1868), which introduced Western literature; Hashizume Kan'ichi's, *Kaichi shinhen* (pub. 1869), which compiled accounts of
the West by assorted repatriated Japanese and introduced Western customs and culture;
Asō Tadakichi *Kiki shinwa* (pub. 1869), which explained the wondrous machines of the
ages, such as the steam train and the magic lantern; and Fukuzawa Yukichi's works, *Kaei
tsūgo* (1860), *Seiyō jijō* (1866–77), *Seiyō tabi annai* (1867), *Jōyaku jūichi kokki* (1867), *Raijū
sōhō* (1867), and *Shōchū bankoku ichiran* (1869).

Japanese nation has so thoroughly, and, thus far, so successfully conducted: nothing less than that of breaking up its ancient civilisation and recasting the fragments thereof in a European mould.

After having heard and read so much about Japan and its people from Europeans, it may prove interesting to hear what Japanese themselves have to say about Europe and Europeans in relation to this metamorphosis of the laws, customs and political institutions of their country. . . .

As a mere translator and editor of others' work, I might have permitted myself, without incurring the charge of fatuity or vanity, to say a few words in its praise, to touch on its points of utility, interest, humour or other excellence. I have not done so: for reasons which the intelligent reader will not find it difficult to guess, and with which the unintelligent reader need not be troubled.

Matters which are merely of domestic interest to the writers of these letters, or which relate to their private affairs, have been excluded from the translation; that only has been retained which appeared to possess general interest. In the process of translation certain surface peculiarities have disappeared of themselves, others have been toned down purposely. If something of the flavour of the original has thus been lost, a more than countervailing advantage has been gained, for peculiarities which are entertaining merely because they are strange or uncommon become tiresome by repetition. But for this word of explanation the ingenious reader might almost have suspected the writers of the following letters to be children of the editor's imagination.

Although this work is *entirely* a child of Berkeley's imagination, it shows us that the Japanese impression of the West was a topic on which more than just the Japanese themselves mused.[13]

But on a more serious note, Japanese did travel to the West, and they did write of their experiences. Happily, travel literature in Japan met Westernization and adapted to it. Meiji Period travel writers created a dynamic new type of travel literature, one that had solid foundations in traditional Japanese *kikōbungaku*, yet also showed the influence of the West. This is the story of the writers and their works.

---

13. Hastings Berkeley, *Japanese Letters: Eastern Impressions of Western Men and Manners* (London: John Murray, 1891).

This book is not a comprehensive study of all travelogues written between 1860 and 1912, nor is it an anthology of translations of works. Rather, it is a study of works from that period chosen for their lyricism and poesy. Because my goal is to examine overseas travel writing as a genre and trace trends within it, there are numerous works excluded here for the sake of literary sensibility. Most conspicuously, Fukuzawa Yukichi's (1835–1901) work *The State of the West* is not addressed here, not because it is a work of little significance but rather because it is a collection of descriptions and not a travelogue. Many of the diaries of early governmental officials who participated in diplomatic missions to the West are omitted because they lack in literary sensibility, and also because three excellent studies already exist of them.[14] I have omitted a number of works because they recount only the ocean voyage from Japan to Europe, leaving off where the author goes ashore; however, records of such a voyage have been included if the travelogue (or a subsequent travelogue) goes on to describe Europe. I have made efforts to include a variety of works and authors to present an accurate view of the genre.

The flavor of any work is altered by its intended audience, and these overseas travelogues are no exception. In the earliest travelogues, the intended audience was often a small coterie of officials or acquaintances—most were not meant for mass consumption. Sometimes, however, the works did undergo a wider distribution, as in the case of Mori Ōgai's diary of his time in Germany. In many cases, the intended audience is unclear—many texts lack colophons, indicating a private printing, one that was by chance later reprinted.[15] After the 1870s, printing of travelogues became more common and standardized. Many were distributed by popular publishing houses in single volumes, and still more were published serially in newspapers and

---

14. W. G. Beasley, *Japan Encounters the Barbarian: Japanese Travelers in America and Europe* (New Haven: Yale University Press, 1995); Masao Miyoshi, *As We Saw Them: The First Japanese Embassy to the United States* (New York: Kodansha International, 1979); Peter Duus, *The Japanese Disocvery of America: A Brief History with Documents* (Boston: Bedford Books, 1997).

15. Correspondence with Yumani Shobō, the publisher of *Meiji Ōbei kenbunroku shūsei*, reveals the randomness with which modern editors have chosen to reprint this material. When asked what standards were used in choosing among the many *kenbunroku*-type works, a representative of the publisher replied, "There was no clear standard. The editor in charge of the project at the time went to the National Diet Library and other sources and chose the selected books from indexes and original manuscripts."

magazines for mass consumption. This transition from private record or report to public reportage certainly affected the content of the works—writers still produced informative travelogues, but often had one eye toward entertainment. Indeed, the criticism that *kikōbungaku* gave way to Western travel writing sensibilities (and consequently lost connection with traditional aesthetics) could be partially attributed to this change in venue. The attention given in late Meiji periodical travelogues to the personal experience, trials and tribulations, and logistics of travel for the author(s) mirrors those of Western travelogues from the same period. In other words, in copying venue, the Japanese also copied style.

Ideally I would have constrained the parameters of this study to works with similar intended audiences, but the dearth of popular works in the *bakumatsu* and early Meiji made that impossible. Instead, I have chosen (of the early travelogues) works that transcend the category of government reportage by including lyrical passages—works that, had they been produced a few decades later, may have appeared in a more popular medium.

The reader may wonder why all the authors in this study are male. Certainly there were female travelers from Japan to the West during the period 1860–1912; some of the earliest on record were five girls who were sent in 1872 by the Japanese government to the United States for study as part of the overall educational reforms of the early Meiji period.[16] However, the ratio of female to male travelers was low and, to my knowledge, the number of travelogues written by them even lower (the five girls mentioned above, for example, did not write travelogues). An example of a woman writer who is not included here would be Yosano Akiko (1878–1942), who went to Europe in 1912 and who wrote a handful of travelogues from London and Paris, published in 1914.[17] Given her skill at composing *waka* poetry and her prominent place in the literary establishment, one might expect her travelogues to be rich with natural and nostalgic poetic imagery;

16. An excellent biography of one of these girls, Tsuda Ume, is available in English: *The White Plum: A Biography of Ume Tsuda, Pioneer in the Higher Education of Japanese Women* by Yoshiko Furuki (New York: Weatherhill, 1991).
17. These works, "In Paris", "Paris from a Traveler's Window", "From London", "A London Inn", and "First Impressions of Paris", are available in the *Yosano Akiko zenshū*, vol. 9 (Tokyo: Bunsendō shoten, 1972).

rather, she writes mostly of women's lives and how the West compares
to Japan. In other words, her work is more a political commentary
than a travelogue. To include women's works here simply to provide
a female voice among many male voices would be artificial and incon-
sistent with my effort to examine the works that best reflect the inte-
gration of traditional motifs with a modern world. The reader should
rest assured that I eliminated many more male writers than female
writers on these grounds, and that the works chosen for this study
are representative of the field.

Let us begin then with the story of *kikōbungaku* itself, with its
defining characteristics in Japan and how those characteristics evolved.

CHAPTER ONE

❧❧

A Brief History of Japanese Travel and Travel Writing

When Japanese travelers, particularly writers, went abroad, how did they digest what they saw? What informed their interpretations? How do those influences appear in their travelogues? There are many variables in the mixture: the writer's background and education, the intended audience, the writer's purpose in both traveling and writing, and the time period in which the journey takes place. General cultural trends also affect the style and voice of each work. In particular, the strong national identity fostered in the Tokugawa period still flavored the views of the Japanese abroad in the *bakumatsu* era. Although those writers were in awe of the relatively unknown world of the West, aesthetically they could not assess or integrate what they saw in their own traditions. When sentiment turned pro-Western in the mid-Meiji period, travelers wrote of a world relatively separate from Japan, a world in which Japanese sensibilities had little place. The experiences of the traveler were focused on the Western context; as before, East and West were not integrated, but at least the Japanese traveler by this point was familiar enough with Western history and civilization to appreciate its accomplishments and beauties. In the end of the Meiji era, a return to pro-Japanese attitudes, blended with a familiarity with the West, was reflected in the comparison of Western poetic locales to similar locales in Japan, such as Anezaki Chōfū's association of Tuscany with Musashino in the epigraph of this book. By that time, writers accepted that Japanese literary tradition could be applied outside of its traditional borders and through that transcendence a new, albeit short-lived, art form was born.

Of course, literature rarely conforms neatly to theory, and the trends outlined above do not apply absolutely to each and every work of *kikōbungaku*. There is, however, a common thread that helps bring this disparate genre (which contains both domestic and international, and classical and modern works) together. It is the essence of traditional *kikōbungaku*: the *uta makura*, or "poetic pillow."

UTA MAKURA

Uta makura were originally codified poetic references, some of which became, over the centuries, strongly connected with specific *meisho* ("famous places") around Japan.[1] Most Japanese travel literature deals with famous places in some capacity, whether by being exclusively on a famous place, or by incorporating the poetic images associated with famous places. The establishment of famous places began in the earliest times of Japanese literary history—the first examples come from the poetry anthology *A Collection of Myriad Leaves*, compiled in late Nara period (712–85), and the imperial histories *Record of Japan* (c. 720), and *Record of Ancient Matters* (c. 712). In these poems and histories, the mention of a famous place and what aspect of it was most prominent or noteworthy—in other words, the creation of an *uta makura*— often established the precedent to be followed from that point forward throughout Japanese literary history.

As a simple example, let us look at one of the earliest *uta makura*: in *A Collection of Myriad Leaves*, which contains over 4,000 poems, there is a clear development of *uta makura*, as when poem #456 makes direct reference to poems #288–90. The latter poems, by Kakinomoto no Hitomaro (died c. 708–15), tell of the unhappy dilapidation of the once glorious capital at Sasanami:

Tamadasuki	From that hallowed age
Unebi no yama no	When the monarch Suzerain of the Sun
Kashihara no	Reigned at Kashihara

---

1. This description suffices for my purposes here but certainly does not encompass the whole of *uta makura*. For an excellent detailed discussion of *uta makura*, see Edward Kamens' *Utamakura, Allusion, and Intertextuality in Traditional Japanese Poetry* (New Haven: Yale University Press, 1997).

Hijiri no miyo yu	By Unebi, called the Jewel-sash Mount,
Aremashishi	Each and every god
Kami no kotogoto	Made manifest in the world of men,
Tsuga no ki no	One by one in evergreen
Iyatsugitsugi ni	Succession like a line of hemlock trees,
Ame no shita	Ruled under heaven
Shirashimeshishi o	All this realm with uncontested sway:
Sora ni mitsu	Yet from sky-seen
Yamato o okite	Yamato did one depart—
Aoni yoshi	Whatever may have been
Narayama o koe	The secret of his sage intent—
Ikasama ni	And passed across
Omōshimese ka	The slopes of blue-earth Nara Mountain
Amazakaru	To a land, remote
Hina ni wa aredo	Beyond the distant heaven,
Iwabashiru	The land of Ōmi
Ōmi no kuni no	Where water dashes on the rocks,
Sasanami no	To the palace of Ōtsu
Ōtsu no miya ni	In Sasanami of the gently lapping waves;
Ame no shita	And there, as it is said,
Shirashimeshikemu	He ruled this realm beneath the sky:
Sumeroki no	That sovereign god,
Kami no mikoto no	August ancestral deity—
Ōmi ya wa	His great palace stood
Koko to kikedo mo	Upon this spot, as I have hears;
Ōtono wa	Its mighty halls
Koko to iedo mo	Rose here, so all men say;
Harukusa no	Where now spring grasses
Shigeku oitaru	Choke the earth in their rife growth

Kasumi tachi	And mists rise up
Haruhi no kireru	To hide the dazzling springtime sun;
Momoshiki no	Now I view this site
Ōmiyadokoro	Where once the mighty palace stood,
Mireba kanashi mo	And it is sad to see.[2]

Poem 456, by Takechi no Kurohito (fl. ca. 700), alludes to the sad state of affairs at Sasanami:

Kaku yue ni	It would be like this,
Miji to iu mono o	I knew, I told you I'd no desire
Sasanami no	To see the old palace
Furuki miyako o	At Sasanami of the lapping waves
Misetsutsu motona	But you'd show it, you gave me no peace.

Edwin Cranston comments that "the peculiar effect of no. 456 depends on a knowledge of the events at Sasanami, depends indeed for its plenitude on a reading of Hitomaro's series on the fallen capital (nos. 288–90). . . . In a poem such as this, the existence of a poetic tradition begins to take on shape and force. The primary emotional field associated with a place can now be assumed; the place has entered the vocabulary of the art, or in Japanese parlance has become a 'song pillow' (*uta makura*) on which the poet can share the dreams of generations past."[3] In this way, *uta makura* references to famous places were carried from one generation of writers to the next, adding layer upon layer of reference to the same referent.

Let us look at another example, one that spans many more centuries. The following is poem #4097 from *A Collection of Myriad Leaves*:

Sumeroki no	Let our Sovereign's reign
Miyo sakaemu to	Open now in glorious flower:
Azuma naru	In the Eastern Land,

---

2. Translation of poem by Edwin A. Cranston, *A Waka Anthology*, vol. One: *The Gem-Glistening Cup* (Stanford: Stanford University Press, 1993), pp. 190–91.
3. Translation of poem 456 and comment in *A Waka Anthology*, vol. One: *The Gem-Glistening Cup* p. 263.

| Michinokuyama ni | In the mountains of Michinoku, |
| Kogane hana saku | The golden blossoms bloom.[4] |

Here the author, Ōtomo no Yakamochi (718–85), refers to Kinkazan, an island off the coast of present-day Sendai. Almost a millennium later, the haiku poet Matsuo Bashō (1644–94) traveled to the same location and wrote:

> The port [of Ishinomaki] was located in a spacious bay, across which lay the island of Kinkazan, an old goldmine once celebrated as "blooming with flowers of gold."[5]

Here Bashō is clearly referring to Kinkazan with the same phrase as Ōtomo had chosen.[6] One could give thousands of examples of such referents/references, but the point remains the same: over the centuries *uta makura* were perpetuated by Japanese poets and travelers. Also, the *uta makura* has two functions: it evokes an image for the reader, and it inspires and directs future travelers.

These *uta makura*, although often only a few syllables long, were laden with imagery; thus they would not only remind the reader of the general location itself but also of the specific flora or fauna—the special character or *hon'i*—for which the location had become famous. For example, the author, when invoking the name of Maki no Shima, would evoke the image of attractive trees. Seta was known for its bridge; Miyagino was known for bush clover; Yoshinoyama was known for its cherry blossoms, and so on. And once an *uta makura* was established for a famous place, travel writers had a literary obligation to correctly invoke it.

These *uta makura* were so clearly established that there were numerous published lists of them, to aid the writer in choosing the correct phrasing to describe specific places.[7] Once a well-known

---

4. Translation by Cranston, *A Waka Anthology*, vol. One: *The Gem-Glistening Cup*, p. 460.
5. Translation from Matsuo Bashō *The Narrow Road to the Deep North and Other Travel Sketches*, Nobuyuki Yuasa, trans. (London: Penguin Books, 1966), p. 117.
6. Matsuo Bashō, *Oku no hosomichi* (Tokyo: Iwanami shoten, 1979), p. 39.
7. *The Princeton Companion to Classical Japanese Literature* mentions the following four *uta makura* lists as "among the best": *Nōin Utamakura* (Heian period) by Nōin, *Godaishū Utamakura* (c. 1126) by Fujiwara Norikane, *Yakumo Mishō* (c. 1221–42) by Juntokuin, and *Meisho Hōgakushū* by Sōgi. See *The Princeton Companion to Classical Japanese Literature*, Earl Miner, Hiroko Odagiri, and Robert E. Morrell, eds. (Princeton: Princeton University Press, 1985), p. 434.

writer, usually a poet, established an *uta makura* for a famous place, successors followed in kind. It was expected of great poets that they would properly employ *uta makura*, combining the traditional imagery associated with a place with a fresh perspective of their own. Thus it was with great anticipation that readers awaited the poem by Matsuo Bashō written on his visit to the famous Matsushima—known for its many islands and beautiful scenery—and some disappointment and dismay when the venerable master, perhaps unable to face the monumental task of writing yet another sublime poem on this famous place, declined to put pen to paper.

Allusions to famous places had the unfortunate tendency to become hackneyed after centuries of writers had used the same *uta makura* over and over again. Moreover, one modern critic of Tokugawa period travelogues laments that the Japanese traveler who was well read in travel literature, and thus versed in *uta makura*, would have such a strongly preconceived notion of what a famous place should look like that he would fail to see the true landscape despite standing right in front of it.[8] Such a vicarious familiarity with place lent itself to the creation of what I term "pseudo-travelogues," works that describe famous places even though the author had never been to them and had based all his writing on previous travelogues. A popular writer in his day, Akizato Ritō, published a series of works on famous places between 1780 and 1815, each of which blended poetry and illustrations, although it is doubtful that Akizato had really visited all the places that he describes.[9] Akizato's works were part of the so-called *meisho zue* ("picture guidebooks") genre; these works were gazetteers that recorded the famous sights, landmarks, shrines, temples, etc., of specific localities, and had accompanying landscape paintings. They were not records of actual journeys to these famous places, though, and so will not be examined here.

By their dominant presence in literature, *uta makura* also inadvertently stifled innovation. For Japanese travel writers, there was no draw in going to a famous place and writing of something other than what it was famous for; the place was known for a specific thing, be

---

8. Suzuki Tōzō, *Kinsei kikō bungei nōto* (Tokyo: Tōkyōdō shuppan, 1974), p. 5.
9. Some of the titles Akizato published are: *Tomeisho zue, Yamato meisho zukai, Izumi, Tōkaidō meisho zue, Settsu, Miyako rinsen meisho zue, Kawauchi, Kisoji meisho zue,* and *Ōmi.* See Suzuki Tōzō, *Kinsei kikō bungei nōto,* pp. 6–7.

it a flower, tree, sunset, mountain or whatnot, and that was its *raison d'être*. For perennial *uta makura*, a journey could be made at any time, but if a place were famous for a seasonal occurrence, such as the bloom of a specific flower, one would schedule one's journey to see that flower at its height; arriving at any other time would be disastrous. For the Japanese traveler, the entire purpose of a journey was to see what had been seen, to do what had been done, to relive the experiences of previous travelers, in short, to experience the familiar. Japanese travelers, particularly in the Tokugawa period and later, have traditionally chosen to keep to the beaten track; it would seem that exploration of new, unknown territory was never a great attraction.

For writers, a familiarity with famous places and the *uta makura* associated with them was the driving force behind choice of destination; it was much more tempting to travel to a place where one could employ an artistic use of *uta makura* than to explore an uncharted region. The attraction for travel writers was not in writing something of a place that had never been said before but rather in writing of the same images while adding a slight variation or improvement. Even Bashō, noted for his improvisation, spent much of his time retracing the steps of the poet-priest Saigyō (1118–90), and making allusions to his poetry of five centuries earlier. Of course, in order for there to be familiar territory, someone at sometime must have been the first to explore it, but that onerous responsibility was taken on by the earliest travelers, most of whom were journeying on official business first and artistic voyage second. So the establishment of *uta makura* was at first incidental, but once done, codified rather strongly.

Uta makura have, however, remained an exclusively domestic product. They are as much a celebration of the Japanese archipelago as they are anything else. And, as mentioned, it took centuries to establish fully the *uta makura* canon after the seventh century "pioneers" first composed *waka*. So when Japanese went to the West, they were in a land of no *uta makura*, and they could not easily and instantly create a new large set. But to observe that Japanese travelers abroad were stymied by a new landscape that did not afford them the traditional flora and fauna is elementary. What we must then ask is, when the Japanese traveled to the West in the mid-nineteenth century, was the *uta makura* tradition abandoned as a remnant of a feudal civilization, or was it modified for a new set of circumstances? In the context of overseas travelogues, did the earliest travelers have to create *uta makura* for later writers? There does not exist a codified list of such *uta makura* as is found in domestic literature. However, a broader examination does show a sort of modern Western *uta makura*. These *uta makura* tend to be associated with places not initially made famous by the Japanese traveler but rather places that already existed in Western fame and lore, and that were then appropriated by the Japanese writer. And unlike Japanese *uta makura*, which are predominantly nature-based, Western *uta makura* are often associated with the manmade world.

In a 1909 essay titled "Uta makura," the writer Ueda Bin (1874–1916) muses on this topic. He writes that there are many places in the West that could, indeed, should, qualify as *uta makura*:

> The landscape on the continent [of the United States] differs tremendously according to the region. One cannot generally sum it up. For those who have never done so before, going to a Pacific paradise like Hawai'i in which the four seasons are all alike and seeing a complete change of scenery can be extremely interesting. The sea over the shoals is a piercingly clear green, and the appearance of the palm tree groves is so much more beautiful than that one would see in a painting as to have an element of mystery about it. I think that future travelers will certainly designate it as an *uta makura*. I remember how, when I was visiting the gardens at Kapiolani'i [in Hawai'i], there were peacocks left loose to roam beneath the branches of the verdant banyan trees— their bright and glossy feathers resembled flowers. And when I approached San Francisco by sea, I gazed out from our ship, accompanied by countless wild geese fluttering alongside, and saw the breakers at Golden Gate Bay roll into the harbor. Like a folding screen of water they roiled up, and made it seem as if there were a waterfall on the surface of the sea. I think one would be remiss not to call this an *uta makura*. It goes without saying that the tropics have a special charm compared to Japan, but the American and European landscape also has such a charm. That is, other countries have fewer flora than our country. One after the other, the mountains one sees are not covered with pines and cypresses as they are in Japan. Rather, they are like mountains of sod; occasionally, among the rocky peaks one sees the sight of dozens of lush trees growing closely together.

Japanese are inclined to be proud of the many verdant landscapes in their own country, but this is a biased view—of
course there are various beauties to be had in both places.
However, rock-strewn terrains cannot be considered a good
landscape. In one part of America that I traversed, there was
one place which was especially withered in the winter; it
made me feel like I was traveling through a vast, lonely desert
with not a soul in sight. On the whole the trees there were
all straight, not gnarled, and a few feet up from the ground
the branches pointed in all directions, properly spreading
their hands out wide. This straight, proper formation of
branches may somehow seem to be an impoverished sight,
but actually such was not the case. In any event, if I were to
propose one or two *uta makura* in America, one would be the
vast plains of Wyoming. There is not one thing as far as the
eye can see. Sometimes, amidst the blowing snow, a flock of
sheep roams near the railroad tracks, and although this is
short of a superiorly beautiful vista, it has a sort of grandeur
about it. Along the long Lucin road which cuts across the
eponymous Great Salt Lake, hillocks undulate across the
broad prairies, and the landscape which reflects rocky patches
of snow in the morning sunlight also must have the quality
of an *uta makura*.[10] Also, in northern Colorado [*sic*], there is
a part of the so-called Grand Canyon which winds along odd
rock formations in such a way as to evoke the work of some
magical, mischievous force. This scenery also must be called
an *uta makura*. Now, I would like to propose that we broaden
the meaning of the word "uta makura" a little bit. That is to
say, we should not limit it to natural landscapes, but further
it to include city streets full of dust and sights of factories
spouting smoke—I think it would be interesting to incorporate these images in poetry. For example, buildings like New
York's skyscrapers do not hold any architectural beauty, but
within them is a sort of new charm of thoroughness. If one
gazes at New York from the Brooklyn suspension bridge, the
skyscrapers, all lined up, soar above the clouds and the lights
in the windows twenty or thirty stories up, especially in the
early evening, shine like stars in the sky. The morning mist
and the evening colors of the harbor entrance at Hoboken
are found in no other land. And if we take this one step further and include landscapes of human emotion, we will have

10. Lucin, a city to the west of the Great Salt Lake near the Nevada state line, was on the
South Pacific rail line.

even more proper *uta makura*. New York's Madison Square
is located at the bustling nexus of world prosperity. There,
listening to the Italian immigrants play plaintive tunes on
their barrel organs, one hears in their reedy voices the keen
music that sings of the vices of recent civilization. Then,
when one walks along Wall Street during business hours, one
gets the feeling that the crazed blood-shot eyes of everyone
working for money are more wretched and tragic than those
one sees in the gambling houses. In contrast, when one goes
to the countryside in winter and sees children running and
kicking through the snow beneath rows of maple trees
denuded of their leaves, one feels like raising one's voice and
crying "Long Live Young America!" The countryside landscape in New England makes one relaxed, rejuvenated, and
somehow nostalgic.

    If one is asked where amongst the great cities of Europe
and America is good, anyone would reply that Paris must
surely be the best. In addition to the beauty of the markets
and the order of the streets there is the clement weather and
the refined manners. Living in a place like that, anyone
would want to compose poetry in its praise, I think. The
Champs-Élysées is truly like Chang An in its heyday; it is
the most graceful and beautiful city in the world. Within the
city, there are *uta makura* lying about at every turn. The
height of civilization is France, or rather, Paris. And within
that extremely beautiful city there is an air of saintliness.
Along the banks of the Seine with their ceaseless horse cart
traffic are hermits who hang up boundless lengths of silks.
Below the bridges, there are grooming shops for dogs. On
the stone dikes along the river are old, familiar used book-
stores. And the exemplary gothic architecture of Notre
Dame shows a remarkable transformation in the morning
and evening sun. I have spent full days and nights gazing at
these transformations of Notre Dame, but the most beautiful time is in the evening, looking from the San Michel
bridge at the golden waves of color bathing the landscape.
There and then one can savor the fine shadows of colors
from a pearly, cloudy white to a lively rose hue. There are
also old women who sell flowers; they wear a *charlotte*, grasp
their baskets and walk by the storefronts, selling their wares.
The manner of the packhorse drivers who lead horses larger
than oxen; rain falling on the after-theater crowd near midnight; the reflection of thousands of street lamps on the cob-
blestones; the honking of automobiles; the creaking of horse

carts in the grandeur of this nightless city; the patina of the spirit of the age in full view; these all have the charm that makes them *uta makura*. Few people praise London as a scenic locale, but the change of seasonal colors and the richness of the palette is like that in Turner's paintings, and although there is little cultural beauty, there is some merit in savoring the change of the light. However, I think that even if they view the scenery in the same way, all travelers would praise Paris for its accommodating nature. It's just that in London, and along the banks of the Thames near Richmond, the scenery has the special beauty of England. In addition to these beautiful sights are the windmills, red roofs, and neat dikes of Holland, and the dream-like scenery near Naples, Italy. Switzerland is a country famous for its scenic beauty and anyone would praise it as such, but I prefer southern Germany. The scenery around Salzberg is very much like that in Japan. In sum, it is hard to decide which country has the overall most superb scenery. Every place in creation—no matter what sort, no matter what locale—has a fitting beauty in the eye of the beholder. England's wave-driven seashore viewed from a ship, the unbearably hot Red Sea viewed from a ship's cabin—each evokes its own beauty according to the viewer. Fundamentally, when it comes to designating *uta makura*, and questioning whether such a thing is wrong, I wonder if everything under creation isn't an *uta makura*. My journeys are not taken for the purposes of academic research, nor are they connected with a special mission. They are simply random wanderings, and so I can only offer my impressions as such.[11]

Here Ueda explicitly states what some earlier writers implicitly stated: beauty is not limited to the Japanese archipelago, nor is it limited to the natural world. If one is to travel, it is only natural to find and record particular sights of beauty. By focusing on potential new *uta makura*, Ueda suggests that in future more travel writers pay attention to the sights of beauty around them and incorporate their observations in their writing in a way that directly reflects the travelogues of old. But Ueda himself falls short of the task: he does not compose poetry using the proposed *uta makura*, nor does he develop particularly

11. "Uta makura" in *Ueda Bin zenshū* (hokan) (Tokyo: Kaizōsha, 1931), pp. 219–22. This essay originally appeared in *Kokoro no hana*, vol. 13, no.1 (January 1909).

poetic terminology to capture the special characteristics embodied therein. We are left knowing of special sights, but bereft of the encapsulating phrases necessary to make them real *uta makura*. One may conclude that Ueda suggests an application of a poetic tradition that was already so ossified as to prevent appropriation and modification. But if we consider that Ueda suggests radical modifications to what an *uta makura* is—such as his suggestion that the term be broadened to include urban scenes—then his appropriation seems plausible.

We should remember that Ueda Bin came on the coattails of many earlier writers for whom these sights were unusual and unfamiliar. He has not randomly chosen these sights but rather has focused on them both for their beauty and for their familiarity. The first Japanese overseas travelers who saw these sights did not react in the same way; for them, it was all they could do to objectively describe what they saw. Likewise, the first Japanese domestic travelers were seeing new, unfamiliar sights, and could not have known that their descriptions would dictate poetic imagery for generations to come. Thus we see that in any context, domestic or overseas, the creation of *uta makura* is not consciously done; only the codification and invocation of them is a conscious act.

Indeed, if we look to the imagery of the late Meiji period overseas travelogue, we see that there was a set of favorite images repeated in the works of disparate authors. The form in which these images appear, mostly in a prose context, differs from the poetic form of domestic *uta makura*, but the intent of the authors to evoke a nostalgia is the same. By this time, travelers knew what to expect abroad, and were pleased when they, too, were able to walk along the famous Champs Élysées, to see the infamous Tower of London, to thrill at the sight of the street lights of New York, and to ride the transcontinental railroad across America.

TRAVEL EAST AND WEST

This aesthetic of *kikōbungaku* contrasts dramatically with Western travel literature, which emphasizes the exploration of new lands. There is no such thing as an *uta makura* in the Western tradition; the writer-traveler is not as much an artist as a communicator of strange facts and fictions, and his narrative is not as much a celebration of place as it is of self. Thus, Western travelers write of experiencing profound emotions at certain sights, or of maturing over the course of their journey; the narrative tends to be an individualistic one, centered on the author, and not on the place. In contrast, the Japanese travel writer hesitates to talk of his/her own impressions or emotional developments beyond being moved by the appropriate sight in the appropriate famous place.

The importance of *uta makura* and a familiarity with place demonstrates the centrality of nostalgia in Japanese travel literature. A traveler, domestic or overseas, may never have set foot in a place before, but if he has read of another's journey prior to his own, he may experience a kind of vicarious nostalgia, and with that nostalgia comes a warm, pleasant longing for times past, a longing that, in the case of domestic literature, is closely associated with the aesthetic values of the short-lived and the ephemeral. In this sense, the aesthetics of travel literature are the same as the traditional literary aesthetics of Japan, and may account for why travel literature can stand alone as a legitimate genre in Japan when it is often dismissed as nonliterary journalism or reportage in the West. This nostalgia is not always vicarious: firsthand nostalgia for the traveler's distant home also plays a role in the travel aesthetic. In *Tosa Diary*, Ki no Tsurayuki (ca. 872–945) records a number of scenes in which he or his fellow travelers long for their home, or at least a familiar landscape.[12] In the following passage, Tsurayuki's party has been trapped by high winds for days aboard their ship at Ōminato. If they were in the capital, they would be feasting with friends, but instead their distance from home leaves them feeling forlorn and isolated:

> The Seventh Day came, with the boat still in the same harbor. People thought in vain about the White Horse Banquet being held that day; for us, waves were the only white things in sight.[13]

---

12. Ki no Tsurakyuki writes *Tosa Diary* in the voice of a woman, but there is no doubt among scholars of his authorship. Thus, the narrator here is referred to as a female, whereas Ki no Tsurayuki himself is referred to as a male.
13. Translation by Helen Craig McCullough in *Classical Japanese Prose: An Anthology* (Stanford: Stanford University Press, 1990), p. 76.

In another scene, the travelers find themselves at sea on the "Day of the Rat," on which people traditionally picked greens from the fields. The narrator tells us:

> The boat was taken out. We were rowed along in bright sunlight. Noticing that my nails had grown excessively long, I reckoned up the days and found that it was a Day of the Rat; thus I refrained from cutting them. Since it was the First Month, people began to talk of the Day of the Rat in the capital. "Wouldn't it be nice to have a little pine tree?" someone said. But that was scarcely possible on the open sea. One of the women jotted down a poem, which she showed around:

obotsukana	How unreal it seems!
kyō wa ne no hi ka	Is this the Day of the Rat?
ama naraba	Were I a fisher
umimatsu o dani	then I might at least uproot
hikamashi mono o	pine of the sea, but alas . . .

> What shall we say of that as a Day of the Rat poem composed at sea?
> Someone also composed this:

Kyō naredo	Though it is today,
wakana mo tsumazu	I cannot even pick greens,
kasugano no	for on the beaches
waga kogiwataru	I pass in this rowing craft
ura ni nakereba	there is no Kasuga Plain.

The boat proceeded on its way amid such talk. Presently, we approached a beautiful spot.
"Where are we?" someone asked.
"Tosa Harbor."
Among the passengers there was a woman who had once lived in a place called Tosa. "Ah," she sighed. "It has the same name as the Tosa where I lived long ago." She recited this poem:

toshigoro o	It bears the same name
sumishi tokoro no	as the place in which I lived
na ni shi oeba	while the years went by,

| kiyoru nami o mo | and thus I feel affection |
| aware to zo miru | even for its approaching waves.[14] |

In this passage, the passengers long for both traditions and lives left behind. There is a distinct loneliness in these poems, a forlorn quality that emphasizes the difficulties of travel in the tenth century. Yet the landscape is not entirely forbidding; when passing the shores of Uda, the narrator and her fellow travelers are profoundly touched:

> Presently, the boat passed the pine woods of Uda. It was impossible to imagine how many trees might be standing there, or how many thousands of years they might have lived. The waves came up to their roots, and cranes flew back and forth among the branches. Too deeply moved to admire the spectacle in silence, one of the passengers composed a poem that went something like this:

miwataseba	They must think of them
matsu no ure goto ni	as friends for eternity—
sumu tsuru wa	those cranes far away
chiyo no dochi to zo	dwelling wherever a pine tree
omoubera naru	offers a bough for a home.

The poem was not the equal of the scene.[15]

These passages reflect the strong sensitivity to nature so prominent in early travel writing; they also show the sadness that permeated the hearts of the isolated travelers. This was a journey made of necessity, and was not a source of joy.

As in Japan, travel in the West began as an unpleasant, trying activity and emerged by the late sixteenth century as something one chose to do, such as in the case of the upper class in England, where travel was "thought of as an essential part of a young gentleman's education."[16] And despite the contrast between place and individual, there

14. McCullough, *Classical Japanese Prose*, pp. 91–92.
15. McCullough, *Classical Japanese Prose*, p. 81.
16. John Julius Norwich, *A Taste for Travel* (New York: Alfred A. Knopf, 1987), p. 5.

is an element of similarity between Western and Japanese travel: Westerners may not have a set of *uta makura* committed to memory, but they do have a literary and cultural history that inspires their travel. An Englishman who traveled to Greece during the nineteenth century may have gone as much to see modern Athens as to see the Parthenon and imagine the glory days of ancient Greece, much in the same way that a Japanese traveled to Yoshinoyama to see the cherry blossoms and thus imagine past blossoms, as described in traditional poetry. This similarity between Japan and the West, however, is inverted in the case of Japanese abroad; in the West, early travel literature tends to be accounts of exploratory journeys, such as Bernal Diaz Del Castillo's (c. 1492–1581) *The True History of the Conquest of New Spain* or Marco Polo's (c. 1254–1324) *Travels.* Only once the world had been well traveled could Westerners begin to write travelogues that hearkened back to the past and find familiarity in foreign places. The age of the "Grand Tour" (the seventeenth and eighteenth century) saw British travelers setting off to famous places in continental Europe for the purpose both of joining legions of other travelers in seeing famous places and also experiencing their own cultural past by visiting the sources of Western civilization. The age of exploration was by no means over, but the world was certainly a more familiar place by the nineteenth century, and travel writing reflects that. Conversely, in Japan, early travelers stayed in the familiar domestic setting and journeyed to famous places, while later travelers traversed borders and set off to *terra incognita.* It is the older travel literature that covers the familiar, the fully explored "famous places"; it was not until the nineteenth century that Japanese travelers began to explore the unknown.

There was also a distinct class difference in the Japanese traveler abroad in comparison to his Western counterpart. Western travelers during the age of the Grand Tour and beyond tended to be moneyed, and people of leisure. Paul Fussell, in describing later Western travel books, calls them "pastoral romances" and goes on to explain:

> If William Empson is right to define traditional pastoral as a mode of presentation implying "a beautiful relation between rich and poor," then pastoral is a powerful element in most travel books, for, unless he is a *Wandervogel* or similar kind of layabout (few of whom write books), the traveler is almost always richer and freer than those he's among.

He is both a plutocrat pro tem and the sort of plutocrat the
natives don't mind having around.[17]

Indeed, the same was true of Japanese travelers until the seventeenth
century; only the wealthy had the ability to travel about the country,
and they often described the poverty and indigence they encountered
on the road. However, when the Japanese began to travel overseas,
specifically to Europe and the United States, in the nineteenth century, they were certainly not more wealthy than the natives, nor were
they "freer" in a political sense. Fussell says that travel of the twentieth century is "a celebration of the Golden Age. . . . One travels to
experience the past, and travel is thus an adventure in time as well as
distance."[18] But if Westerners traveled to see the past, nineteenth century Japanese traveled to see the future, an unfamiliar world without
poetic precedents, a world that they imagined would someday soon
become their own. And although at first the travelogues that resulted
from these journeys were full of foreign terms and concepts, the strong
influence from traditional Japanese travel literature soon reestablished
itself in the writer's mind, making what was unfamiliar familiar.

THE PRECEDENTS IN *KIKŌBUNGAKU*

In premodern Japan, travel was arduous enough to prevent much in
the way of leisure jaunts, and thus journeys made in those times were
more often pilgrimages made out of religious fervor or obligatory trips
made in conjunction with one's occupation. *The Tosa Diary* is an
example of the latter; it is the narrative of a governor's journey from
Tosa (in central Shikoku) to the capital (present-day Kyōto) in an official capacity. Religious pilgrimages also date back to the Heian period
(795–1185), when members of the aristocracy made regular journeys
to designated shrines; the Fujiwara went annually to the Kasuga
Shrine in Nara, the Minamoto clan to the Yawata Shrine, and the
Taira to Itsukushima.[19]

17. Paul Fussell, "Travel and Literary Imagination" in *Temperamental Journeys: Essays on the Mod-
    ern Literature of Travel*, ed. Michael Kowalewski (Athens and London: The University of
    Georgia Press, 1992), p. 86.
18. Fussell, "Travel and Literary Imagination," p. 86–87.
19. Herbert Plutschow, "Japanese Travel Diaries of the Middle Ages" (Ph.D. diss., Columbia
    University, 1973), p. 75.

In addition to these annual journeys, imperial court members also made religious pilgrimages to other location, and often recorded their journeys (mostly in Chinese), as was the case with Emperor Sutoku's *Account of the Imperial Pilgrimage to Mt. Kōya* (1124).[20] Other prominent travel literature of the Heian period includes Zōki's (dates unknown) *The Hermit*, portions of Sugawara Takasue no Musume's (b. 1008) *Sarashina Diary*, Enchin's (814–91) *Notes of Travel*, and Jōjin's (1011–81) *A Record of a Pilgrimage to Mt. Tendai and Mt. Wudai*.[21] The latter two works are of journeys abroad to China, as were a number of Heian and Kamakura works written mostly by Buddhist scholars and pilgrims, and they represent the small number of foreign travelogues extent before the Tokugawa period.[22] Generally speaking, Heian travelogues were either written in literary Chinese, the standard language of official documents at the time, or in *kana majiribun*, the written language reflective of indigenous Japanese. Many were written in a mixture of prose and poetry, a form that would persist through the centuries.

One would be remiss not to mention that some travel writing, notably that of Saigyō, is primarily poetry. There were also travelogues of "accompaniment," written by poets who attended officials or high-ranking travelers. In the Heian period, accompaniment writers composed in Chinese. In later eras, they wrote in Japanese, often including poems along with prose. In a sense, these poetic sidekicks were entertainers—it was their responsibility to provide an appropriate poem, which meant utilizing the correct *uta makura* for a given place. If an official could not be bothered with memorizing *uta makura*, or was not particularly adept at composing poetry, an accompanying poet would provide the service, thus making the journey more enjoyable for all. These accompaniment poems focused on the official, not the poet, and so resulted in more of a celebration of the former, not a personal account of the latter, and in that sense lack in lyricism.

---

20. See Plutschow, "Japanese Travel Diaries of the Middle Ages," p. 25, for more examples of court travelogues of pilgrimages.
21. Alternate titles for *The Hermit* are *Zōki hōshi shū* and *Ionushi*. Donald Keene discusses this work in detail in *Travelers of a Hundred Ages* (New York: Henry Holt & Co.,1989), pp. 32–39.
22. See Joshua A. Fogel, *The Literature of Travel in the Japanese Rediscovery of China: 1862–1945* (Stanford: Stanford University Press, 1996), pp. 20–33, for a more complete account of early Japanese travelers to China.

Tosa Diary, first and representative of the early travelogues, is primarily a poetical text of longing. The author sees little of the surrounding landscape without it reminding her/him of the capital, which she/he misses terribly.[23] The journey is unpleasant and full of the sadness that accompanies her/his grief at the death of her daughter while away in the provinces. Perhaps because there were not yet many "famous places" established in the literary tradition, the author takes little joy in seeing specific regions or sights. Poems of lamentation abound, such as the following two:

makoto nite	If, true to its name,
na ni kiku tokoro	this place consisted of wings,
hane naraba	how nice it would be
tobu ga gotoku ni	to return to the city
miyako e mo ga na	like a flock of flying birds.

yo no naka ni	Ponder as we may
omoiyaredomo	the sorrows of this bleak world,
ko o kouru	we find none more sharp
omoi ni masaru	than the grief a parent feels
omoi naki ka na	mourning the loss of a child.[24]

Perhaps such a doleful tone in *Tosa Diary* is to be expected, given the conditions under which the author journeyed. Travel during the Heian period was strenuous at best. There was no well-developed road system, nor were there inns in which travelers could rest. This meant that travel was slow, and that although refuge at night could sometimes be found in a temple, some nights were necessarily spent out of doors on the ground. Travelers journeyed by horse, palanquin or foot. Although there were relay stations along the major roads, travel

23. The narrative voice claims to be that of a woman in the opening passage of *Tosa Diary*, but it is that of Ki no Tsurayuki, a man. Helen McCullough notes that "Tsurayuki's assumption of a feminine persona pays lip service to the view that Chinese was the appropriate prose medium for a man. The device is, however, a transparent one—for example, the narrator tends to indulge in masculine locutions and crack masculine jokes—and the contemporary reader must have been intended to see through it." McCullough, *Classical Japanese Prose*, p. 71.
24. McCullough, *Classical Japanese Prose*, p. 83.

remained an activity undertaken by few, and consequently the traveler would quickly find himself in rural areas where his currency,
often gold, was a foreign and unfamiliar item useless to purchase the
necessary supplies and food.[25]

As a result of these hardships, the concept of "travel weariness"
or "travel tedium" (ryojō) became a common part of kikōbungaku
rhetoric. Travelers mention suffering from it, and being relieved of it
(at least temporarily). This conceit continues over the centuries,
regardless of improvements in amenities. That is to say, even in the
modern age aboard a jumbo jet one can experience ryojō. It is inherent in the act of traveling, not in the particular circumstances of the
traveler. This term is found in a number of classical sources, including the early Heian kanshi poetry collection Glories and Graces and
the Muromachi period travelogue Journey to the North Country by
Gyōe. Its etymological origins can be traced as far back as the works
of Bo Zhuyi (772–846), the Chinese poet.[26]

Nonetheless, in the early and mid-Meiji travel writers' works it is
conspicuous by its absence. What is ryojō and why is its use here of
note? The word is defined as "the poignant feeling one has on a journey," but that still leaves the term vague. Its usage indicates a feeling
that encompasses any number of emotions, including melancholy,
tedium, and nostalgia. More specifically, it indicates a sadness at separation from the familiar, a longing for home, and occasional despair
at one's difficulties on the road. All of these emotions require some
reflection; they also assume that the journey is being made to a place
that is less desirable than one's home. Perhaps we can say that the
early Meiji travelers shelved ryojō, at least temporarily, for it had no
place amidst the comforts of the industrial revolution.

In the Kamakura (1185–1333) and Muromachi (1336–1573) periods, travel conditions improved. Inns appeared for the first time, and
brought with them the services demanded by travelers, including
those of prostitutes who served the weary male traveler. In particular, the Tōkaidō road, which runs north-south along the east coast of
Japan, became more heavily traveled after the Kamakura government

---

25. See Plutschow, "Japanese Travel Diaries of the Middle Ages," chapter iii, for more details
    on the roads systems, relay stations, government subsidies, etc.
26. The poem by Bo Zhuyi reads in part, "Packing my bags in the early morning, I lament in
    thoughts of travel."

established government administrative offices along it in the late twelfth century. The division of power between the imperial court and the shogunate also naturally caused some unrest and consequently, more travel. People traveled on the Tōkaidō and other roads in both public and private capacities.

Not surprisingly, the increase in travelers also brought an increase in travelogues; authors included the companions of aristocrats who were privileged to travel, refugees who fled the chaotic cities for the countryside, and men of letters who were summoned by aristocratic families from distant provinces. Most authors were skilled poets, intellectuals, and/or priests. Whereas in the Heian period, Japanese was seen as a woman's mode of writing and Chinese a man's, in the Kamakura period men began to use Japanese when writing, although some aristocrats and priests still wrote in Chinese. Their Chinese evolved from a standard form to assorted converted forms, sometimes with *kana* interspersed in the text.[27]

The medieval period saw a gradual increase in travelogues, which can be broken down into four categories: "grass hut" literature, "traveler" literature, "pilgrimage" literature (all three of which have a religious aspect), and the "poetic diary".[28] The religious travelogues tend to reflect Buddhist aesthetics more than employ *uta makura* for the sake of literary art. "Grass hut" literature is that written by one who forsakes the comforts of the city for the solitude and penitence of a life in a hut far from civilization. Although such a self-imposed hermitage was not permanent, like Henry David Thoreau's retreat to

---

27. Here, "standard form" is 本格的な漢文 and "converted form" is 変体 or 変格な文章. *Nikki, kikōbungaku, Kenkyū shiryō Nihon koten bungaku,* vol. 9, Ōsone Shōsuke et al., ed. (Tokyo: Meiji shoin, 1984), p. 110.

28. Major travelogues from the medieval period include (in chronological order) *The Record of Ise, Record of the Kaidō, The Diary of Shinshō, Journey to the Eastern Barrier, A Record of Wandering in the Southern Seas, The Diary of Asuka Imasa'ari,* portions of *The Diary of the Waning Moon, An Unsolicited Tale, Record of a Pilgrimage to the Great Shrine, A Souvenir from the Capital, A Tune from Ojima, Traveling on the Road, Record of a Pilgrimage to Itsukushima, A Comforting Pillow of Grass, Journey to Mt. Fuji, A Record of Viewing Mt. Fuji, A Diary of Viewing Mt. Fuji, A Journey to Ise, Journey to Zenkōji, Journey to Shirakawa, A Record of Fujikawa, On the Road in Tsukushi, Record of a Journey to Arima, Journey to the North Country, Record of Viewing Historical Mt. Fuji, Around Sano, Diary of a Pilgrimage to Mt. Kōya, Record of the Road to Azuma, Journey to the East Country, Record of a Pilgrimage to Yoshino, Record of Jōha's Journey to View Mt. Fuji, Saga Journal,* and *Record of a Journey to Kyūshū* This is a partial list compiled primarily from Plutschow's "Japanese Travel Diaries of the Middle Ages" (pp. 518–19) and *Nikki, kikōbungaku* (pp. 110–213). For more details on these travelogues, the reader is encouraged to refer to the latter source, which provides synopses and bibliographic information for each travelogue.

Walden Pond centuries later, it was a momentary respite from common, secular concerns. Likewise, "pilgrimage" literature is a record of
a religious pilgrimage to a holy site, such as a shrine or temple. The
time spent away from others was a personal, spiritual journey, lend-
ing itself more to meditation on the state of the world than to poetic
responses to nature. "Traveler" literature is a record of a journey taken
for spiritual solace, but without a particular sacred destination. In this
sense, these medieval travelogues may be some of the most personal
travel literature written before the modern era. The authors were not
forbidden to write poetry or use standard allusions, but such was not
the sole purpose of their writing. This is not to say that the Buddhist
travelogues are void of poetry—far from it—but that the poetry, when
recited, expresses an admiration for Buddhist ideals more than the
beauty of nature. These religious categories overlap to some extent—
On the Road in Tsukushi, *A Souvenir from the Capital*, *The Diary of
Shinshō*, and *A Comforting Pillow of Grass* all contain elements of both
the "grass-hut" tradition and the "traveler" tradition.

The "poetic diary" category contains anthologies of poetry written
on a journey, works that mixed prose with poetry written on a journey,
and diaries that contained "travel passages." Poetry anthologies are usually private (as opposed to imperially commissioned anthologies) and
contain poems in a chronological order that reflects a journey taken by
the author. These works also contain some prose, but the bulk of the
text appears in verse. *The Diary of the Waning Moon* is an example of a
private poetry anthology, as well as a combination travelogue and diary
(see below). Another example is *Record of Viewing Historical Mt. Fuji*,
in which the author, Asukai Masayasu (1436–1509) records his journey of 1499 to Mt. Fuji, including ten poems on Fuji, and forty-five
other poems. *Journey to the Eastern Barrier* is an example of mixed prose
and poetry. In this work, the unknown author travels from Kyōto to
Kamakura and back again in 1242. The text makes many references to
classical Chinese and Japanese poetry, and also makes full use of established *uta makura*. *The Diary of the Waning Moon* is an example of a diary
with travel passages; in the first part of the work, the author, the nun
Abutsu, writes of her journey to Kamakura. This work contains a number of poems, in both the *chōka* and *tanka* styles.

Overall, the number of travelogues increased during the medieval
period, and we see a continuation of the *uta makura* convention, as

well as a growing number of religious travelogues. Yet lengthy travel remained outside of the common man's realm, and that, combined with a relatively small readership, resulted in a dearth of popular travelogues.

The improved roads and infrastructure of the Tokugawa period provided for an even greater variety of travelers, and by extension a greater variety of travelogues.[29] Another reason behind the burgeoning of travel literature in this period was the development of an urban culture, one that spawned much popular literature. Travelogues from the Tokugawa range from the lyrical and poetic *Narrow Road to the Deep North* by Matsuo Bashō to the fictional and often perverse *Chikusai's Progress East* by Tomiyama Dōya (1583–1634).[30] The Tokugawa period also saw the development of a new genre, the travel guidebook (*dōchūki*). Like its Western counterpart of *Baedeker's* or *Fodor's*, the Tokugawa travel guidebook provided travelers with practical information, absent artistic and lyrical consideration. A guidebook might tell a traveler of auspicious and inauspicious days for setting out on a journey, and also equally auspicious or inauspicious days for returning home. It might provide names of towns, post stations, and the important landmarks in between. Price lists for the sorts of services a traveler would avail himself of—inns, horses, food, etc.— would also help the outsider avoid being swindled.[31]

There was some crossover between travel guidebooks, travelogues, and fiction, such as in Nakagawa Kiun's (1636–1705) *Child of the Capital*, Asai Ryōi's (1612–91) *A Record of Famous Places on the Tōkaidō*, and Jippensha Ikku's (1765–1831) *Shank's Mare*, all of which

29. For an excellent study of travel in the Tokugawa period, see Constantine Vaporis' *Breaking Barriers: Travel and the State in Early Modern Japan* (Cambridge, Mass.: Harvard East Asia Monographs, 1994).

30. For a translation and commentary of this work, see Laurence Bresler, "The Origins of Popular Travel and Travel Literature in Japan" (Ph.D. diss., Columbia University, 1975), pp. 189–288. Bresler notes in chapter IV, n. 12 (p. 198) that the authorship of this work has long been wrongly attributed: "The identification of Dōya [as the author] was based on evidence gained from a genealogical table of the Tomiyama family in the archives of the Ministry of Education (Monbushō shiryōkan). In 1956, Sasano Ken had named Isoda Dōya as the author of *Chikusai*, and until 1965, this had been accepted by most scholars. The source of Sasano's error was apparently the fact that Dōya's brother had been adopted into the Isoda family. . . . Because of Sasano's mistake we find Isoda Dōya's name as the author of *Chikusai* in Ichiko and Noma, eds., *Otogizōshi kanazōshi*, 1963, and in Maeda Kingorō and Morita Takeshi, eds., *Kanazōshi-shu*, vol. 90: *Nihon koten bungaku taikei* (Tokyo: Iwanami Shoten, 1965)."

31. For entertaining and informative details on the growth of the travel industry during the Tokugawa period, see Vaporis *Breaking Barriers*.

fall into the category of *meishoki* ("famous place records"). Naka-gawa's work, one of the first *meishoki*, told the story of a priest who travels to the capital to show around a young, intelligent youth. It includes some poetry and focuses more on the customs and conditions of the capital than on the scenery. In *A Record of Famous Places on the Tōkaidō*, Ryōi used the information found in the guidebook titled *Journey in the Year 1616* written by Hayashi Razan (1583–1657) to create a realistic story of a monk, Rakuami, who wanders along the Tōkaidō with a companion and experiences a number of mishaps, all told in a humorous voice.[32] The book was presumably read by both "armchair travelers" and those who had traveled or planned to travel themselves along the road described, as the information on the route was relatively accurate.

Shank's Mare is a similar work, in which the two protagonists travel the Tōkaidō at a leisurely pace, having various escapades in the process. Because it specifically referred to stages of the Tōkaidō, and provided some information that might have been of use to real travelers, the work should be considered a hybrid of fiction and guidebook. Above that, it is bawdy and ribald, and enjoyed great popularity in its time despite the low-brow nature of the narrative.[33] However, in keeping with my definition of travelogue—that it is necessarily the record of a physical journey from one place to another—*A Record of Famous Places on the Tōkaidō* and *Shank's Mare* cannot be considered part of the travelogue genre.

Another type of travel literature popular in the Tokugawa was the *meisho annai* ("famous place guide"), which gave the traveler practical information about famous places without the fictional framework of *A Record of Famous Places on the Tōkaidō*. The Neo-Confucianist Kaibara Ekiken (1630–1714), best known for his treatise *Greater Learning for Women*, also wrote a number of famous place guides. His titles include *Record of An Excursion to All Provinces*, *Record of An Excursion to Japanese Provinces*, and *A Record of My Wife's Travels* (published posthumously). In *A Record of An Excursion to Japanese Provinces*,

---

32. Ryōi's work has some Meiji period counterparts, such as Suehiro Tetchō's (1849–96) novel *Journey of a Deaf Mute* (1891) and Kanagaki Robun's (1829–94) *Hizakurige of the West*. See discussion in chapter 3 for more details.

33. *Shank's Mare* is available in English translation: Jippensha Ikku, *Shank's Mare*, Thomas Satchell, trans. (Rutland, Vt.: Tuttle Books, 1960). This is a reprint of Satchell's 1929 translation, which was published in Kobe.

Ekiken forgoes recording the mundane details of a diary, such as the weather and distance traveled, and simply provides practical information for the traveler.[34] Ekiken's travel works are not commonly included in lists of Tokugawa travel literature, however, probably because of their lack of poetic sensibility.

The Tōkaidō was made famous and popular not only by writers such as Ryōi, but also by artists, most notably Andō Hiroshige (1797–1858), in his series of woodblock prints *The 53 Stages of the Tōkaidō*. Travelers were no longer only the wealthy or religiously pious; the growth of the merchant class prompted a dramatic increase in the lower classes traveling along Japan's roads. Of course, a merchant traveling to peddle his wares was far less likely to record his journey than a poet traveling to view famous sites. There were also tourists, people who traveled for the sake of enjoying those same said famous sites, but who were not intent on writing their own impressions of the journey.

It was primarily for these latter two groups, merchants and tourists, that the travel guides were created. The trend away from a strong literary sensibility and toward a general audience evident in the Tokugawa travelogues accounts for the judgment of some literary critics that later travel writing "collapsed" or at least changed substantially from a distinct genre to a blend of essay writing.[35] The change is undeniable, but to call it a "collapse" ignores the positive, albeit different, attributes of Tokugawa and modern travelogues, as we shall see.

The Dutch, Portuguese, and Spanish arrived in Japan in the late sixteenth century. This was the first exposure that the Japanese had to Westerners; as an indirect result, a few Japanese began to travel abroad during this period, to new locations (other than China and Korea) and for reasons other than study or diplomacy. Because the main focus of this study is on foreign travelogues, it seems pertinent to give particular attention to these "pioneers."[36] Takayama Ukon

---

34. Suzuki Tōzō, *Kinsei kikō bungei nōto*, pp. 8–9.
35. Narugami Katsumi titles his chapter on Tokugawa travel writing, "The Collapse of Travel Arts," in which he vaguely criticizes the authors of failing to imitate the masters, such as Saigyō, satisfactorily (Narugami Katsumi. *Nihon kikō bungeishi* [Tokyo: Tsukuda shobō, 1943], pp. 298–311). Herbert Plutschow, in his entry for "travel diaries" in the *Kodansha Encyclopedia of Japan*, says that "*kikō* continue to be written today, but compared with traditional models, they tend to resemble the genre known as *zuihitsu*, or the personal essay" (*Kodansha Encyclopedia of Japan* [New York: Kodansha, 1983], vol. 6, p. 106).
36. For a list of and biographical information on all travelers from Japan to the West from 1551–1897, see Tomita Hitoshi, ed, *Umi o koeta Nihonjinmei jiten* (Tokyo: Nichigai asoshieetsu, 1985).

(1552–1615), a *daimyō* from Takatsuki and an ardent Christian, left the country in 1614 after Tokugawa Ieyasu (1542–1616) issued an edict expelling all Christian missionaries from Japan. Ukon fled by ship from Nagasaki to Manila, where there was a small Japanese community. But the voyage and life in Manila proved too strenuous, and he died on February 5, 1615, a mere forty days after arriving in his new home. Neither he nor any of the other nameless Japanese merchants in Manila left a travelogue for posterity.

There was a considerable number of Japanese in Southeast Asia during this period, mostly a result of the vermilion seal ship trade, established by putative *shōgun* Toyotomi Hideyoshi (1536–98) in the 1590s. Toyotomi and his successor, Tokugawa Ieyasu, saw fit to license some Japanese ships for trade in Southeast Asia, verifying their authorization with a document that had the shōgun's vermilion seal, hence the name. This system was set up in response to the growing number of "Japanese pirate" vessels that terrorized shipping on the high seas; it also possibly was an attempt on Ieyasu's part to strengthen his political legitimacy at home.[37] The growth of trade in Southeast Asia resulted in the growth of small Japanese communities that were homes to both traders and Japanese Christian converts who had left a less-than-hospitable homeland. The most prominent of these communities were in Manila, Ayutthaya (Thailand), Tourane (Vietnam), Faifo (also Vietnam), Pnompenh, and Ponhealu (Cambodia). But the inhabitants of these communities were emigrants, not travelers; they did not return to Japan, nor did they write down their experiences in a foreign land for the sake of their compatriots back home. The most infamous of these overseas Japanese was Yamada Nagamasa (d. 1630), who lived in the Ayutthaya community in Thailand. Yamada supported the Thai king and led Japanese forces in battle for his sake, but he was eventually poisoned by a rival royal faction. Although a Japanese writer saw fit to record Yamada's exploits, that record postdated the man by two centuries, and due to its biographical (as opposed to autobiographical) nature and journalistic tone, it hardly qualifies as travel literature.[38]

---

37. For more information on Japanese piracy during this era, see Kwan-wai So's *Japanese Piracy in Ming China During the 16th Century* (East Lansing, Mich.: Michigan State University Press, 1975).
38. The piece mentioned here is by Saitō Masakane, titled "Kai gai i den" and translated by Capt. J. M. James in *Transactions of the Asiatic Society of Japan*, vol. 8 (Yokohama, 1879; reprint Tokyo: Yushodo Booksellers, Ltd., 1964), pp. 191–204.

Yamada and Takayama may have traveled abroad, but they did not travel to the West. One of the first Japanese to leave Asia and the first to visit the Americas officially was Hasekura Tsunenaga (1571–1622), a Christian convert who traveled to Mexico and then to Spain on a journey that lasted over six years (1614–20). Hasekura met with the Mexican viceroy, the Spanish King Philip III, and Pope Paul V, and also worked to facilitate better trade between Japan and Spain. When he returned to Japan in 1620, he was in direct violation of Tokugawa Ieyasu's prohibition on Christianity, but he was granted dispensation and allowed to retain his faith. However, like Yamada and Takayama, Hasekura did not write of his journeys.

Thus the few intrepid Japanese who traveled far from home before the Tokugawa period did not leave a legacy of travel literature. Travel abroad was too young and underdeveloped an undertaking to produce a canon of works. In any event, with the coming of the Tokugawa period and the closed-country policy, the stream of Japanese traveling abroad waned to a trickle. It was illegal to leave the country. It was also illegal, if one did leave the country in some manner, to be repatriated. There were a few Japanese who broke this edict, but most were involuntary criminals—they were shipwrecked sailors who landed outside of their national borders. Some of these men wrote about what they had experienced and seen in foreign lands, although their works lack much literary value. These works invariably have the word *hyōryū* ("drifting") in the title, and often have a combination of text and illustrations; poetry is conspicuously absent from these works.[39]

The most notable examples of Tokugawa ship-wrecked Japanese, at least in terms of travelogues, are Daikokuya Kōdayū (1751–1828) and Hamada Hikozō (1837–97), both of whom were shipwrecked in foreign waters and spent years abroad before being repatriated. The former set sail from the town of Shiroko (modern day Suzuka) in Ise aboard the *Shinshō maru* in 1782. Shortly thereafter the ship was

39. Modern studies of these *hyōryū* works include: Katherine Plummer's *The Shogun's Reluctant Ambassadors* (Portland, Ore.: Portland Historical Society Press, 1991), Arakawa Hidetoshi's *Ikoku hyōryūki shū* (Tokyo: Furukawa Hirobumi kan, 1962), *Nihon hyōryū hyōchaku shiryō* (Tokyo: Kizō kenkyūjo, 1962), *Ikoku hyōryūki zoku shū* (Tokyo: Kizō kenkyūjo, 1964), and *Kinsei hyōryūki shū* (Tokyo: Hōsei daigaku shuppan, 1969); Ishii Kendō's *Hyōryū kidan zenshū* (Tokyo: Hakubunkan, 1900) and *Ikoku hyōryū kidan shū* (Tokyo: Fukunaga shoten, 1927); Mishima Saiji's *Nanban kibunsen* (Tokyo: Shuhōkaku, 1926), which contains Arai Hakuseki's *Seiyō kibun*, Nishikawa Joken's *Nagasaki yowasō*, and Sugita Genpaku's *Yasōdokugo*. See Ikeda Akira, *Kankai ibun*, vol. 2: *Kaigai tokōki sōsho* (Tokyo: Yūshōdō shuppan, 1989), pp. i–ii, for more details.

shipwrecked off Suruga with a broken mast and no oars. Eventually she drifted northward toward Hokkaidō and the Aleutian islands beyond. The crew, including Kōdayū, landed on Amchitka island (not far from Attsu island), where they spent the following four years among the native hunters and Russian fur traders. Eight of the original seventeen crew members succumbed to the harsh conditions, but the remaining nine men collectively built a ship out of driftwood and were able to reach the Kamchatka peninsula, where the Siberian winter and starvation took the lives of three more crew members.

Kōdayū and the others continued on, crossed the Sea of Okhotsk and arrived on the mainland. There, with the aid of money donated by the Russian government, they bought warm furs and gloves and headed toward Irkutsk. By the time Kōdayū reached Irkutsk, six years had passed since he had left Japan, but he still longed to return to his homeland. He appealed to the Russian government for permission to be repatriated, but was initially refused. A second appeal, one that took him personally to Petrograd and involved an audience with Catherine II at her detached summer palace outside the city, eventually resulted in the granting of the long-awaited permission in 1791. Kōdayū reached Japanese shores in 1792, and after convalescing in Nemuro traveled to Edo, where he was subjected to an investigation of whether he had violated the "closed country policy" and was subsequently sentenced to house arrest for life.

A record of Kōdayū 's journey overseas can be found in *A Sketch of Things Heard on a Raft in the North*.[40] This eleven-volume work is an objective account of the voyage and of Russia, as best as could be comprehended by Kōdayū. The first volume recounts the full names of all passengers aboard the *Shinshō maru*; the second and third cover the voyage; the remaining chapters narrate, in great detail, aspects of life abroad. Section headings include: funerals, medicine, writing, taxation, weights and measures, arithmetic calculations, schools, hospitals, kindergartens, food, drink, commerce, shipping, weapons, musical instruments, lacquer wear, paper, housing tiles, umbrellas, glass, soap, candles, grasses, trees, birds, beasts, fish, insects, etc. Particularly for the last few categories, the text provides only a glossary of

---

40. This work was annotated by the Dutch Learning scholar Katsuragawa Hoshū (1751–1809), and revised by the historian Kamei Takayoshi in 1937. It was originally published in 1794 and has gone through several reprints since, one as recent as 1993.

terms, giving the Russian and the Japanese for familiar flora and fauna. A poetic work this is not, although fascinating reading nonetheless for the window it provides on eighteenth century Russia.[41]

Hamada Hikozō was a peasant sailor who set sail from Hyogo Harbor on a ship named the *Sumiyoshi maru* in 1850. Hamada's ship encountered a turbulent storm and was left disabled and adrift for two months before an American vessel rescued her crew. The young Hamada was subsequently taken to San Francisco, where he worked at a few menial jobs. After an abortive attempt to return to Japan that took him as far as Hong Kong, he returned to the United States and found a benefactor in a Mr. B. C. Sanders, a customs collector from Baltimore. Hamada adopted an American name, "Joseph Heco," and remained in the United States until 1860, when Lieutenant John M. Brooke of the U.S. Navy hired him as a secretary on a survey voyage to Japan. Back in his home country, Hamada became a translator for the American consulate in Yokohama, although after almost ten years abroad, he admitted that "it was no trouble for me to use the language and the figures of the foreign land while those of Japan would give me trouble at every turn unless I learned them again."[42]

Although Hamada was certainly not the only Japanese to leave his country during this era, he was one of the only Japanese to record and publish his experiences, both in Japanese and later in English. His travelogue is written in a diary format, and dedicates most of its space to explaining the strange land of America to a Japanese audience. The aspects of American life that catch his attention are below the notice of travel writers fifty years later, but for an audience completely unfamiliar with life in other lands, the details were undoubtedly fascinating reading. Hamada describes a masquerade dress ball, the various new and strange foods, architecture, and such modern technological innovations as the telegraph and the use of electricity. The final sections of the travelogue are dedicated to providing further details about the country,

41. For commentary on Daikokuya Kōdayū 's journey, see *Umi o watatta Nihonjin* in *Nihonshi tanbō*, vol. 18 (Tokyo: Kadokawa shoten, 1985) pp. 157–81.
42. Hamada Hikozō, *Floating on the Pacific Ocean* (Los Angeles: Glen Dawson, 1955) p. 63. There are several versions of Hamada's travelogue: the first Japanese edition, titled *Hyōryūki* (A Record of Being Adrift) was printed in Japan in 1863. The 1955 English translation (cited above) is of this earlier text. Another expanded English version of the travelogue was published later, titled *A Narrative of a Japanese* (James Murdoch: Yokohama, 1892). *Hyōryūki* was reprinted in Japan with the new title *Ikoku hyōryū kidanshū* (A Collection of Strange Tales from Foreign Countries). Ishii Kendo, ed. (Tokyo: Fukunaga Shoten, 1927).

details that could not easily conform to a diary-formatted text but that the author felt were of importance nonetheless. The 1927 edition added the following descriptive section headings: "A History of the American Government," "Legal Proceedings and Lawsuits," "On Religion in America," "Marriage," "Holidays and Sports," "A Diagram of European Chess," and "Drawings of American Devices" (which includes a steam carriage, a telegraph, an artificial leg, an iron bridge, and iron ships).[43]

A contemporary of Hamada's was Nakahama Manjirō, aka John Mung or John Manjirō (1827–98), a fisherman who was shipwrecked in 1841 and landed on a deserted island south of the Izu peninsula with four shipmates. After forty days, the men were rescued by an American whaling ship, the *John Howland*, captained by William H. Whitfield. When the ship reached Hawai'i, it was decided that Nakahama would remain in Whitfield's care and head for the mainland, while his shipmates stayed in Hawai'i to make lives for themselves. Nakahama went to Fair Haven, Massachusetts, and attended school there. After finishing his studies, he pursued assorted occupations, including whaling and gold prospecting, eventually returning to Japan in 1851. In the following years, Nakahama worked as an interpreter for the Japanese embassy staff who traveled to the United States, for his English, although not fully fluent, was certainly better than almost any other Japanese at the time.[44]

Like Hamada, Nakahama recorded some of his experiences, and this work, *A Record of Manjirō's Shipwreck*, was one of the very few works by shipwreck survivors permitted publication during the Tokugawa Period.[45] Other overseas travelers from the later Tokugawa

43. Hamada, *Floating on the Pacific Ocean*, 64–89.
44. Nakahama has captured the interest of many biographers. There are three books on him in English: *Manjirō: The Man Who Discovered America* by Kaneko Hisakazu (Tokyo: Hokuseidō Press, 1954); *Voyager to Destiny: The Amazing Adventures of Manjiro, the Man Who Changed Worlds Twice* by Emily V. Warinner (New York: Bobbs-Merrill Co., Inc., 1956); and *The Life and Times of John Manjirō* by Donald R. Bernard (New York: McGraw-Hill, 1992). Also, the modern fiction writer Ibuse Masuji (1898–1993) wrote a novel based on Nakahama's life entitled *Jon Manjirō hyōryūki* that has been translated as *Castaways: Two Short Novels* (New York: Kodansha International, 1987). In addition, Nakahama is mentioned in a number of Japanese works, and is the subject of numerous biographies, such as *Tsubaki to hanamizuki: Manjirō no shōgai* (Tokyo: Yomiuri shinbunsha, 1994); *Yūhi no umi: koshoga ga kataru Jon Manjirō no shōgai* (Kōchi-shi: Kōchi shinbunsha, 1991); *Nakahama Manjirō* (Tokyo: Ōhashi Shintarō, 1900); and *Jon Manjirō no subete* (Tokyo: Shin jinbutsu Ōraisha, 1992).
45. According to Arakawa Hidetoshi, there were only five accounts of shipwrecked Japanese published in Japan during the Tokugawa period: *A Record of Manjirō's Shipwreck*, *A Record of Joseph Heco's Shipwreck*, *A Record of the South Seas*, *A Pumpkin's Account*, and *Strange*

period include Mogami Tokunai (1754–1836), an explorer who traveled in northern Japan and who became fluent in Ainu and Russian, and Mamiya Rinzō (1775–1844), an explorer and cartographer who charted much of Sakhalin Island. In the early nineteenth century, Mamiya traveled up the Amur River in Manchuria, despite his country's edicts against such a journey, and recorded his experience in two works, *The Sakhalin Region* and *Travels in Tartary*.[46] A contemporary of Mamiya's was Inō Tadataka (1745–1818), a cartographer and surveyor who studied Western calendar making and who, at the request of the Tokugawa shogunate, was the first to fully survey the island of Hokkaidō. Inō published numerous maps, and a few diaries of his work.[47]

But how do these men's experiences affect traditional travel writing? Exposure to a land of no preset *uta makura*, and to which travel was often serendipitous, left the traveler with no tradition upon which to fall back. The establishment of famous places known to all was viable in a small country whose boundaries were clearly demarcated by the sea (other than the northern climes of Hokkaidō, there was little in the way of unexplored territory in premodern Japan). But the world is a much larger place, and thus daunting to the poet who is dependent on the familiar. The only example of premodern Japanese travel writers applying traditionally domestic aesthetics to overseas travel writing is seen in travelogues of China and Korea. These travelers were certainly not explorers; rather, they were scholars who went to well-known locations to study well-established subjects, mostly Buddhism in some form. When they wrote about China, they referred to places that were familiar to their fellow Japanese either through

---

Tales from Overseas. Arakawa Hidetoshi, comp., *Kinsei hyōryū kishū* (Tokyo: Hōsei daigaku shuppan, 1969), p. 188.

Katherine Plummer notes that the account of captain Jōkichi, who drifted to southern California in 1813, *A Captain's Diary*, was "published underground." Another account of a shipwrecked Japanese is *Stories of Barbaric Places*, about captain Jirōkichi of the *Chōjamaru*, who landed in Alaska in 1838. Katherine Plummer, *The Shogun's Reluctant Ambassadors*, p. 78 and 136, respectively.

46. These two works, originally published in 1811, have been reprinted in Mamiya Rinzō, *Todatsu chihō kikō*, Hora Tomio and Tanizawa Shōichi, eds. (Tokyo: Heibonsha, 1988). It should be noted that Mamiya dictated the narrative to an amanuensis, Murakami Teisuke (1780–1846).

47. Among his cartography works are *Map of the Waterways and Lands of Japan* (*Dai Nippon enkai yochi zenzu*), *A Record of an Actual Survey of the Earth* (*Yochi jissoku roku*), and *Logarithm Tables for Time in All Districts* (*Kokugun chūya jikoku taisūhyō*).

other texts or through art.[48] They admired China, and they saw themselves as students, not conquerors, as some of those Japanese involved
in the vermilion-seal ship trade may have. In the premodern era,
China was seen as a glorious place, perhaps superior in many ways
to Japan. It was the seat of a great civilization, and had a national literature that stretched back much further than Japan's.

Consequently, Japanese travelers treated some parts of China
with the same literary finesse as they did their own famous places.
Although China was foreign, it was simultaneously familiar, and so
did not pose the same problem that the unknown West posed for Meiji
period travel writers.[49] Thus, a Japanese such as the Tendai monk
Ennin (793–864), could travel to China and record the ceremonies
and events of his journey and safely expect his audience to understand
the political structure of China and the activities associated with a

---

48. The act of alluding to famous places in literature has a strong parallel in art; artists in the
    Muromachi period often chose Chinese landscapes over Japanese landscapes as their sub-
    ject matter, regardless of whether they had actually seen the true landscape. A predeces-
    sor's painting would provide the inspiration and model, and through the act of re-painting
    the landscape the artist, like the writer, would sense a vicarious nostalgia for place other-
    wise outside of his grasp for lack of personal experience. Paintings of famous places
    (*meishoe*) depicted both Japanese and Chinese landscapes.
49. For a summary of premodern travelers and travel writing (from Japan to China), see Fogel,
    The Literature of Travel in the Japanese Rediscovery of China, 1862–1945, pp. 20–33. Inter-
    estingly, the tradition of travel writing in China focused on some of the same values as that
    of Japan: Chinese travelers preferred visiting famous locales over unbeaten tracks. In China,
    texts that spoke to the beauty of the place were engraved by early travelers at these famous
    sites for future travelers to appreciate, and over time, travelers journeyed more to see the
    engraving than to see the site. Richard Strassberg describes this phenomenon:

    > A further form of transmission [of travel writing], one perhaps unique to Chi-
    > nese travel writing, was accomplished by engraving texts at the original sites
    > of their inspiration. By incorporating a text into the environment, the trav-
    > eler sought to participate enduringly in the totality of the scene. He perpet-
    > uated his momentary experience and hoped to gain literary immortality
    > based on a deeply held conviction that through such inscriptions, future read-
    > ers would come to know and appreciate the writer's authentic self. At the
    > same time, the text altered the scene by shaping the perceptions of later trav-
    > elers and guiding those who sought to follow in the footsteps of earlier tal-
    > ents. Often, local figures would request of commission such inscriptions by
    > notable visitors to signify the importance of a place. Certain sites thus
    > became virtual shrines in the literary culture, eliciting further inscriptions
    > through the centuries. [Richard E. Strassberg, trans. and ed., *Inscribed Land-
    > scapes: Travel Writing from Imperial China* (Berkeley: University of California
    > Press, 1994), pp. 5–6.]

    Although the convention of onsite inscription never took root in Japan, the close tie
    between place and verse did. Japanese travelers carried their inscriptions in their minds,
    in the form of memorized poems, and then inscribed their own poems, written and pub-
    lished upon return, on others' memories. So China was not only a familiar place, it had a
    familiar literary tradition.

Buddhist temple.[50] Even when explaining a ceremony unique to the mainland, Ennin conveys an air of familiarity:

> At night they burned lamps in the private homes along the streets to the east and west. It was not unlike New Year's Eve in Japan. In the monastery they burned lamps and offered them to the Buddha. They also paid reverence to the pictures of their teachers. Laymen did likewise.
>
> In this monastery they erected a lamp tower in front of the Buddha Hall. Below the steps, in the courtyard, and along the sides of the galleries they burned oil. The lamp cups were quite beyond count. In the streets men and women did not fear the late hour, but entered the monastery and looked around, and in accordance with their lot cast coppers before the lamps which had been offered. After looking around they went on to other monasteries and looked around and worshipped and cast their coppers.
>
> The halls of the various monasteries and the various cloisters all vie with one another in the burning of lamps. Those who come always give coppers before departing. The Wu-liang-i-ssu sets up a "spoon-and-bamboo lamp." I estimated that it has a thousand lamps. The spoon-and-bamboo lamp is constructed like a tree and looks like a pagoda. The way in which it is bound together is most ingenious. It is about seven or eight feet in height. [This festival] lasts for a period of three nights from this night to the night of the seventeenth.[51]

Ennin does not—indeed, needs not—describe the architecture of the temple buildings, who or what the Buddha is, or the meaning behind the offerings of coppers at the temple; these are all things he could safely assume his audience already knew. And although Ennin predates the Tokugawa period, later Japanese travelers to China were in the same semifamiliar cultural situation, and followed suit in their records.

However, men like Daikokuya Kōdayū, Hamada Hikozō, and Mamiya Rinzō found themselves in an unfamiliar setting, one that had

---

50. Ennin recorded his journey in *Nittō guhō junrei kōki* (A Record of a Journey to China in Search of the Law), a four- volume work. This work has been translated by Edwin O. Reischauer, *Ennin's Diary: The Record of a Pilgrimage to China in Search of the Law* (New York: Ronald Press Co., 1955).
51. Reischauer, *Ennin's Diary*, p. 71.

no firmly established poetic images on which to build (at least from the Japanese tradition). These travelers to the West were faced with a much more monumental literary task than their predecessors, and it shows in their narratives. First, they had to explain even the most basic aspects of their destinations before proceeding any further; for their own sakes, as well as their readers', these men had to find the terminology to grasp the concepts of the outside, unfamiliar world, and only then could they reflect on the psychological impact that being in such a world had on them. The result, as seen in so many early overseas travelogues, is a highly structured and organized account, one that reads more like a summary or inventory of events than of one's personal experiences. Lyricism is rare, as is poetic description of the scenery—landscapes for which there were no established *uta makura*.

One may argue that a shipwrecked sailor would naturally lack the poetic sensibility of a well-read scholar, but even the early scholarly travelers reflected this tendency (see chapter 2). The early author of foreign travelogues on the West was reduced to prosaic, objective depictions of what he saw. Many of the travelogues from this period (roughly 1860–70) carry the title *kenbunroku*, or *bunkenroku*, both of which mean "a record of things seen and heard." The term has a distinct connotation of reportage, and does not infer the inclusion of lyrical responses. The reader learns what was seen and heard, but not what was felt. Nonetheless, even those works with a *kenbunroku* title sometimes contain commentary and insight; it would have been hard for an author to detach himself so entirely from passing judgement on such a strange world. Not surprisingly, the driest travelogues from this period are embassy reports, the purpose of which was to inform the Japanese government of conditions overseas.

Another reason why some travelogues, such as Nakahama's, lack the literary quality and interpretive insight that one might hope for is that the traveler spent too much of his youth away from home. Nakahama left Japan at the age of fifteen, so a good number of formative years were spent abroad. It is unlikely that someone of his social status in Japan would be even remotely familiar with the literary travelogue tradition, and so it is not surprising that when he sat down to record his experiences, his writing reflects none of that heritage. Also, Nakahama's extended stay abroad made it more difficult for him to recognize the profound differences between his homeland and the West; indeed, by the time of his repatriation he had spent over one-third of his life abroad and had forgotten much of his native language and customs. Such an intimacy with the 'foreign' (America) prevented him from being a true traveler. A traveler is necessarily a stranger, an outsider, an interloper; but if he stays long enough in his destination, he ceases to be a foreigner, and his account of that land loses the patina of the exotic.

Decades after Nakahama's journey, another Japanese travel writer, Sakurai Ōson (1872–1929), addressed this in the preface to his travelogue of Europe:

> "Guido Fridolin Verbeck of Japan" came to our country before the Meiji Restoration and remained here for about forty years. He came before the treaty revisions, and among the foreigners, he alone maintained the special right to live freely on our soil. But he never wrote even one volume about Japan. When someone asked him the reason for this, he replied, "I have been living in Japan for too long, and I know Japan too well, so it has become impossible for me to put pen to paper. If one wants to write of the state of Japan and her customs, one must not stay longer than eight weeks."[52]

Although Sakurai is trying here to establish the legitimacy of his own travelogue, written after a short seven month stay in London, his point about travelers who have become expatriots is well taken. Intimacy with the landscape can be detrimental, as well as beneficial. It is good to know of a place—indeed, to know it inside and out through the literature written on it and the art produced by it—but Sakurai warns us that physical proximity should be limited to prevent one from becoming inured to its charms.

---

52. Sakurai Ōson, *Ōshū kenbutsu* (Tokyo: Teibi shuppansha, 1909), p. 9. Guido Fridolin Verbeck (1830–98) was a Dutch-born American missionary for the Dutch Reformed Church. He went to Nagasaki in 1859, then moved to Tokyo in 1869, where he taught at university and later became an advisor for the Meiji government. In the course of his time in Japan, he taught and worked with many of the prominent figures of the Meiji Restoration, such as Itō Hirobumi (1841–1909) and Ōkubo Toshimichi (1830–78). There is an English biography of Verbeck: *Verbeck of Japan: Citizen of No Country* by William Elliot Griffis (New York: Fleming H. Revell Co., 1900).

The midnineteenth century saw dramatic change in Japan; it began with the arrival of the American Commodore Matthew Perry (1794–1858) in Edo bay in 1853. Perry, sent by President Franklin Pierce (1804–69), demanded that Japan open her doors to the Western world, a demand to which she reluctantly acquiesced. Over the following fifteen years, opposition to the Tokugawa shogunate grew as rival samurai factions, particularly those from the domains of Satsuma and Chōshū, rebelled against a government that they saw as weak and ineffectual, especially in the face of the new foreign threat. However, no amount of political unrest would prevent the West—both physically in the form of expatriates (who were given the right to reside in Japan in 1858), and figuratively in the national consciousness—from taking a firm root in Japan. In 1868, the shogunate relinquished its grasp of the central government, to be replaced by a monarchy headed by the emperor Meiji (1852–1912).

Gradually, as Japan entered an era of rapid modernization and familiarity with the West, the nature of foreign travelogues of the West changed. Although the occupation of the writer still had a strong influence over style and content, generally speaking writers began to assume their audience no longer needed fundamental explanations; surely they would know what foreign light fixtures were, the fundamentals of motor-propelled transportation, and other basics of everyday life. Writers' attention focused instead on the poetic nature of their experiences—what emotions were evoked, what beauty or ugliness sprang before their eyes—and the historical significance of the places they visited. Writers also often expressed a longing for home, for which there was certainly precedent even in the earliest of domestic Japanese travelogues.

Meanwhile, on the domestic literary front, travelogues began to show some influence from Western literature. Although a careful study of these changes would amount to a monograph in itself, suffice it to say here that in reflecting on the Japanese landscape and their own psychological state, the authors are not "visiting the future" as their colleagues traveling overseas were. Representative of the domestic Meiji travel writers are Narushima Ryūhoku (1837–84), Aeba Kōson (1885–1922), Kōda Rohan (1867–1947), Chizuka Reisui (1866–1942), Tayama Katai (1872–1930), Ōmachi Keigetsu (1869–1925), Ōhashi

Otowa (1869–1901), Kawakami Bizan (1869–1908), and Kubo Tenzui (1875–1934).

What were critics thinking and saying about travel literature during this period? What expectations did they have of the genre? The earlier categories such as "pilgrimage literature" and "accompaniment literature" had fallen into obscurity with the coming of the modern age. In surveying the state of travel literature during the Meiji period, Takasu Yoshijirō divides domestic travel literature of the Meiji period into three periods: the first (1868–87) owes much to Tokugawa travel literature but has some modern tenor to it. The second (1888–97) has an increased modern influence but still lacks in artistic quality due to the scientific flavor of the detailed Western descriptive passages. In the third period (1898–1912), Takasu claims, modern travelogues came into their own.[53] We shall see some carry over of these trends in the foreign travelogues, but perhaps a more useful set of categories was presented by Tayama Katai. Katai identifies four kinds of travelogues: the first type he says records the journey "as is" without embellishment, the second type offers some information on locales, the third is centered on the author's emotions, and the fourth type has an added flavor of exploration or discovery.[54] Although Katai has only domestic travelogues in mind when he sets down these categories, they are also

53. Takasu Yoshijirō, "Meiji no kikōbun," in Meiji kikō bungaku shū, in Meiji bungaku zenshū, vol. 94. (Tokyo: Chikuma shobō, 1974), pp. 374–78.
54. Katai's fourth category was new. By the late Meiji and early Taishō periods, a number of Japanese had begun to explore the far reaches of the world—undeveloped places where nature ruled over man—much in the same way that Westerners had done and were still doing, and their travelogues have very little in common with Japanese literary tradition. Nakamura Naokichi traveled to over sixty countries and produced at least three travelogues in the process: A Discussion of Exploring South America's Amazon (1909), Exploring the World: 150,000 Miles (1915), and A Record of Exploring the Amazon (1915). The novelist Emi Suiin (1869–1934) boarded a Japanese fishing vessel in 1906 and observed whaling in the Korean Straits. He also traveled to Norway to observe whaling practices there, and wrote of his experiences in the travelogue Exploration on Site: The Whaling Ship (1907). Tada Keiichi traveled to the South Pole on an expedition with Lieutenant Shirase Nobu in 1910; both men authored records of the journey. Tada published A Personal Record of the South Pole Expedition (1912) and A Souvenir from the South Pole (1912), while Shirase published The South Pole Expedition (1913). These men's accomplishments are not to be belittled; they ventured on dangerous journeys, often using technologically advanced machinery and transportation, to far away places only a generation after their country had opened her doors to the outside world. But their travelogues fall outside of our focus, which is on settled, civilized areas, specifically Western Europe and the United States. See Tayama Katai, "Gendai no kikōbun," in Meiji kikō bungaku shū, in Meiji bungaku zenshū, vol. 94. (Tokyo: Chikuma shobō, 1974), p. 370.

applicable to foreign travelogues; the first type is typical of the earliest records of journeys to the West, the second gradually replaced the first, and the third appears throughout the Meiji period on an irregular basis. These categories, however, are broad and open to concentricity. Certainly a travelogue can do more than one thing, as we shall see. In any event, Katai and Takasu's comments raise the question of how exactly travelogues of the West compared to domestic works, if at all, and it is my intent to answer that question here.

This abbreviated history of the travelogue in Japan should provide the reader with the background knowledge necessary to appreciate the form and changes of modern foreign travelogues of the West. Because both the writers' familiarity with his subject and his expected readers' familiarity with the same subject strongly influences the tone of the travelogue, it seems to make most sense to me to take up these works in (more or less) a chronological order, as the more time passed, the more the average Japanese knew of the West. In the early years of Meiji, travelers expressed a reserved curiosity about the outside world, but it was a curiosity tempered by lack of full knowledge. Often language barriers and misinformation caused these early writers to make errors of judgement, and thus false conclusions about the outside world. Over the years problems were overcome: there was more opportunity to learn a rudimentary amount of a foreign language before traveling abroad (alleviating many language barriers); accounts written in Japanese of the political, social, and cultural structure of foreign countries were more reliable and available before departure for the prudent, studious traveler; and small communities of expatriates were established in many foreign urban centers, thus providing both a place of respite from the foreign, and a source of reliable local information for the traveler.

By the end of the Meiji period, the Japanese felt themselves full citizens of the world, even if the world refused to treat them as such. There had been a number of setbacks in this vein, including the "Triple Intervention" by Russia, France, and Germany in 1895, that forced Japan to renounce her claim on the Liaotung Peninsula, territory that she claimed as part of the spoils of the Sino-Japanese war of 1894–95. Also, in 1906, the United States passed anti-Japanese legislation in the wake of increased Japanese immigration (particularly in California), such as exclusion from further immigration, denial of land ownership, and segregation of school children. Still, Japan remained determined to be accepted by Western nations as an equal. As a side effect of this determination, the travelogues in the mid to late Meiji show an almost unnatural persistence in portraying the unfamiliar as familiar. While travel books on Japan written for Americans repeat *ad nauseam* the same rudimentary observations as the previous generation(s)—explanations of annual festivals, daily customs, etc.—Japanese travelogues of the West assume the reader knows the basics of the topic and focus on particular twists or changes evident to the author, much in the same way that Japanese writers centuries ago focused on the minute twist of an *uta makura*.

CHAPTER TWO

New Lands: The Early Travelogues, 1860–80

The earliest travelogues are authored by students, scholars, and diplomats. They reflect the wonder felt by these men at the Western world, and bear little resemblance to the seminal travelogues of the Heian period. Most are exclusively prose, and they limit reflective statements to the prologue or afterword, the only place in which the author indulged in expressing personal impressions. Some did contain poetry, however, and are represented in this study because their literary quality merits attention. The education of the author had some bearing on the nature of the work, as did his occupation while abroad. In the end of the Tokugawa period and the beginning of the Meiji period, most Japanese did not have the financial ability nor the political clout necessary to travel abroad for leisure purposes; furthermore, although a strong curiosity about the West would be expected in a Japanese, the West still represented a foreign, possibly hostile place, one devoid of the poetic attractions of domestic locales. Consequently, the travelers from this period were students, either literally or figuratively, sent to learn what the West was, and to transmit that knowledge back home, not to enjoy the experience or be tourists. Most of them transmitted knowledge of abroad by way of returning to Japan and conveying their experiences through verbal means, although a few published accounts of their journey. These early travelers were as much ambassadors to their own people as to the West, as they helped explain the outside world to their compatriots, and promoted a further understanding of and interest in Western culture.

A note seems in order regarding the routes and means taken by these travelers. For those going to Europe, regardless of whether it was their first or final destination, the standard route took them by sea through Southeast Asia, the Indian Ocean, then through the Mediterranean to Europe. More specifically, the usual ports of call were Hong Kong, Singapore, Colombo, Aden, and Suez—all English-controlled territories. Moreover, they usually booked passage on Western (usually British) ships and were surrounded by mostly Western passengers. The culture on board was dominated by Western traditions—food, pastimes, etc. Thus, even though these early Japanese travelers were traveling through Asia on the first legs of the trip, it is important to remember that they were already enveloped in the West, and seeing Asia through lenses tinted by the imperial experience. Of course, they were Asians, but by merit of their status as tourists or travelers, their mode of transportation, and the select places they visited, their European experience can be said to have begun long before they arrived in Europe.

TRAVELOGUES BY STUDENTS

Before the Meiji Restoration, some *han* (provincial governments) chose to send students abroad to study the West in anticipation of the coming Western influence soon to be felt on home ground. The students numbered 152, and came from Fukuoka, Shizuoka, Kaga, Chōshū, Mito, Saga, Sendai, Kagoshima, Izu, Aizu, Sakura, Karatsu, Ina, Hamamatsu, Echizen, Sadowara, Kurume, Ōgaki, Tsuyama, Nagasaki, Toyoura, Okayama, Nakatsu, Kumamoto, and Sanuki. They journeyed to the United States, Germany, the Netherlands, England, France, Russia, and Hong Kong.[1] Many of them became educators or government officials upon repatriation, but only three—Nakai Hiroshi (1838–94), Nomura Fumio (1836–91) and Shibusawa Eiichi (1840–1931)—published a record of their experiences.[2]

1. Names, dates of travel, place of origin, destination, and specialties of these early overseas travelers can be found in Ishizuki Minoru, *Kindai Nihon no kaigai ryūgaku shi* (Tokyo: Chūō kōronsha, 1992), pp. 443–86. Of the 152 students, only two went to Hong Kong, one to pursue British Studies and the other to study surveying, both Western disciplines.
2. It should be noted that there were other students, such as Itō Hirobumi (1841–1909), who traveled to England in 1862–64 and who wrote on the West. Itō's works, however, are not travelogues of that experience but rather commentary on the West at large.

Nakai Ōshū

Nakai Hiroshi, aka Nakai Ōshū,[3] published *A Journey West: A New Discourse on a Voyage* in 1870, in which he records, in diary fashion, his trip from Yokohama to Paris in 1866.[4] Both *A Journey West: A New Discourse on a Voyage* and Nakai's other work, *Setting Off on a Tour*, were republished by Nihon hyōronsha in 1928 in the series *Meiji bunka zenshū*, vol. 16. Nakai was from Kagoshima and traveled to England with Yūki Kōan (dates unknown), who also came from southern Japan. Unlike most of his peers, Nakai was not sponsored by his *han*, nor by the Tokugawa shogunate; rather, he had a benefactor in a man named Gotō Shōjirō (1838–97). Gotō was a *han* official from Tosa, who took a liking to Nakai, seeing in him much promise. With the help of Yoshida Genkichi (dates unknown) and Sakamoto Ryōma (1835–67), both prominent men of the *han*, Gotō financed Nakai's studies abroad. Presumably Nakai was expected to learn about a variety of topics on his journey in order to become a well-rounded man. He was not enrolled in any organized academic program, nor did he have a clear political agenda for the trip. But Nakai was an astute observer, and apparently deeply interested in what he saw; he commented on shipbuilding, Parliament, medical advances, the navy, education, transportation, and more.

Nakai spent much of his time abroad with other Japanese travelers, some of whom were fellow students and some of whom were businessmen. It was common for Japanese travelers to keep each others' company, even in later periods, a fact that seems natural when one considers that many travelers could not speak the local language, and so other Japanese provided a valuable source for local information. Nakai could not speak English and depended on his friends to interpret for him. Surprisingly, he tells us that a good number of non-Japanese passengers on the ship from Japan to Europe could speak

---

3. In this case, Nakai's alias is a *nom de plume*, but several of the other students who traveled abroad had nonliterary aliases, as was common at the time. For authors whose works I discuss in detail, I provide aliases; for those who receive only passing mention, I provide only the most common name by which they were known.

4. The 1870 edition was published out of Tokyo. There was an earlier edition, published in 1868 in Ōsaka titled, *A Record of Things Seen and Heard on a Journey to the West*, which had a limited circulation among the author's friends and acquaintances. There were numerous editorial changes in the second edition. [Kobayashi Kaoru, "Seiyō kikō: Kōkai shinsetsu kaidai," in *Meiji bunka zenshū*, vol. 16, Yoshino Sakuzō, ed. (Tokyo: Nihon hyōronsha, 1928), p. 15.]

at least some Japanese, something that perhaps lulled in him a sense of comfort and familiarity.

The naval leg of his journey lasted two months, during which time Nakai records his experiences in a style reminiscent of domestic travelogues, such as *The Tosa Diary*. *A Journey West* is written in a diary format that mixes Japanese prose and Chinese poetry. The prose is reflective, sensitive, and personal, almost devoid of any political commentary; the poetry is redolent with nostalgia. Nakai tells us how he feels—both physically (he was seasick much of the time) and mentally—without didactically imposing his thoughts on the reader. His first poem, written on the occasion of embarkation from Nagasaki reads:

> I head to lands distant from Japan
> Where are the three mountains and five peaks?
> The steam ship flies like a bird through the waves at full speed,
> Cutting through the giant waves and leagues of foamy water.[5]

The "three mountains and five peaks" here refer to both real and fictional locales in China, and it is thought that Nakai is reflecting on the fact that his journey is a more formidable undertaking than famous difficult journeys to China made by his predecessors.[6] The journey was indeed arduous, and he was right to consider the gravity of the undertaking, as is evidenced by an event recorded days later:

Fifth Day of the Month.

Last night an Englishman died. He will be buried at sea. He had fallen ill while living in Calcutta, India, and died while on his way home to England to convalesce. How truly pitiful! In the morning, A great wind blew from the west, and

5. Nakai Hiroshi, *Seiyō kikō: Kōkai shinsetsu*, in *Meiji bunka zenshū*, vol. 16, Yoshino Sakuzō, ed. (Tokyo: Nihon hyōronsha, 1928) p. 281.

    For the translation of this and all other poetry, I have not attempted to recreate the prosody of the original poem, for fear that forcing the poems to have appropriate alliteration and rhyme in English would alter them too far beyond their original forms in Chinese or Japanese.

6. Nakai, *Seiyō kikō: Kōkai shinsetsu*, p. 281. Commentary and gloss for this poem is found in Kawaguchi Hisao, comp., *Bakumatsu Meiji kaigai taiken shishū* (Tokyo: Daitō bunka daigaku tōyō kenkyūjo, 1984), p. 38. The "three mountains" are the fictitious Peng Lai, Wan Zhang and Ying Zhou. The "five peaks" are Dong Yue Tai Shan, Xi Yue Hua Shan, Nan Yue Heng Shan, Bei Yue Heng Shan, and Zhong Yue Gao Shan.

waves angrily pounded against the deck; it was as if we had
run into a sudden storm. I do not enjoy ships.[7]

Such is the nature of most entries in the first half of the travelogue.
The hardships on board accentuate the pathos of life. The tragedy of
the Englishman's demise so far from home is reminiscent of that
expressed in the poetry of the *Collection of Myriad Leaves*, in which
many poets lament the pitiful situation of those whose corpses are
left at the side of the road, far from home.[8] The environment of the
ship was initially foreign and at times unpleasant, but it remained the
same throughout the journey, so that by the end of the trip, it provided the author with an environment free of the sorts of political,
social, and cultural distractions that awaited him on land in England
and France.

On land in Southeast Asia, the culture and customs were unfamiliar but the flora and fauna were still commonplace to the Japanese traveler, and had a place in his comments, as in the following
passage from Singapore:

Second Day of the Month.

At dawn, we anchored in front of the British Coal Company.
The coast adjoining Singapore for a mile in either direction
is like that of Bakan and Chinzei [in Japan]. The hills are
not high, and in the level distance grow green grasses. The
people of this land are mostly dark, and wear red and white
kerchiefs on their heads. They wear yard-lengths of cotton
cloth [on their torso] and wrap another piece of cotton cloth
around their waist, and go about bare-footed. There are
many British, and many Chinese coming and going. I went
to the Port of Singapore in a horse cart I shared with a
Briton, and that seemed to fly through the air. In the port,
there was a church. It was extremely grand. I ate lunch with
the Briton, and toured about in the horse cart. At dusk, I
returned to the steamer. There is a French ship anchored
here that carries a number of Shogunate officials. We depart
at sundown. A small boat with tens of boys aboard came
alongside our ship; the passengers threw silver coins, which

7. Nakai, *Seiyō kikō: Kōkai shinsetsu*, p. 289.
8. See poems 220–22; 415; 434; 1800; and 3339–43 in the *Man'yōshū* for examples of poetry
   on roadside corpses.

sunk to the bottom, and the boys dove to retrieve them. The
earth is red here, and among the many trees are banana,
palm, and another that extends a stick, like a betelnut tree
does. There are barracks for "black soldiers." They guard
against the vicissitudes of the Asian sea.[9]

Certainly this account differs from one of the Japanese countryside,
but there is still an assumption that the reader knows what banana
trees are, what the Chinese look like, and the basics of Western-style
architecture.

Nakai gives more consideration to Southeast Asia than to South
Asia, and almost no mention is made of the journey from the Suez
Canal through the Mediterranean. By then, familiar landscapes and
histories were no longer available to the author; the unfamiliarity left
him unable to evoke the poetic muse. The Chinese poetry in the first
half of *A Journey West* focuses on nature, history, and the visual images
before the passenger—waves, sky, exhaust smoke, etc. But by the time
the ship reached the Gulf of Arabia, Nakai was so distanced from the
familiar that most of the stock poetic images were no longer service-
able. It was difficult to make the poetic transition that his environment demanded, and he seems happiest when he can, at least
temporarily, block out the foreign world:

> Here we are, surrounded by the Sea of Arabia
> The continent of Africa is lost in the fog.
> My body feels as if far away in the blue sky,
> As the migratory wild geese, who entrust themselves to the
>   flock.[10]

The fogbound ship is blissfully separated from the unfamiliar by the
enveloping mist, leaving Nakai with the opportunity to dream of himself in another place or state. Nakai uses the foreign names "Arabia"
and "Africa" in the first two lines, and then in the third and fourth
lines, he evokes a familiar image from *Zhuangzi*—the migratory *peng*
bird symbolic of transcendental bliss. One critic notes that the use of
the place names emphasizes the exotic nature of the locale, and that

9. Nakai, *Seiyō kikō: Kōkai shinsetsu*, pp. 282–83.
10. Nakai, *Seiyō kikō: Kōkai shinsetsu*, p. 286. See also Kawaguchi Hisao, comp., *Bakumatsu Meiji
    kaigai taiken shishū* (Tokyo: Daitō bunka daigaku tōyō kenkyūjō, 1984), p. 46.

the travelogue was not written, as so many domestic travel guides of the Tokugawa period were, by someone sitting comfortably at his desk, but rather by the true traveler on the road.[11]

Once Nakai arrives in England, his writing changes dramatically. No longer does he express himself in poetry—the only poem in this part is one he wrote while in Singapore—or see the beauty of nature around him. Suddenly he centers his narrative on the nature of civilization, on what he views as right and wrong, and on the new technological advancements that he saw for the first time. This change is jarring, because it is so abrupt and parallels the drastic change from ship-board life to life on land. Initially, Nakai was more interested in reflecting on the East than the West. He sees the portrait of Lin Cexu (1785–1850) in a London gallery next to the portraits of such great leaders as Bismarck, Napoleon I, Peter the Great, and George Washington, and he explains Lin's role in resisting the British in Guangdong, China, adding that he admires Lin's efforts. The other great leaders get no further commentary. Nakai also comments at length on rectitude and evil, in the context of Confucianism and other traditional ideas. But even this focus is no match for the sensory overload Nakai must have experienced in Europe. After a while, his commentary is abandoned.

The last part of A Journey West, which recounts diurnal events in London, focuses on who went where to visit whom. Nakai was visited by Sugiura Kōzō, aka Hatakeyama Yoshinari (1843–76), a Ministry of Education official who had arrived in England in May of 1865 and subsequently enrolled in the University of London to study a variety of disciplines. Nakai also toured about with a number of other Japanese residents, many of whom are only identified by their surnames. These men undoubtedly served as a source of information on England, and helped Nakai understand his surroundings.

The remainder of the travelogue covers Nakai's further movements, but with little reflection on that which he saw as a result. He seems distrustful of the West and disinterested in what pleasures it has to offer. In one of the final passages, he tells us that the source of the epidemic of syphilis in China at the time had been revealed to him: it had been spread by Europeans to the four corners of the earth

11. Kawaguchi, *Bakumatsu Meiji kaigai taiken shishū*, p. 46.

after they themselves had spread it amongst themselves as a result of wars and pillaging in the Middle Ages. He is silent about the source of this "knowledge" but asserts its veracity. It is an unpleasant picture of the West that he presents, but it is on that note that *A Journey West* abruptly ends, with a quick authorial disclaimer about the quality of a work written ostensibly to calm the author's soul while at sea for the homeward voyage.

Nakai returned to Japan in 1867, and in 1870, he went to his home town of Kagoshima. Later, through the kind offices of Kirino Toshiaki (1838–77), a Satsuma *han* official, he went to Tokyo as an accounting attaché to the military. In May of 1872, he was headed toward becoming a fourth-class official in the government, but in July, he changed his mind and became a legation secretary. From 1874 to 1876, he worked as a secretary in the Japanese legation in Britain, and then he traveled through France, Germany, Russia, and Turkey. In 1878, he published another travelogue about his experiences there, entitled *Setting Off on a Tour*.[12] Unlike *A Journey West: A New Discourse on a Voyage*, *Setting Off on a Tour* was a serious publication that carried prefatory remarks by such notables as Itō Hirobumi, (1841–1909), Ōkubo Toshimichi (1830–78), Nakamura Masanao (1832–91), Narushima Ryūhoku (1837–84), and Yoda Gakkai (1823–1909). Like *A Journey West: A New Discourse on a Voyage*, the first two parts of this work are written in a diary format and follow the author's journey in a chronological fashion. The third part is a collection of miscellany, in a loose chronological order, that covers not only Europe but the Americas as well. Here, too, Nakai composed in a mixture of Japanese prose and Chinese poetry.

Setting Off on a Tour begins with a description of the author's send-off in Liverpool England. Like Ki no Tsurayuki in *Tosa Diary*, Bashō in *Narrow Road to the Deep North*, and countless other travel writers before him, Nakai chose to begin his travelogue before his departure, telling of his planned itinerary—the route would take him through Russia, across the Black Sea, to Constantinople, Greece, Egypt, India, and China—and the colleagues who came to the train station to bid him farewell. Once en route, he describes his movements, what he

---

12. The title is a play on words: the word *kitei* ("setting off on a journey"), normally written with a first character that means "occurance," is written with a first character that means "record," to imply a written record.

sees, and whom he meets, but quickly seems to realize that his narrative will mean nothing to the reader without the historical and cultural background of the places visited.

At first this information is given in small portions. When he crosses an iron bridge over the Neman River near the Russian border, for example, he notes casually that on June 24, 1807, Napoleon I and the Russian Czar met on a raft on said same river and shook hands to show "friendship." Actually, this off-hand remark refers to the signing of the treaties of Tilsit that ended the War of the Third Coalition and in which Russia, Prussia, and Austria were defeated, giving Napoleon I almost complete control over Europe. The Russian Czar, Alexander I, met with Napoleon I on a raft on the Neman to negotiate this treaty, one that ultimately ceded control of territory to France. In other words, there was a much larger story behind the meeting on the Neman River, but Nakai omits it, despite the fact that all but the most educated Meiji audience would be unfamiliar with the events of the Napoleonic Wars and may have found further information helpful if not interesting. Later in the same paragraph, Nakai describes the French advance on and occupation of Moscow in 1812, a move that would end in disaster for Napoleon I, who lost thousands of soldiers before escaping a surrounding enemy and retreating back to French territory. Nakai mentions this, he tells us, because there is

House where Napoleon lived on the Neman River

a historical marker in Kaunas, upon which is briefly engraved the historical significance of the place.[13]

His casual references to the Napoleonic wars are puzzling in their brevity. One wonders: given Nakai's lack of foreign-language ability and the long history of Europe virtually unknown in Japan until the Meiji Restoration, is the information he provides here terse not because the author can assume a common understanding among his audience, but because he himself can offer no information beyond the short explanations gleaned from historical markers or a guide's passing remark? In either case, however, references of historical significance are important first steps; Nakai was breaking ground for foreign travel writing, even if the impressions he recorded were rehashed histories and not flavored by his own impressions. Compared to the bewildered descriptions of Western technology found in the travelogues of Nakahama and Hamada, Nakai's text shows an acceptance of and interest in the West that goes beyond such magical items as the telegraph and railroad.

In his poetry, also, he alludes to famous places and events that transpired there. He notes that these events are recorded in European epic histories, so he cannot be credited with originality, but by putting these events in a poetic form, he perpetuates their legendary quality. For example, while in Russia, he composed the following two poems on Peter the Great (1672–1725):

> His authority and force was known in his time throughout the
> world,
> His tyranny ruled, and all he wanted was in the palm of his
> hand.
> Even for such a hero, there are those who skillfully carve his
> image
> Even now, there are hand-made boats in that ancient house.

> The weak can control the strong, and the soft can defeat the
> hard
> His plan was a great work; it was not to eliminate the common
> man,

13. Nakai Hiroshi, *Man'yū kitei*, in *Meiji bunka zenshū*, vol. 16, Yoshino Sakuzō, ed. (Tokyo: Nihon hyōronsha, 1928), p. 305.

But to put the poor houses within the castle walls,
Where the old and young will burn incense for the soul of their
    great king.[14]

The poems elucidate the character of Peter the Great: he was a great ruler, and his memory has been perpetuated as such in the West. Furthermore, Nakai tells us that he and his traveling companions composed these poems after having visited the czar's palace; these men reflected on the history and meaning of the sights they had seen, simultaneously celebrating it in verse and disseminating the significance of the moment to the reader. To round out the experience, two more poems are written that reflect the physical appearance of the palace:

Rays of sunlight shine bright gold light upon the tower,
We arrive before Peter's tomb in the morning snow,
Generations of czars' sarcophagi have lain peaceful in these halls,
How the world has changed in two hundred years!

The czar's palace soars beyond the river
In the forbidden summer gardens snow flurries about
The river ice is thick, and is flat as a plain
We rode our sledges across it to visit the czar's palace.[15]

Omitted are the mundane observations of mirrors, furniture, linens, and the like found in earlier travelogues of the palaces of Europe. Nakai and his companions had come to see the historical places of Europe, to imagine history unfolding before their eyes. They were familiar enough with Western culture by this point to admire refined exhibitions of it instead of criticize it at every turn.

Clearly Nakai and his companions had a feel for the history of Europe, and what sort of civilized place it was. However, this preconception was occasionally met with discordant images, as Nakai comments in a poem written on the train to Kiev after having toured the Kremlin in Moscow:

14. Nakai, *Man'yū kitei*, p. 306. See also Kawaguchi, *Bakumatsu Meiji kaigai taiken shishū*, pp. 64–65.
15. Nakai, *Man'yū kitei*, p. 306. See also Kawaguchi, *Bakumatsu Meiji kaigai taiken shishū*, pp. 62–63.

I travel a thousand miles by night and day to the hinterlands
The moon floats along across the vast barren fields
If not for the Caucasians living all along the route,
Who would know that this place is Europe?[16]

For Europe was a place of imposing architecture, bustling cities, artificial lights, telegraph wires, and steam trains, not a wasteland of uncultivated fields. Nakai denies Europe the possibility of having unique or inspiring natural sights; he closes his eyes to them and refuses to see the latent beauty of the untamed landscape. The remainder of his poetry is on themes of civilization, including European literature, archeological sights, and the railroad.

All of this emphasizes that Nakai's motive on this journey was to visit places in Europe that were famous for their role in political, not natural, history. Unlike Japanese "famous places," these locales are not noted for their natural elements—flowers, trees, birds, mountains, etc.—but rather for human events that transpired there. Kronštadt is noted for its strategic military position between Russia and Finland and its batteries; Odessa is noted for being attacked by British and French troops during the Crimean war; Greece is noted as the seat of Western civilization and the home of Homer. When Nakai describes the physical appearance of Odessa, he tells us that there is a railroad near the port, that the roads are paved with stone and lined with trees like those in Paris, and that there are innumerable masts in the harbor, visible against the vast horizon.[17] Not another word is said of the natural landscape.

Nakai was intent on becoming familiar with Europe, with seeing beyond the surface of cultural prosperity. He writes:

> [Japanese] travelers who pass through Europe arbitrarily travel to those regions where the grasses are lush and the songs thick, and thus return home discouraged and dazzled, and speak, charmed, of the good and beauty they saw. If one contemplates and deliberates, and journeys about each state in Europe, then for the first time one will necessarily wake from the dream of prosperity and experience many deep emotions.[18]

16. Nakai, *Man'yū kitei*, p. 308. See also Kawaguchi, *Bakumatsu Meiji kaigai taiken shishū*, p. 69.
17. Nakai, *Man'yū kitei*, p. 309.
18. Nakai, *Man'yū kitei*, p. 311.

He goes on to discuss the power structure of European states. The operative word here is *discuss*; whereas most of Nakai's peers *described* the political structures of the West, Nakai interprets them in a more thoughtful manner. He dedicates much thought to the political problems that arose with the fall of the Ottoman Empire, going so far as to enumerate events in an organized fashion for the unfamiliar Japanese reader.[19] He was particularly concerned with the British acquisition of control over the Suez Canal Company in 1875, which he describes in such detail as to include the number of shares involved in the takeover.

Nakai is usually an impartial observer; he has no illusions of grandeur, and clearly has awakened from his own "dream of prosperity" when he describes conditions in Turkey:

> Walking is difficult due to small stones loose in the road. Moreover, mud sinks into our shoes. The people's houses are all made of wood, and one can see stone roofs between them. Most are unclean and foul smelling. Men in red hats mill about in the streets, and along with howling dogs hamper visitors' progress. Beggars stand at the side of the street and beseech visitors for money. One look at that filthy state and one cannot but flee. I was surprised at the outer beauty of this place, which I gazed at from the sea, and now I am surprised and disappointed at this filth and uncleanliness.[20]

Here Nakai hints at the disdain that many Japanese travelers had for the lesser European powers. Although England was not a pristine land, it was cleaner than Turkey, and Nakai held British standards, despite the fact that a mere two decades earlier his own country lacked the modern conveniences that he now took for granted. Moreover, Nakai's attitude toward Turkey—that its outward appearance was attractive but that below the surface it lost its charm—echoes the earlier passage on Japanese travelers abroad. He was disappointed in much that he found but insisted on digging nonetheless.

The narrative is absent of banal comments on Western culture—we are spared a discussion of eating utensils, for example—for Nakai distinguishes himself from those "arbitrary" visitors awed by what they

19. Nakai, *Man'yū kitei*, pp. 320–21.
20. Nakai, *Man'yū kitei*, p. 313.

see. The West, he tells his compatriots, is scrutable. In some passages, Nakai is gently didactic by using the adjective "famous" before proper names, driving home to the reader that the subject is a potential "famous place" or famous person. In almost all cases, after distinguishing a place or a person as "famous," Nakai goes on to explain the source of fame, such as in the case of Ferdinand Marie Lesseps (1805–94), the Frenchman responsible for the building of the Suez Canal, the commercially successful Rothschild Family of England, and the fourteen-kilometer-long Mont Cenis tunnel, completed in 1871, that runs between Italy and France.[21]

In comparison, one can say that *Setting off on a Tour* is a more informative travelogue than *A Journey West* and provided its contemporary audience with a wealth of information about the West. In some cases, where Nakai refers to some significant item without explanation, interlinear text provides additional information, as in the case of Mohammed (the interlinear text notes mistakenly that he is the God of Islam) and Paris (the text notes that it is in France).[22] In essence, Nakai was establishing famous places and persons on two levels; he alludes to historically famous entities—those with which Westerners would also be fully familiar as part of their cultural idiom, such as Paris and Mohammed—and also to contemporarily famous entities, such as Lesseps and the Mont Cenis tunnel, urging upon the Japanese reader the importance of both sets.

This awareness of contemporary events and accomplishments is noteworthy because it is absent in so many other travelogues. Japanese travelers are strangely selectively aware of such events. For example, no mention is given in any of the travelogues examined here of the American Civil War, even though it prevented shogunal missions after 1860 and certainly had a profound effect on the world. There are two ways of looking at this blindness toward the contemporary: on the one hand, one could criticize the writers for being ignorant, for not reading newspapers and other accounts of the affairs of the day, for depending on strange, subjective sources and first impressions

21. Nakai, *Man'yū kitei*, pp. 323, 319, and 321, respectively. The tunnel under Mt. Cenis is particularly pertinent, as that mountainous passage was notoriously difficult and had been described by many a traveler on the Grand Tour a century earlier as an arduous journey. See Jeremy Black, *The British and the Grand Tour* (London: Croom Helm, 1985), pp. 20–21, for excerpts of British travelogues concerning Mt. Cenis.
22. Nakai, *Man'yū kitei*, pp. 314 and 322, respectively.

in their descriptions of the West. On the other hand, one may say that writers who focus on the past and not the present are simply following the *kikōbungaku* tradition.

Ki no Tsurayuki is, for example, not much interested in the country folk along the way from Tosa to the capital, although he does cite some of their poems. Nor is the nun Abutsu (in *The Diary of the Waning Moon*) interested in the local people along her journey. Bashō gives passing mention to a few individuals—an orphaned child, some prostitutes—but they were likely fictionalized and not representative of place. For traditional *kikōbungaku* writers, contemporary events and people of place were irrelevant. The point of traveling and writing was to experience the beauty of the natural landscape, a private nostalgia, and a sense of the old and familiar. The trick for Nakai, who wanted to write of both the historically established and contemporarily dynamic events of the day, was to impress upon his audience the difference between the two, because for them it was *all* new. For this modern Western reader, the differentiation is not difficult to discern, but for the contemporary Japanese reader, one cannot help but suspect that past and present blended into a confusing pastiche.

Indicative of the novelty to the Japanese of all these subjects, both old and new, is the lack of codified terminology and orthographic representation. In an age when foreign terminology was being imported into the Japanese language at a dizzying rate, it was common for one entity to have multiple "names," the choice of which was left to authorial prerogative. For example, "Paris" is alternately written in two different ways in this work. Nakai used *katakana* phonetics to write the names of lesser known entities, such as Lake Erie, the Place de Concorde, the River Thames, and the Louvre, but the lack of consistency could only further frustrate a studious reader.

The third section of *Setting Off on a Tour* covers both Europe and the United States. Section titles indicate the subject matter: "London," "Assorted Poems on London," "Assorted Poems on Paris," "Assorted Poems on the Environs of Paris," "The Bamboo Sticks of Paris," "Assorted Poems on Switzerland," "Switzerland," "Entering Italy," "Bavaria," "Napoleon I," "On the Road from New York to San Francisco," "Niagara: The World's Premier Waterfall," "Three Assorted Poems on the Americas," "San Francisco," "The Pacific Ocean," "A Short Biography of Julius Caesar," and "Miscellany on the Environs of London." The entire section covers a mere fourteen pages. Most subsections begin with a Chinese poem, followed by explanatory commentary. It is geographically focused, leading the reader through various locales, noting their physical features (with the exceptions of the "Short Biography" and the "Miscellany"). It is the most complimentary of the three sections. The opening passage is representative:

> London
>
> I escaped the heat in the gardens, where the sun hung low
> in the sky
> On this outing I rode a light carriage pulled by a stout horse
> The poet dissipates in the purity
> Of viewing the flowers at the Crystal Palace

The Crystal Palace is located in the suburbs about three and a half *li* south of the city. It is built on the old exhibition site, and has a main hall that is two hundred seventy and a half *ken* long, thirty three *ken* and three *shaku* tall, and is structured entirely out of iron pillars and eaves covered with glass. Inside are arranged goods from every country—unique famous stone sculptures from each land and models of ancient architecture. Trees and flowers from each country are cultivated, their verdant leaves open in the sun, their flowers tempting the nose. Outside are fountains and reservoirs

Crystal Palace daguerreotype

where geese swim about and fish jump splashing in the water.
Inside there is nothing that the various shops and tea rooms
do not provide. I feel that perhaps the saintly paradise could
not hold a candle to this.[23]

Nakai is enamored of the Crystal Palace and its offerings, to the
point of making superlative comments. In later poems, he notes the
beauty of the urban landscape in London and Paris, finding the glow
of gas street lights appealing amidst the mist and fog. He admires the
opulence of the wealthy, he celebrates the verdancy of the city parks,
and he is moved by the sight of Mt. Blanc in Switzerland. Indeed, his
poetic response to the Swiss countryside is flavored with a latent pathos:

> The sun moves on after a time
>
> The railway winds through the rocky cliffs like a thread
>
> I have come visiting to this lakeside villa
>
> Where the spring snows from Mt. Blanc blow through the
> blinds.[24]

Mont Blanc

23. Nakai , *Man'yū kitei*, p. 331. See also Kawaguchi, *Bakumatsu Meiji kaigai taiken shishū*, p. 90.
24. Nakai , *Man'yū kitei*, p. 332. See also Kawaguchi, *Bakumatsu Meiji kaigai taiken shishū*, p. 96.

Here for the first time Nakai appreciates the beauty of Nature in Europe and leaves political commentary off to the side. The blowing spring snows emphasize the desolate yet beautiful scene, far away from the hustle and bustle of the city. But the image could easily be from indigenous or Chinese poetry—indeed the final line of the poem, "Where the spring snows from Mt. Blanc blow through the blinds" is reminiscent of a line from a poem by the Tang poet Du Fu (712–70): "This window holds the snow that for a thousand years has capped the Western Mountains."[25]

The poem he writes on his journey from New York to San Francisco laments the hardship of the trip, in much the same voice as many of the poems in *A Collection of Myriad Leaves*, written by forlorn travelers:

> My wife and children cannot know the hardship of my journey
> I have crossed waters, traversed fields, and climbed over
>   mountains
> The European Continent is off in the far distance
> These seven days and nights riding the train, bathed by wind and
>   moonlight[26]

Nakai paints a lonely picture of himself, enduring the tedium and loneliness of travel (*ryojō*). No matter that he traveled in relative comfort aboard swift trains that brought him from coast to coast in the span of a week, or that the rail line was a recent feat of modernization (the transcontinental railroad was only finished in 1869). He is true to the conventions of *kikōbungaku* in *Setting Off On a Tour*: travel is an occasion to experience certain emotions, not an occasion to explore *terra incognita*.

Was this approach to travel writing remarkable? It would seem so: much more typical of the early Meiji *kenbunroku* genre was that of Nomura Fumio, who was an astute observer but incapable of the lyricism of Nakai.

---

25. As noted in *Bakumatsu Meiji kaigai taiken shishū* the original line from Du Fu is 窗含西嶺
千秋雪. Nakai's line is 白山春雪入簾来.
26. Nakai, *Man'yū kitei*, p. 335. See also Kawaguchi, *Bakumatsu Meiji kaigai taiken shishū*,
pp. 105–6.

Nomura Fumio

Nomura Fumio, aka Murata Fumio, was a newspaper reporter from Hiroshima who left Japan for England in 1864 and remained there until 1868. When he returned to Japan he did so via the United States, and thus made a complete circumnavigation of the globe. Before leaving on his journey, he had studied "Dutch learning" in Ōsaka and "English Learning" in Nagasaki. While in England, he studied Western technology, and after returning to Japan he taught "Western Learning for his *han*, the same organization that had sponsored his trip abroad. Nomura, a keen observer of the West, recorded what he saw in detail in his work *A Record of Things Seen and Heard in the West*, published in 1869.[27] This work is a deliberative record, primarily of England but touching on other parts of the West; it begins with the climate and geography, moves on to government, and includes an exhaustive list of topics, including education, medicine, religion, architecture, cuisine, and shipbuilding. Nomura tried to give the reader an impartial report on the West. He was also meticulous in his record-keeping, which results in a much longer work than Nakai's, approximately twice again as long. There is no poetry, and the prose is flat and objective, without a hint of the author's opinion in all but a few places. Nomura's interests are revealed, however, by the items he chooses to mention. He tells of the high standard of living in Britain, of the ice houses that provided ice in the height of the summer heat, and of the vessels used for food and cooking—in sum, the sorts of things Nakai criticizes Japanese for being "dazzled" by. Indeed, Nomura rarely sees anything he dislikes, and even when he does, he finds something sanguine to say about it. In an uncharacteristically editorial passage, he repeats the old canard that everything in the West is the opposite of that in the East.[28] He gives as examples vertical versus horizontal writing, beginning books from the left side versus

---

27. This work was originally published by Tenminkan in two volumes. It was reprinted, in a photostat copy of the original manuscript, in 1987 by Yumani shobō in the series titled *Meiji Ōbei kenbunroku shūsei*, vol. 1.

28. This canard dates back to Father Luis Frois' treatise of 1585, "Contradictions and Differences of Custom Between the People of Europe and This Province of Japan," in which he noted such opposites as, "We pick our noses with our thumb or index finger; the Japanese use their little finger because their nostrils are small." It was repeated through the ages by Western scholars of Japan, including Basil Hall Chamberlain (1850–1935), Ruth Benedict (1887–1948), and Rutherford Alcock (1809–97), who observed in 1863 that "Japan is essentially a country of paradoxes and anomalies, where all, even familiar things, put

the right, putting ladies first versus not, the significance of wearing black versus white in each culture, the usage of posthumous names, etc. Nonetheless, Nomura states that Japan and the West have many similarities too: he mentions the children's game "Blind Man's Bluff," equating it with its Japanese counterpart, *kakurenbo*. He notes that although the British often call the Japanese "Chinese" upon sight, his own countrymen were guilty of the same sort of error when they called all foreigners in Edo "American" or all foreigners in Nagasaki "Dutch." Clearly the four years spent overseas helped Nomura see the folly of man as a whole.

Undoubtedly due in part to the earlier publication date of this work as compared to *Setting Off On a Tour*, Nomura assumes little prior knowledge on the readers' parts. If a place is introduced, its significance (or at least its location) is clearly explained. Nomura tells us that Windsor Castle is

> . . . eleven Western miles distant from London, was constructed by William the Conqueror, added to by Henry I and Henry II, and has been the home of successive generations of monarchs of England. If one wants to take a look at this castle, one must go to London, get a ticket, and go; there one will be able to look around at all the rooms, save those used inhabited by the royal family. There are approximately 80 *ken* of hallways, and a tower of 30 *ken* in circumference. Inside are hung famous paintings of old and new, and it is most beautiful and gallant. There is an armory, in which a veritable forest of weapons of old and new are lined up in rows. The air of the place is profound and remote. There is a garden, in which flowers and vegetables are grown.[29]

Similarly detailed descriptions are given for the Parliament building, London Tower, St. Paul's Cathedral, and Buckingham Palace.

---

on new faces and are curiously reversed. Except that they do not walk on their heads instead of their feet, there are few things in which they do not seem, by some occult law, to have been impelled in a perfectly opposite direction and a reversed order" (Rutherford Alcock, *The Capital of the Tycoon: A Narrative of a Three Years' Residence in Japan* [New York: Bradley, 1863], vol. 1, p. 357). My thanks to Henry Smith at Columbia University for the lineage of this idea.

29. Murata Fumio, *Seiyō kenbunroku*, in *Meiji Ōbei kenbunroku shūsei*, vol. 1. (Tokyo: Yumani shobō, 1869, 1987), pp. 135–36. Page numbers refer to those of the Yumani reprint, not the original. A *ken* is approximately 1.82 meters.

Nomura, in contrast to Nakai, is more concerned with the present than the past, and with physical characteristics more than human events. Like Nakai's manuscript, Nomura's work has interlinear text that gives the uninformed reader enough information to understand the significance of place; it tells us that the Canary Islands form an archipelago in the "African Sea," and that Gibraltar is located in the sea between land.[30] Everyday items are afforded the same sort of annotation: we are told that "piano" is the name of a harp, a "coffee house" is where morning tea and sweets are taken, a "dining room" is for the afternoon meal, and a "supper room" is for the evening meal.[31] Nomura's editors were more sensitive to reader context than Nakai's, hence the inclusion of this information. Their contribution also indicates that the authorial and editorial intent in this case was more geared toward the dissemination of pragmatic information than the expression of emotional responses to travel.

Some portions of *A Record of Things Seen and Heard in the West* read more like an almanac than a travelogue, such as the list of offices in the British government and the current listing of all members of the British monarchy, as well as the appendix to the work that lists all the countries of the world and their type of government, capitals, area, population, and products. Overall, the reader concerned with travel literature must search long and hard through Nomura's work to find the poesy of Nakai's travelogues, and even then he will undoubtedly be disappointed. Nomura stands between the ship-wrecked sailors of the 1850s and the literary travelers of the 1870s; he certainly recorded information about the West in a more infor-mative fashion than Nakahama or Hamada, but he was prevented from literary musings by the still foreign nature of his subject matter.

Why even look at Nomura's travelogue, then? Put plainly, it is rep-resentative of most travelogues of this period. The other works included in this chapter are largely exceptions to the rule. Truly aes-thetically sensitive travel writing was not easily adaptable, and as a result, it experienced a hiatus when the Japanese first went overseas.

---

30. Murata, *Seiyō kenbunroku*, pp. 117 and 122, respectively.
31. Murata, *Seiyō kenbunroku*, pp. 112 and 203, respectively. It should be noted that the great-
    est incidence of interlinear text are notes on conversions of weights, measures, and
    currencies.

Behind Nomura stand dozens of other similar works, works that sadly have little lyricism in them.

Shibusawa Eiichi

Shibusawa Eiichi, one of the luminaries of the Meiji industrial revolution, traveled in France 1867–68 under the sponsorship of the shogunate. Shibusawa wrote three travelogues of this journey: *Diary of a Westward Voyage, Diary of the Imperial Residence in Paris,* and *Record of the Imperial Tour.*[32] As the latter two titles indicate, Shibusawa's official capacity on this journey was more than that of a mere exchange student; he was one of the representatives of the sixth and last official missions sent to the West by the Tokugawa shogunate. This mission marked the shogunate's participation in the Paris Exposition of 1867; there were also nonshogunal (*han*) participants, notably from the provinces of Satsuma and Hizen. The shogunate's party had over twenty members, many of whom were samurai "who seem to have been chosen for their unrelenting lack of enthusiasm for the West."[33] There are voluminous records of this and prior missions to the West that will be discussed later, but Shibusawa's record stands out in that he was considered a "student" in addition to being a government dignitary; thus his travelogue has less of an official air about it.

The Tokugawa mission was headed by Tokugawa Akitake (1853–1910), whose older brother, Tokugawa Yoshinobu (1837–1913), was the last Tokugawa *shōgun.* Akitake, although only fourteen years old, was accorded the diplomatic favor of a full ambassador. His nominal duties were to represent Japan, but in order to gain a further understanding of the West, his party toured more than just the Paris Exposition. The mission left Yokohama in February 1867, arriving in

32. All three works are included in Shibusawa Eiichi, *Taifutsu nikki,* in *Nihon shiseki kyōkai sōsho,* vol. 126 (Tokyo: Tōkyō daigaku shuppankai, 1928). Sections of *Diary of a Westward Voyage* are translated in *The Autobiography of Shibusawa Eiichi,* Teruko Craig, trans. (Tokyo: University of Tokyo Press, 1994), pp. 152–71. Donald Keene discusses *Diary of a Westward Voyage,* which he translates as *Voyage to the West,* in *Modern Japanese Diaries: The Japanese at Home and Abroad as Revealed through Their Diaries* (New York: Henry Holt & Co., 1995), pp. 77–89.

　　Shibusawa also wrote another travelogue of the West, entitled *Ōbei kikō,* but this was published much later in 1903.

33. W. G. Beasley, *Japan Encounters the Barbarian: Japanese Travelers in America and Europe* (New Haven: Yale University Press, 1995), p. 115.

Paris two months later. They toured Switzerland, Holland, Belgium, Italy, Malta, and Britain, and ended their peregrination of Europe in December of the same year. Of the three travelogues mentioned above, *Diary of a Westward Voyage* has received more attention than the others. *Diary of the Imperial Residence in Paris* is more of an official record of the mission than it is a personal diary, and *Record of the Imperial Tour* is essentially a redundant version of the events recorded in *Diary of a Westward Voyage*.[34]

Diary of a Westward Voyage was a compilation after the fact; Shibusawa, at the urging of his friend, Date Munenari (1818–92), compiled and edited memoranda from his diary and published them in 1870. A third party, Sugiura Aizō (1835–77), a manager of the foreign magistrate, assisted Shibusawa, although to what extent is unclear.[35] (Shibusawa did not have a scholar's training, so the editing of his diary was perhaps prudent.) The work is written entirely in prose—no poetry—and in a diary format, with daily headers for each entry. What is remarkable about *Diary of a Westward Voyage* is its celebration of quotidian events and details; Shibusawa focuses on those things most noteworthy to an entrepreneur such as himself. What fascinates him about his surroundings is the dynamism of places undergoing rapid change and the excitement of being in such a place at such a time. He shows none of the reflective pathos of Nakai, nor does he follow a methodical presentation like Nomura.

Diary of a Westward Voyage begins with the departure of Akitake's company from Yokohama. Shibusawa describes the French ship *Alphée* in detail, focusing particularly on the cuisine (Western and thus a novelty to him) and service, which impressed him greatly. Perhaps

34. The official record of this trip is *Tokugawa Akitake tai-Ō kiroku*, in *Nihon shiseki kyōkai sōsho*, vols. 146–48 (Tokyo: Tōkyō daigaku shuppankai, 1932). Beasley notes that this record "needs to be supplemented by the journals kept officially and privately by Shibusawa Eiichi while in Europe" (Beasley, *Japan Encounters the Barbarian*, p. 237, n. 6). One more record of the trip is found in *Kawakatsu ke monjo*, in *Nihon shiseki kyōkai sōsho*, vol. 57 (Tokyo: Tōkyō daigaku shuppankai, 1930). Kurimoto Jōun's (1822–97) works *Enpitsu kibun* and *Gyōsō tsuiroku*, later published together with other miscellany under the title *Hōan jisshu* (Kurimoto Jōun, *Hōan jisshu*, in Narushima Ryūhoku, Hattori Bushō, Kurimoto Jōun shū, in *Meiji bungaku zenshū*, vol. 4 (Tokyo: Chikuma shobō, 1969), are also a result of this trip.
35. Keene notes that the work is ". . . based on the notes Shibusawa took on his journey, but he had the literary assistance of Sugiura Aizō. It is unclear which man was responsible for individual sections of the diary." Onishi Shirō also mentions that Sugiura Aizō contributed his efforts to Shibusawa's work. (See Keene, *Modern Japanese Diaries*, pp. 87–88, n. 1, and Onishi Shirō, "Kaidai," in *Taifutsu nikki*, p. 496.)

as a result of posh surroundings on the high seas, the hustle and bustle of Shanghai was distasteful to Shibusawa. His descriptions of the crowded streets, poor sanitation, and veritable animal-like quality of the Chinese show both a contempt for his fellow Asians and a certain vivification in response to the tumult of human activity around him. Coming from a culture in which commerce was viewed as the work of the (socially, not economically) lowest class, Shibusawa's mind was naturally surprised and stimulated by the frenetic nature of commercial Shanghai. Occasionally he makes reference to traditional imagery associated with place, as when, at the mouth of the Yangtze River, he notes that the scene reminds him of a scene from classical Chinese literature in which fish from the Yangtze are offered.[36] However, these allusions are rare; in China, Shibusawa found more inspiration in the modernizing influence of the West than in the vestiges of a past, great civilization. He writes,

> China is an old country of renown. No country of Europe or Asia, even in olden times, could match China in breadth, population, fertility of the soil or richness of products. However . . . it has fallen behind in this age of world advancement.[37]

After Shanghai, the entourage continued on to Hong Kong, Saigon, Singapore, Ceylon, and through the Suez Canal, arriving in the Mediterranean Sea. Once in Europe, Nomura's narrative covers a variety of subjects, including museums, such as the Louvre and the Tuileries, the Bois de Boulogne—where he spent much time in recreation—political events of the day—he gives a lengthy description of the attack on the Russian czar by a Pole—hospitals, morgues, newspapers, military arms, national currencies, oil painting, etc.

At first glance, Shibusawa appears to record many of the same things that Nomura did. However, whereas Nomura avoids personal comment and provides statistics, Shibusawa gives a richer, more entertaining description of what he sees. Compare the two on the subject of zoological gardens:

36. The reference is apparently to the Chinese work entitled *Sui-Tang jiahua*, although Shibusawa writes the title with a homophonous third character. See *Taifutsu nikki*, p. 6.
37. Shibusawa, *Taifutsu nikki*, p. 10.

Cascade at Bois du Boulougne

This is a most strange looking, vast garden in which animals
are collected for the purpose of animal research. In understanding the reason behind such a place, one must realize that
during the period 1860 to 1861—one calendar year—293,915
people came to see it. This place was originally annexed to
the Animal Research Society, and was established in 1828.
Since that time they have been exhibiting birds, beasts, and
fish from all countries, including many from the tropics of
Africa, India, and New Zealand. For the likes of rhinoceros,
elephants, tigers, leopards, and lions, they have built cages and
view the animals for amusement. As for otters and sea lions,
they have built a large pond into which they have drawn sea
water and thus domesticate the animals. There are many apes,
all of which are placed behind wire nets. There were also beautiful birds that caught the eye, and great beasts that threat-
ened one's being; I can only say that I do not have the time
to mention those strange birds and odd beasts, but they are
wondrous sights of the world. [Nomura][38]

38. Murata, *Seiyō kenbunroku*, pp. 158–59.

On the southern bank of the River Seine there is a large zoological garden. It is much like the previously mentioned botanical garden, except that it holds varieties of lions, tigers, leopards, elephants, jackals, wolves, bears, brown bears, and foxes. The beasts are all kept in iron enclosures. They have a "hippopotamus" that comes from southern Africa, and for which there is no comparison. It is an unsightly aquatic animal. It is large, like an ox, has short, fat legs, and the entire body is hairless. It has skin like a toad's—thick and extremely strong. It has a big mouth, the sort that would come in use at the Gion Festival. It has a head like a lion's. It usually stays in the water, but if a keeper throws some bread, it will come out of the water to eat it. There are also many kinds of vipers, that, all coming from the same region and liking warmth, are put in a box and wrapped in a blanket, all in an enclosure that can not be but a [square] foot. Occasionally, they thrust out their necks and their tongues slither out. There are also varieties of shark. Each and every one is quite beastly. There are skeletons on display of great whales and great snakes, that, it was said, are used as educational tools. [Shibusawa][39]

Nomura tells us which varieties of animals are kept in the zoo, but beyond declaring them "strange" or "beautiful," refrains from expressing his opinions. Shibusawa, holding forth on the appearance of the hippopotamus, is opinionated and comic. Shibusawa clearly had fun at the zoo; Nomura, it would seem, was either overwhelmed and unable to digest all that he had seen, or simply saw the zoo with an impassive eye more suited to describing Parliament than a menagerie of exotic animals, the likes of which he had probably never seen before. Nomura is interested in presenting a clinical depiction, but Shibusawa allows himself the indulgence of noticing small details, details that may not contribute much to the overall description of the item but are of interest to the author. Compare the two authors' description of hospitals:

There are many prosperous hospitals in London. Each illness has its own institution, such as a hospital for the insane, or a hospital for fevers. There are also hospitals for

39. Shibusawa, *Taifutsu nikki*, p. 62. Shibusawa's reference to the "Gion Festival" refers to an annual festival held in Kyoto, Japan.

general illnesses. There are 12 hospitals for general illnesses,
and they have a total of 3,500 beds. The annual number of
patients who receive treatment in the hospital but stay else-
where is approximately 400,000. These hospitals receive
£110,000 (333,000 *ryō*) annually in taxes. These are all
large hospitals. As for small hospitals, it is said that there
are some 30 of those. Total annual revenues for all general
hospitals and penury hospitals is £1,120,000 (3,360,000
ryō). In the winter time, the added expenses of the general
hospitals are approximately £200,00 (360,000 *ryō*). If there
are excessive financial losses due to the cold weather, the
large hospitals often receive building money from rich families and thus build [new buildings]. In the large hospitals,
there are libraries, safes, and lecture halls. Some students
enter this hospital, and every month or every year their abil-
ities are tested and rewarded by the government. All of the
nurses are women, and they are taught nursing by the doc-
tors. They care for the patients and are deliberate in their
nursing.

One of the big hospitals is called Saint Bartholomew's.
It has 650 beds and in one year treats six or seven thousand
patients. Outpatients number 70,000. The cost of drugs
totals approximately £2,600 (7,800 *ryō*).

There is also a hospital called Saint Thomas', that was
built with funds from the bookseller Thomas Guy and the
wealthy merchant Hunt. In that hospital there are statues
and paintings of these two men displayed, and their gra-
ciousness is extolled. The bookseller donated £18,800
(56,400 *ryō*) and also bequeathed £219,500 (658,500 *ryō*).
From the wealthy merchant was received £119,000 (357,000
ryō), and it is said that every year they treat 50 or 60 thousand patients.

There is an annex to the school where there is a hospital in which student patients convalesce. There are 200 beds
there.

There is also a boil clinic. Every year they cure 2 to 3
thousand persons.

There is also a hospital that treats people who are sailors
or whose work is of a maritime nature.

There is also a convalescence ship. This is a discarded
ship that cannot be used in battle. It has been made a military ship and is used as a hospital. It is on the River Thames.
The ship is called the *Dreadnought* hospital. It is a place that
treats sailors from around the world who suffer from illness,

and those ill sailors from all nations number 2 to 3 thousand a year. Except for on Sundays, they always see patients. [Nomura][40]

6th Day of the 5th Month of Keiō [June 8, 1867]

Clear weather. At 1PM went to see a new inn. At 4PM accompanied the prince to see a hospital.

This hospital is next to the city center and is situated on a high, level plot of land, and is surrounded by an iron fence. It is a multi-storey building. It has a guard at the entrance. The rooms are divided by type of patient, and upper and lower classes are separated. Each room has tens of patient beds lined up, and each bed has a number. The linens on the beds are made of white cloth to indicate their cleanliness. The nurses all do the work of nuns. There are plenty of locations that dispense pharmaceuticals and food. There are places where a stream has been installed and one can receive water or bathe. There are steam pipes running beneath the beds that are used in the winter months to warm each room. There is also a darkened room. Here corpses lie on six or seven beds, and each has a wooden board on top of it. The sides are shrouded with cloth, and there is a placard on one side. This placard states the doctor's doubts about any unclear cause of illness in a patient, and on that placard is clearly written the deceased's name, age, and symptoms. As the days pass, necrosis necessarily comes forth from the place where the illness resided in the patient's body, and this is one way of conducting an autopsy. Behind the hospital there is a place for doing laundry. A number of people who go there for that purpose stroll about in the flower garden of the hospital. It is good exercise for the patients to wander about on the grounds. This hospital was built with funds donated to charity by a wealthy widow who lived in the Paris city center, so there is a large photograph of her at the entrance.

Most illnesses are cured by the administering of medicines and recuperation. Medical treatments are initially done in accordance with the practice dictated by medical research, but if there is a suitable method of nursing and recuperation

40. Murata, *Seiyō kenbunroku*, pp. 167–70. A *ryō* is a premodern unit of currency for which there is no easy equivalent. The conversions given are in interlinear text.

that would assist and in turn hasten recovery, then this hospital will follow it as a method of treatment. They are very precise about the propriety and amount of food in a restorative diet, and they measure dryness and humidity, and modulate the air to such a climate as to be suitable for the patients. They also make the patients exercise, which is fitting for recovery. They carry this on until the day when the patient is recovered, and thus learn from the experience. However, the average people stay in their homes and ask for a doctor's care, having their families lovingly nurse them, massage them, and look after their needs, being trusted with all recommendations therein. Perhaps, in these cases, they over eat, or are malnourished, and their care is incorrect, resulting in a lack of spirit and eventually this forces their spirit to exert effort. Consequently, contrary to expectation, there are many people whose illness becomes worse and who blame the physician when they do not become well. This causes everyone do be at quite a loss, and so in this land the ill are always put in the hospital where they receive care and medical attention, and do not die an unnatural death but rather live to the end of their natural lives. [Shibusawa][41]

Both passages are rather prosaic, but they do demonstrate that Shibusawa was more interested in the welfare of the sick, and the rationale for the state of the medical profession and the health care it provided. Nomura seems obsessed with the cost of building and maintaining hospitals but never mentions the care provided patients. In sum, Shibusawa notices human events and accomplishments more often than Nomura. Whether it be grand, such as the tree-lined Champs-Elysées, or small, as in the individual trials of a patient in a hospital, Shibusawa focuses on the human element. Nomura, even when telling us that funds for a hospital were donated by a philanthropist, gives the impression that such an event happened without a human touch.

When it comes to describing the ostensive objective for Akitake's visit to Europe, the Paris Exposition, Shibusawa describes the various displays set up to show different countries' wares, products, and specialties. If he had been in the mind to write a travelogue that established the famous natural characteristics of place, this would have been a prime opportunity; it was the purpose of each country's dis-

41. Shibusawa, *Taifutsu nikki*, pp. 75–77.

play to present those things that distinguished the nation. However, Shibusawa forgoes this chance and instead emphasizes the general: he tells us that there is a hothouse, in which various things are displayed, such as the cultivated plants of each nation, and the strange flowers and plants from the tropics, but his descriptions lack specifics and the objects remain disassociated from any country. Still, the detail with which he describes the technological advancements establishes the West as a place where industry thrives, and thus he conveys that, at least in early Meiji, "modernization" is an *uta makura* for the West.

Nakai, Nomura, and Shibusawa all spent their stints abroad before the Meiji Restoration. After the Restoration, the number of students overseas increased dramatically. In the first seven years of the new era, hundreds of students went abroad to Europe and the United States, sponsored both privately and by the government. As did their predecessors, they went to study the West and to transmit information and technology back home. Upon repatriation, many of them became prominent figures in the new Meiji government. Others became scholars, journalists, and industrialists. A few published works resulting from their experiences, such as translations of foreign works and commentaries on the West.[42]

TRAVELOGUES BY DIPLOMATS

The most prolific group of travelers to the West during the waning years of the Tokugawa Period and the beginning of the Meiji period were

---

42. For example, Iizuka Osamu (1845–1929), a journalist, went to France as an exchange student in 1870 to study law. He arrived in Paris in the midst of the Franco-Prussian war, and gained admittance as a scholar who held highly advanced Social-Democratic views to a well-reputed private school. When Prussian troops surrounded Paris, he fled to Switzerland; he later returned to Paris after the end of the war. As a young man in Japan, Iizuka had studied the Chinese classics under the Confucian scholar Amemori Seisai (1811–82); in Europe, he endeavored to write Chinese poetry on the European landscape and profess the wonders of Tang poetry to the French. He returned to Japan in 1880, where together with Matsuda Masahisa (1845–1914), who had also studied law in France, he established *The Eastern Free News*.

Other post-Restoration students who wrote of their experiences include Shiramine Shunme (1836–1909) and Ii Naoyasu (1851–1935). Shiramine Shunme was a shipbuilder who went to America in 1870 to study his craft at Rutgers University. After he returned to Japan, he published *Strange Sights in Many Countries*. Ii Naoyasu, a politician, went to Europe and the United States in 1872 to observe conditions abroad. After his return to Japan in the following year, he authored *A Tour of Europe and America*.

See the second appendix in Ishizuki, *Kindai Nihon no kaigai ryūgaku shi*, for a complete list of students abroad and works they published.

the diplomats. Several missions were sent to the West both by the shogunate and by the Meiji government, and they have been studied in detail.[43] Many of the members of these missions kept copious notes, and although most travelogues were originally meant for private circulation, they have since been reprinted and distributed widely. The first mission was sent overseas by the shogunate in 1860, and its travels were limited to the United States, where mission members exchanged letters of ratification for a U.S.-Japan treaty.[44] The records of this mission are numerous, and because it was the first Japanese mission to the West, it has received more attention than its successors. The second shogunal mission, headed by the commissioner of foreign affairs, Takenouchi Yasunori (1806–?), was in 1862; this group, which went to Russia, France, England, Portugal, Holland, and Prussia, was charged with assorted duties, particularly observing Western technological advancements with the aim of adopting them on Japanese soil.[45] The third mission was to France in 1864; headed by Ikeda Nagaoki (1837–79), its purpose was to settle a number of disputes between Japan and France, including the Japanese proposal to close the port of Yokohama in order to protect the silk trade.[46] The fourth mission, headed by Shibata Takenaka (1823–77), went to France and England from 1865–66 with the objective of gaining the knowledge and connections necessary to open a steel mill in Japan.[47] The fifth

43. English language sources on this topic include Beasley, *Japan Encounters the Barbarian*; Masao Miyoshi, *As We Saw Them: The First Japanese Embassy to the United States* (New York: Kodansha International, 1979); and Peter Duus, *The Japanese Discovery of America: A Brief History with Documents* (Boston: Bedford Books, 1997). For a quick summary of all six pre-Restoration missions, see Numata Jirō, "Bakumatsu no kengai shisetsu ni tsuite: man'en gannen no kenbei shisetsu yori keiō gannen no kenfutsu shisetsu made," in *Seiyō kenbun shū*, in *Nihon shisō taikei*, vol. 66 (Tokyo: Iwanami shoten, 1974), pp. 599–620.

44. This mission was recorded by dozens of its participants. For a comprehensive bibliography of works by the 1860 mission to the United States, see Miyoshi, *As We Saw Them*, pp. 209–11.

45. For a record of the English leg of this mission, see Fukuda Sakutarō. *Eikoku tansaku*, in *Seiyō kenbun shū*, Numata Jirō and Matsuzawa Hiroaki, eds., vol. 66 of *Nihon shisō taikei* (Tokyo: Iwanami shoten, 1974), pp. 477–548. Other records of this journey include Fuchibe Tokuzō's *Ōkō nikki* and Mashizu Shunjirō's *Ōkōki*, both of which are in *Kengai shisetsu nikki sanshū 3*, in *Nihon shiseki kyōkai sōsho*, vol. 98 (Tokyo: Tōkyō daigaku shuppankai, 1930), and Fukuzawa Yukichi, *Seikōki* in *Fukuzawa Yukichi zenshū*, vol. 19 (Tokyo: Iwanami shoten, 1964).

46. One record of this journey is Iwamatsu Tarō, *Kōkai nikki*, in *Kengai shisetsu nikki sanshū 3*, in *Nihon shiseki kyōkai sōsho*, vol. 98, pp. 339–479.

47. Records of this mission include Shibata Takenaka, *Futsu-Ei kō*, in *Seiyō kenbun shū*, Numata Jirō and Matsuzawa Hiroaki, eds., in *Nihon shisō taikei*, vol. 66, pp. 261–476 and Okada Seizō *Kōsei shōki* in *Kengai shisetsu nikki sanshū 3*, in *Nihon shiseki kyōkai sōsho*, vol. 98,

mission in 1866, headed by Koide Hidezane, went to Russia in order to consult with the government on issues of national borders. The sixth and final shogunal mission, headed by Prince Akitake and of which Shibusawa Eiichi was a member, traveled to Europe in 1867.

Of the missions that postdate the fall of the Tokugawa shogunate, one of the most well documented was that in 1871, led by Iwakura Tomomi (1825–83) to the United States and Europe. This mission was chronicled by Kume Kunitake (1839–1931) in *True Account of a Tour of America and Europe*, the voluminous official record of the journey. A complete English translation of this record appeared in 2002 under the title *The Iwakura Embassy, 1871–73: A True Account of the Ambassador Extraordinary and Plenipotentiary's Journey of Observation Through the United States of America and Europe* (Graham Healey and Chushichi Tsuzuki, trans. [Richmond: Curzon Press, 2002]).

Alas, most of these travelogues are dry reportage and not very literarily edifying. They give textbook descriptions of industry, politics, religion, education, trade, economics, military, transportation, etc., often with statistics, making the final product more of a report than a travelogue. Rare is the passage where the reader's opinion shines through; more common is the record of what an official party did, or where they went, on a specific day. As historical material, these records offer a wealth of information, but as works of art, they rank quite low. The authors may have been familiar with the travelogue tradition, but on the whole they remained focused on the job at hand and refrained from waxing poetic on their experiences abroad. This was in keeping with the official objectives of the mission, which were not to gain an understanding of the West or to study her technological advances, but rather to convince the American government that resident consuls on Japanese soil were unnecessary. Furthermore, "The envoys were told to limit their activities to the bare essentials and return home as quickly as possible," which would make lengthy written ruminations hint at immoderate behavior.[48] However, of the works by mission participants, those of Muragaki Norimasa (1813–80)

---

pp. 481–533. For a study of the mission in English, see Mark D. Ericson, "The Bakufu Looks Abroad: The 1865 Mission to France," *Monumenta Nipponica*, vol. 34, no. 4 (1979): 383–407.

48. Beasley, *Japan Encounters the Barbarian*, p. 59

and Fuchibe Tokuzō (dates unknown) stand out as worthy of closer consideration by the literary scholar.

Muragaki Norimasa

Muragaki Norimasa, also known as Muragaki Awaji-no-Kami, was an official of the Tokugawa shogunate whose offices dealt primarily with foreign affairs. He was born the son of a high-ranking shogunate retainer in Edo (present-day Tokyo). In the course of his career, he held the ranks of comptroller, coastal inspector in Ezo, commissioner of Hakodate, commissioner of foreign affairs, and commissioner of Kanagawa. On the 1860 mission to the United States, he held the title of Vice Ambassador. The mission, comprising seventy-seven people, departed Yokohama on February 13, 1860, aboard the USS *Powhatan* and arrived in San Francisco on March 29 after stopping briefly in Hawai'i.[49]

After only a few days, the party continued on by sea, then on land across the isthmus of Panama, then back to sea aboard the USS *Roanoke*, finally arriving in Washington, D.C. on May 14. The mission was brief—after touring Washington, Philadelphia, and New York, they boarded the USS *Niagara* on June 29, 1860 for the return trip to Japan. The group was aided in the Pacific leg of their journey by a dozen Americans, one of whom was John Brooke (who had befriended Hamada Hikozō years earlier); because of the Japanese' relative lack of experience navigating in the open sea, the Americans' knowledge was invaluable. There were also Japanese sailors in the group, but, of course, they ranked below the officials of the mission, who busied themselves with nonnaval issues.

Muragaki's work, *A Record of the Mission to America*, is written in a diary format.[50] It begins with an explanation of the mission's com-

---

49. There were in essence two missions in one: the *Powhatan* mission, which traveled all the way to the east coast of the United States, and the *Kanrin Maru* mission, which sailed to San Francisco at the same time as the *Powhatan*, then returned to Japan. The two are often referred to together, as they were meant to have a diplomatic tie. This figure of seventy-seven members is the number of diplomatic staff aboard the *Powhatan*. The *Kanrin Maru* carried ninety-six men. Beasley, *Japan Encounters the Barbarian*, pp. 58 and 67, and Miyoshi, *As We Saw Them*, pp. 25–26.

50. This work has been reprinted in *Kengai shisetsu nikki sanshū 1*, in *Nihon shiseki kyōkai sōsho*, vol. 96. (Tokyo: Tōkyō daigaku shuppankai, 1928), pp. 1–207. There have also been two

position and purpose, and describes the American warship, the *Powhatan*, aboard which part of the party sailed. Muragaki included poetry written by the mission members and well-wishers at the farewell party for the group. Mention of the farewell parties prior to a journey is reminiscent of traditional travelogues, such as Bashō's *Narrow Road to the Deep North* (c. 1694) and *The Records of a Travelworn Satchel* (1687), in which the poetry composed on the occasion of a farewell party is included. Muragaki's diary from the days before his departure to America reads as follows:

1st Month, 18th Day [February 9, 1860]

Clear skies with a strong northwest wind. My traveling clothes were still cold. Many people came in the morning to bid farewell. If I had not exerted myself and shown an air of bravery in the face of departure, my children would have been despondent. The time to depart will soon be at hand.

USS Powhatan

English translations of the work: *The First Japanese Embassy to the United States of America*, Shibama Chikakichi, ed., Miyoshi Shigehiko, trans. (Tokyo: Nichibei kyōkai (The America-Japan Society), 1920), and *Kōkai Nikki: The Diary of the First Japanese Embassy to the United States of America*, Helen M. Uno, trans. (Tokyo: Foreign Affairs Association of Japan, 1958). The 1920 edition is seriously flawed and inaccurate, and lamentably omits all the poetry of the original. The 1958 edition is faithful to the original.

Entrusting the thread

Of my life both to the gods

And to my liege lord,

I shall leave behind a name

Even in unknown countries.[51]

Upon going to the anchorage where the battleship was, I
found that everyone had gathered there, including Masaoki,
Tadamasa, and Morita, and some petty officials. At about 8
P.M. we boarded small boats and headed beyond the battery,
where the wind was strong and the waves tall. Morita quickly
became seasick.

Rowing out

Into the distant, arresting waves

Of Takeshiba

Such a ship's departure

Is rare in this world.

Reciting such poetry, we arrived at the American battleship
Powhatan, which was moored at the Shinagawa offing. They
played music upon our boarding, and the ship's commodore
came to great us and show us around the ship.[52]

It does not surprise us that Muragaki is somber on the eve of his journey, but such feelings were certainly not unique to Meiji overseas travelers. Bashō expressed similar sentiments in 1687 in the opening lines
of *The Records of a Travel-worn Satchel*:

It was early in October when the sky was terribly uncertain
that I decided to set out on a journey. I could not help feeling vague misgivings about the future of my journey, as I
watched the fallen leaves of autumn being carried away by
the wind.

From this day forth

I shall be called a wanderer,

51. The translation of this poem is by Donald Keene in *Modern Japanese Diaries*, p. 13.
52. Muragaki Norimasa, *Kenbeishi nikki*, in *Kengai shisetsu nikki sanshū 1*, in *Nihon shiseki kyōkai
    sōsho*, vol. 96, p. 7. Shinmi Masaoki (1822–69) was the chief ambassador of the mission.
    Oguri Tadamasa (1827–68) was a vice ambassador. Morita Okatarō (1812–?) was the Chief
    Finance Officer.

Leaving on a journey

Thus among the early showers.

You will again sleep night after night

Nestled among the flowers of sansanqua.

The second of these poems was written to encourage me by Chōtarō, a native of Iwaki, when he held a farewell party for me at the house of Kikaku.

It is winter now,

But when the spring comes,

Your bundle shall contain

Cherry-blossoms of Yoshino

This poem was an extremely courteous gift of Lord Rosen. Other friends, relatives and students of mine followed his example by visiting me with poems and letters of farewell or sending me money for straw sandals, so that I was spared the trouble of preparing for my journey, that normally, it is said, takes as long as three months. In fact, everything I needed for my journey—the paper raincoat, the cotton-stuffed mantle, the hat, the stockings, etc., to keep me warm in the dead of winter—was given me by my friends, and as I was invited to parties on a boat, at my friends' houses, or even at my own hermitage, I became used to the pomp and splendour of feasting unawares and almost fell victim to the illusion that a man of importance was leaving on a journey.[53]

And Imagawa Ryōshun (1326–1414) echoed this trepidation in the opening lines of his travelogue, *Traveling on the Road* (1378), written about a trip to Kyūshū:

Late at night on the twentieth day of the second month I crossed the Katsura River in the shadow of the moon that skirted the mountains in the mist. The sleeves of my traveling robe were drenched with water from the oars, even though

---

53. Matsuo Bashō, *The Narrow Road to the Deep North and Other Travel Sketches*, Nobuyuki Yuasa, trans. (London: Penguin Books, 1966), pp. 72–73. Chōtarō (dates unknown) was a samurai in the service of Lord Rosen. Rosen, aka Naitō Yoshihide (1655–1733), was the feudal lord of Taira in modern-day Fukushima Prefecture. Kikaku (1661–1707) was one of Bashō's disciples.

I departed in the morning. I came to realize how much more
they would be soaked by the oars on the endless waves of my
voyage. I arrived in Yamazaki later that day. Although I knew
this place well, the sight of the unremarkable grasses and trees
were particularly moving—perhaps because I was so loath to
part on this journey.

When I arrived at the Akuta River in Tsū, I felt some
angst about how this old body of mine would fare on the trip.

The indigent in Segawa and Koyano watched us as we
passed. Looking back at the indifferent manner in which
they observed us I now feel an envy for their station.[54]

Muragaki, Bashō, and Imagawa all express misgivings about their
imminent departure; Muragaki and Bashō are comforted by well-
wishers. Their feelings are expressed in words that emphasize the gravity and wonder that travel envelopes. But where Bashō avoids much
in the way of quotidian detail, Muragaki mixes poetics with reportage;
the remainder of Muragaki's entry for that day lists the important
members of the mission by name, the specifications of the *Powhatan*,
and the principal foreigners on the ship. Bashō makes no such mention, but rather continues in a lyrical vein.

Muragaki was diligent about his diary-keeping; even on days on
which nothing of note occurred, he wrote a short entry, with the ship's
location and the number of miles traveled since the previous day. Life
on the ship was certainly different from that on land, as he and his
fellow travelers suffered from constant seasickness and were occasionally confused or surprised by the Westerners' behavior on board.
Still, the relative monotony of the voyage provided Muragaki with the
same somewhat familiar atmosphere as benefitted Nakai in the early
parts of *A Journey West*. Consequently, Muragaki writes more poetry
while on board than he does after landing in the New World, and is
generally more reflective in tone. After arriving in the United States,
he is still able to stand back from the duties and demands of his mission occasionally and write sensitively on subjects of interest, but those
passages are notably scarcer than in the nautical section of the work.
While in Hawai'i, Muragaki took time to notice things visually:

---

54. There is a correlation between the name "Akuta" (dirt) and "old body" (body of dust). See
    Imagawa Ryōshun, *Michiyukiburi*, in *Chūsei nikki kikō shū*, in *Nihon koten bungaku zenshū*
    (new edition), vol. 48 (Tokyo: Shōgakukan, 1994), p. 392.

2nd Month, 15th Day [March 7, 1860]

Clear skies, with occasional clouds threatening to rain. Everybody is improving in spirit and endeavoring to be comfortable. At about 2 P.M. Mr. Taylor came to be our guide, and Masaoki, myself, Tadamasa, and Morita (plus forty-five lesser officials) left the guest quarters by horse carriage. About three or four blocks away we arrived at the king's public hall (which was used for the purpose of greeting foreign guests) and our guides came out to greet us. On both sides of the gate were hedges along a white wall; the entrance was like that of one of our temples. In front of the hall were all sorts of plants and flowers, the reds and whites of them vying with one another. There were many stands about that resembled our stone lanterns (these must have been stands for plants). Climbing the stairs into hall, I was stunned by the large glass mirrors hung on the white walls on all four sides. In front of each mirror there was a table, upon which was a ceramic vase holding assorted flowers. There were beds in the rooms on both the right and left, and upon them were placed thin white cloths. In the front of the building was a carpet measuring about thirty mats and which had many chairs set out upon it.[55]

In this passage, Muragaki describes the two main stimuli that would repeatedly pique his interest: the flora of place and the modern objects that "stunned" the Japanese viewer. The vision of the public hall is a lavish one, one that would appeal to either a Western (the large mirrors, the tables with vases) or a Japanese (the flowers outside and inside the building) aesthetic. By mentioning them in the same paragraph, Muragaki blends the two aesthetics, making the foreign element easier for his Japanese audience to assimilate. The next day Muragaki goes on to comment further on the flora of Hawai'i:

2nd Month, 16th Day [March 8, 1860]

Today, too, rainfall intermittently. A little beyond this municipality there are tall mountains, over which form clouds and from which blows a breeze. This is the rainy season; in the

---

55. Muragaki, *Kenbeishi nikki*, pp. 23–24. Parenthetical remarks in this translation are interlinear text in the original. "Mr. Taylor" is Bayard Taylor, one of the Americans who accompanied the mission. The "king" is King Kamehameha IV (1834–63) of Hawai'i. A "mat" refers to the size of a standard *tatami* mat, approximately eighteen square feet.

winter time the heat remains, and this season is the equivalent of winter here. Nevertheless, the watermelon ripens,
and there are many kinds of fruit; *banana* (the fruit of the
bashō tree) and coconut palms are plentiful. In the morning
and evening, we wear lined kimono, and in the afternoon,
we wear singlets. Yesterday and today I have been composing poems about the scenery all about me. Without spring,
the green leaves grow lush and cool—does the cuckoo sing,
I wonder? The morning and evening wind makes me wonder if autumn is near. This is a landscape that does not
know the four seasons, the occasional late autumn rains, the
rushing of the clouds, the falling of a passing shower.

> A poem that celebrates
>
> Spring and autumn
>
> Makes me feel as if
>
> I follow a simple path
>
> Of dreams.

The crow of the unseen rooster at dusk is no different than
that in my home village.

> The bird's song
>
> Is the same in the East
>
> The breaking of
>
> A spring dawn
>
> On Honolulu[56]

The author's frustration at his inability to use traditional seasonal
imagery in a place that lacks seasonal changes is clear; he wants to
write poetry that employs, if not *uta makura*, some device in keeping
with the tradition of Japanese verse. But a poem on spring or autumn,
a perfunctory exercise that could be done in one's sleep, would indeed
be a poor substitute for what the occasion demands, that being a
poem that addresses a new place in new terminology suited specifically for it. Muragaki finds middle ground in commenting that the
cock's crow is "the same as in the East," thus making some tie to
Japan, but fails to distinguish Honolulu for any specific trait. Indeed,

56. Muragaki, *Kenbeishi nikki*, pp. 24–25.

Keene comments that, "Nothing pleased Muragaki in Honolulu."[57] Although the strange new environment as a whole certainly posed a great number of difficulties, it seems reasonable to surmise that one specific reason for Muragaki's discontent may have been the challenge of writing *kikōbungaku* in a foreign land.

Faced with the inability to find the vicarious nostalgia of place (discussed in chapter one) in his surroundings, Muragaki naturally turns to nostalgia for his home land. Five days out of Honolulu, after recovering from another bout of seasickness, He went out on deck for a bit of exercise. He writes:

> Exercise naturally improved my spirits, and I felt the eternity of the spring day. Since leaving port all there is to see are the same old gulls floating on the water. Today is the third day of the third month.
>
> I see the floating gulls
>
> As my friends
>
> Cherry blossoms adorn
>
> My hometown
>
> Where the little girls play
>
> After I composed this poem, Masaoki came on deck, and as a surrogate for one from my hometown, he composed a poem:
>
> As you,
>
> I am imbued in thoughts
>
> of the flowers and birds[58]
>
> In our hometown
>
> I was cheered upon hearing this poem, and it comforted my soul.

The third day of the third month, on which falls the annual Doll Festival, is something that naturally made Muragaki long for home. The vision of the cherry blossoms in full bloom, underneath which frolicked

57. Keene, *Modern Japanese Diaries*, p. 16.
58. Muragaki, *Kenbeishi nikki*, pp. 37–38.

young children in bright clothing, was undoubtedly a preferable sight to the endless ocean, broken only by an occasional bird floating on the surface. What is particularly interesting is that his desire to be home during this celebration is remarkably similar to those desires expressed centuries earlier by Ki no Tsurayuki and his companions in *Tosa Diary*; aboard a ship, faraway from home, Tsurayuki remarks, "People thought in vain about the White Horse Banquet being held that day; for us, waves were the only white things in sight."[59] Muragaki's imagery here substitutes birds for white caps, the Doll Festival for the White Horse Banquet.

Once he arrived on the American Continent, Muragaki turned most of his attention to describing the movements of the mission. Occasionally he added his own insights, which are generally cautious and reserved. Although editors saw fit to add some interlinear commentary, it is less than one might expect for a record of such a foreign place as the West was to Japan at the time. In Washington D.C., Muragaki tells us of visiting George Washington's grave site, where music was played and all took off their hats in respect. The group toured the city, and met with President Buchanan at the White House to deliver documents for the ratification of the proposed treaty between the two countries. Although they were limited in their movements and under strict orders from the Tokugawa government to focus solely on the assignment at hand, the group did occasionally break from business to attend social functions; ballroom dancing, however, was a shock to see, and the Japanese party quickly excused themselves with their hosts and returned to their hotel.[60]

American customs often perplexed the party. When, during a public appearance, the Japanese found women and children throwing bouquets of flowers into their carriages from third and fourth story windows, Muragaki made it a point to explain that it was a congratulatory gesture, indicating that the Americans respected the mission members.[61] When introduced to an American official's wife and children, he comments that he found this "bringing out of women to be introduced in public places awkward," but then admits that later he

---

59. Translation by Helen Craig McCullough in *Classical Japanese Prose: An Anthology* (Stanford: Stanford University Press, 1990), p. 76. See also chapter one.
60. Muragaki, *Kenbeishi nikki*, p. 92.
61. Muragaki, *Kenbeishi nikki*, pp. 80–81.

came to realize that it was simply a matter of national customs and manners.[62] Repeatedly, he mentions the American's lack of decorum and propriety, particularly as displayed by an assumed equality among peoples, something unacceptable to a man whose home culture, influenced by Neo-Confucianism, was strongly rooted in societal stratification. All in all, the United States was a disconcerting place for Muragaki and his companions, so disconcerting as to prevent them from seeing much of the natural beauty. Another hindering factor was that the mission's movements were closely watched by other Japanese, called *metsuke*, specially sent along with the mission to ensure an adherence to protocol. With the *metsuke* lurking in the background, and the Americans eager to keep their guests busy and entertained, the journey was far from the sort of spiritual retreat that inspired travelogues of the medieval period. It is a wonder that Muragaki was able to compose what he did.

Fuchibe Tokuzō

Two years after the mission to America, the first shogunal mission to Europe was initiated. As with the 1860 mission, many records of the journey were made, but overall they offer little in the way of artistic accomplishment or aesthetics. The exception is Fuchibe Tokuzō's *Diary of a Trip to Europe*, for Fuchibe exhibited the ability to observe the beauty of his surroundings thoughtfully, no matter how foreign. His travelogue is written in diary format, and like Nakai and Muragaki, he mixes prose and poetry (the poetry is composed both in Japanese and Chinese). Fuchibe leaves much to be desired as an historical source, as he is not concerned with documenting Europe as a whole; rather, he records what he sees subjectively, and in the process begins to establish *uta makura* of a sort for the next generation of writers.

Little is known of Fuchibe's background. Although the decision to include him on the mission was sudden, he tells us that he was happy to be chosen despite being given only two days in which to prepare and pack. Fuchibe made the journey to Europe as the member of a smaller group; he accompanied Sir Rutherford Alcock, the British

<hr>

62. Muragaki, *Kenbeishi nikki*, p. 84.

minister, on his journey home from Japan. Alcock, Fuchibe, and an interpreter by the name of Moriyama Takichirō (1820–71) left Japan in March of 1862. After arriving in England, Fuchibe and Moriyama joined the mission group. Fuchibe does not tell us why he was chosen, or what duties he was expected to fulfill on the mission, but such concerns quickly fall to the side as the reader is caught up in the lyrical depiction of the journey. The narrative begins before departure, as he prepares for the long ocean voyage. After a brief comment on how he is anxious about being without Japanese cuisine during his time abroad—a comment that reveals a modicum of sadness—he sends off his luggage to the Dutch ship. This opening entry is typical of future entries in which the author expresses a determined optimism, even in the face of disappointment or discouragement. Whereas other early Japanese travelers kept Western culture at a figurative arms' length or criticized Western customs, Fuchibe finds good in almost everything he sees, at least once he has passed through the Suez canal and left Asia behind.

Fuchibe writes with a balance between description and impression; he often depicts clear pictures of the things he sees, including dimensions, shapes, colors, and general appearance, but he avoids the dry diction of Nomura. Also, perhaps because he was part of a small party on the first leg of the trip, he seems less concerned with putting forth an official appearance in his text and more intent on recording personal impressions. He often chooses to express himself in poetry, both Japanese and Chinese, rather than prose, which reveals his feelings more often than it describes his surroundings. Such a lyrical indulgence is rare among mission members, and it is this that makes Fuchibe's travelogue stand out from the rest. Like many travel writers, Fuchibe dedicates much attention to the ocean leg of his trip, a time when he has little to do but ruminate on what lies ahead, and on the monotony of sea travel. While still in the Inland Sea of Japan, he writes:

26th Day [March 26, 1862]

Light rain, southerly wind. The ship is headed west on a broad reach. In the afternoon a strong southerly wind blew and the boat heeled more than twenty degrees, rolling me out of my seat.

> On the ocean,
>
> Amidst the mountains
>
> Of rising waves,
>
> Flowers may bloom
>
> But their hues have no scent
>
> Drifting upon the waves
>
> Of the great sea,
>
> My transient pillow
>
> Floats along; In this world,
>
> Is there no other such as myself?

According to a Dutchman who has done the calculations, today we part from Japanese territory. We have traveled 120 *li* (in nautical miles, which are about half of a Japanese mile). In the evening there was an easterly wind and rain. The waves hit the hull and there were thunder claps. We moved up, then down, which made me roll as I lay in my berth. In the middle of the night the easterly wind blew fiercely, but the sails had been properly trimmed, and the ship ran quickly along, like an arrow. I fell asleep at 1 o'clock.[63]

This passage shows the curious mix of lyrical poetry and staid prose that is characteristic of the entire work. At times the reader wishes that Fuchibe provided more of an introduction to or explanation of his poetry, as his classical predecessors did, for without it, the emotions appear in a vacuum and lose some of the impact they might otherwise have. Still, it is clear that Fuchibe experienced many of the same anxieties as previous travelers off the coast of Japan; he is lonely, meditative upon his role as traveler (as revealed by the term "transient pillow" in the poem above), and painfully aware of the change of seasons he was and would be missing while at sea. On the twenty-eighth day he writes:

---

63. Fuchibe Tokuzō, *Ōkō nikki*, in *Kengai shisetsu nikki sanshū 3*, in *Nihon shiseki kyōkai sōsho*, vol. 98 (Tokyo: Tōkyō daigaku shuppankai, 1930), pp. 4–5. Remarks made in parentheses are interlinear text.

Clear skies, south-easterly wind. The ship is on a broad reach, headed west.

On the white waves
My thoughts float along
The first cherry blossoms
In my home town
Are surely blooming now[64]

Throughout the remainder of the travelogue, Fuchibe occasionally mentions having his travel weariness relieved, or his loneliness comforted, but this is the only indication that he had found any aspect of the trip unenjoyable. The only apparent physical discomforts he experiences are motion sickness and a bout of beriberi, which was cured in a matter of days, leaving him as fit as before.[65] His homesickness, as expressed in the above poem, appears to have been more the result of him bowing to the literary traditions of experiencing *ryojō* than experiencing true psychological suffering. Unlike Ki no Tsurayuki, Fuchibe had the advantage of traveling in a more modern era on a ship in whose crew he had every confidence. Ki no Tsurayuki was on a return trip to a place for which he longed nostalgically, the arrival in which was never guaranteed; Fuchibe was headed out, to a place he had never seen and that held wonders beyond his imagination, the arrival in which he was certain of. It is no wonder that Fuchibe felt excitement and Ki no Tsurayuki felt mostly dread. Nonetheless, the aesthetic expressed by both men carries a common theme: a longing for one's home. Typical is Fuchibe's poem:

Oh my hometown!
It makes me happy to think
Of remembrances
Of days of old
The bright moon[66]

Fuchibe was an amateur painter, and this affects his travelogues in two ways: first, his descriptions are more visual than emotional, and

---

64. Fuchibe, *Ōkō nikki*, p. 5.
65. Fuchibe, *Ōkō nikki*, p. 15. At sea after leaving Hong Kong, Fuchibe describes symptoms of beriberi, including a weakness in his legs and tightness in his chest.
66. Fuchibe, *Ōkō nikki*, p. 15.

include details that a non-painter might overlook. His attention to detail was further exercised when he sketched landscapes and offered them as gifts to hosts and fellow travelers. Second, he was quick to equate landscapes, especially those of Asia, with those depicted in paintings. Upon arrival in Shanghai, he wrote:

8th Day [April 6, 1862]

A light rain and northerly wind since dawn. We went up river by steam boat, and as the day grew bright I saw the river banks for the first time. The riverside willows and peach trees bloom luxuriantly, and amidst them one can see the houses and temples of those who grow wheat on the dikes and tend rice paddies along the banks. Tile and thatch roofs face each other. Pedestrians carry umbrellas and wear large-brimmed straw hats as they move along the street. We anchored amidst the tangled underbrush and cooked some rice. It is so like what one sees in an ink landscape painting! How extremely graceful; the pagoda and temple gates are all such as are seen in Ming paintings.[67]

Fuchibe is heartened by this romantic image of China. His positive attitude and admiration is still evident when his party transfers to the *Peking*. He notes that it is a beautiful ship, that the passengers are all wealthy merchants and tradesmen, that it is spotlessly clean, and that the meals are delicious, all "somewhat relieving the tedium of the journey."[68] Fuchibe simultaneously focuses on the greatness of Chinese civilization as represented in Ming painting and the comforts and conveniences of modern, Western technology; his fondness and approval of the former eventually gives way to disillusionment in the face of the poverty and destitution he sees in Hong Kong, but he never loses his deep-seated admiration for the West. He writes:

13th Day [April 11, 1862]

Clear. We entered Hong Kong at the hour of the dragon [7–9 A.M.] The inner harbor conditions resemble a rough cape. The mouth of the harbor is crooked, and upon entering it one sees magnificent cliffs surrounding it. Below the

67. Fuchibe, *Ōkō nikki*, p. 8.
68. Fuchibe, *Ōkō nikki*, p. 9.

mountains the people's houses are packed tightly together
and the buildings are of differing heights—just as in a painting. We went ashore in the afternoon and were put up in an
inn. This inn has three stories and walls built of stones piled
one upon another. The construction is entirely of a Western
design. The proprietor is British and runs a shop with the
help of Chinese servants. The members of the Japanese mission last year all stayed in this inn. One hundred and forty-
five years ago this place had a mere forty-five native families
living here, but then it was put under British jurisdiction.
Gradually it opened up, and Westerners came to live here,
and more Chinese also came to settle. It is said that the population is more than forty thousand now. Seven or eight out
of every ten houses are built in a European style, the rest
are built in a Chinese style, and hold no beauty. Mr. Alcock
is staying in a military camp house. In the afternoon the proprietor accompanied Moriyama and myself in a horse carriage to tour the village. The mountains are all rocky but the
climate is warm and so the foliage is lush. Willow blossoms,
morning glories, and moon flowers all bloom in profusion,
making it like June in Japan. The wealthy merchants' houses
are constructed beautifully. There are churches, and these
are also built in a Western style. In the fort there is a hospital, steel forgery, etc., all of which are done in a Western
style. The natives are all stone masons, sedan chair bearers,
or fishermen; some are servant boys who are merely made
to serve the British.[69]

With the contrast between Chinese poverty and British affluence as
seen in Hong Kong clearly laid out before him, Fuchibe reacts in
much the same way that many of his compatriots in the Meiji period
did: he was repelled by the corruption and chaos of life under the Qing
dynasty, and duly impressed by the wealth and ruling power of the
Europeans. Some Japanese, while admiring Western strengths, also
saw the West as a potential threat to Japan, and thus they simultaneously complimented and disparaged Western imperialism. Others,
such as Fuchibe saw little but good in things Western and depicted
the West as a kind of wonderland with only beneficence on offer.

  In later entries from Hong Kong and Singapore, Fuchibe retreats
from describing the modern China before his eyes and instead men-

69. Fuchibe, Ōkō nikki, pp. 11–12.

tions more of the local flora and fauna. Ultimately this traditional focus for the Japanese travel writer also fails him; he admits that the flora are all of a sort he has never seen before, and that they all differ from those found in Japan. He cannot possibly evoke images of blossoms or brilliant colors when he does not even know the names of the flowers he sees. Not one to be easily daunted, Fuchibe tries to describe the new plants he sees. He tells of eating his first banana, describes in detail all the uses of the palm tree, and often enumerates the florae.

On an island in Indonesia, for example, he lists betelnut, nutmeg, black pepper, bananas, coconuts, carambola, and mangosteens. Unfortunately for his Japanese reader, far away from any of these foreign fruits, he neglects to describe their color, shape, or flavor, leaving their names as nothing but vague concepts on the page. Days later near the Red Sea, Fuchibe describes seeing a school of large fish—he guesses tens of millions of them—dancing about in the waves, making the entire surface of the sea a dark color, but he knows not what sort of fish they are. Asking shipmates seems either linguistically impossible or out of the question, and he lets the matter drop. In all these cases, it would seem he knows that what he observes must have some significance, some deeper meaning, but he cannot access it. His valuative tools are anchored—indeed, mired—in the Japanese environment, leaving him artistically unarmed overseas.

The language barrier plays a small roll in shaping Fuchibe's work and impressions. One advantage that Fuchibe and other Japanese travelers had in China over Europe was the ability to communicate relatively freely with the natives through what were known as "written conversations" (hitsudan) in which the participants would write their thoughts in Chinese characters. Fuchibe tried his hand at "written conversations," but he quickly discovered that colloquialisms were a problem and the quality of the conversation suffered as a result. As he traveled further away from Sinicized cultures and lost a common writing system with the natives, written conversations became impossible. His response was to focus on the physical appearance of those whom he met, or to conjecture what thoughts might be expressed if an exchange of words were possible.

In Sri Lanka, for example, he describes the people as all dark-skinned, and thinks the coiffures of those with long hair make them "resemble female demons," an image he most likely took from the *Ramayana*.[70] In the sea of Arabia, Fuchibe finds himself aboard a ship of mostly European passengers with whom he cannot communicate, yet he says that their company comforted his feelings of travel weariness. Isolated by language but surrounded by a relative opulence, Fuchibe was left to imagine conversations and situations; his tendency was to think well of the Europeans, if nothing else because they kept themselves clean and thus presented a semblance of civility. What they were saying was inconsequential, for their accomplishments in the form of grand architecture, immense ships, railways, etc., clearly indicated that they had a civilized society.

After suffering in the harsh conditions of the desert of northern Africa, the group traveled to Malta, Sicily, and finally arrived in Marseilles. Fuchibe's reaction shows his predisposition to admire Europe:

26th Day [May 24, 1862]

Clear. We arrived in the French port of Marseilles at the hour of the rabbit [6 A.M.] This place is located on the seacoast along southern France, and is very prosperous and bustling. The fort has streets lined with thick trees, and along each side are tall buildings. For the first time I saw the prosperity of the West. We went ashore at the hour of the snake [10 A.M.]. We had our baggage inspected in the customs office on the shore, and when that was finished we got into a horse-drawn carriage and went through the city streets. The streets are about thirty *ken* wide, and cherry trees are planted along the street on both sides where one walks in front of the shops. The flowers are small, and unbearably beautiful to behold. Here and there are fountains, just over a *jō* in height. The goods for sale are abundant, and all startle my eyes. We arrived at our inn and ate supper. Not one of the cups, dishes, nor the banquet table could be called inelegant. In the afternoon we boarded a car and went to the mountains. There is a dirt road high up in the mountains that allows one passage. The road is over one *li* long. The lower hills have been cut away to make way for the roads. In the valley the roads are built using stone or iron bridges. Rain fell intermittently today, with thunder and lightning. The day was filled with travel on numerous moun-

70. Fuchibe, *Ōkō nikki*, p. 25.

tainous roads, but when we spotted a level plot of a few paces wide, it was always planted with grapes or mulberries. Stone-riddled grounds where only grasses would grow were used for cattle or sheep grazing. . . . At dusk we arrived in Lyons. This place is extremely prosperous; in the evening the streets are lined with gas lamps, and it is as bright as broad daylight. They have these lamps in their houses, too, and it makes them bright and vivid. We checked in to an inn, where the glasses and plates were unsurpassed and the beds and curtains were all beyond beautiful.[71]

In Paris, Fuchibe was equally favorably impressed, and continued his praise and admiration:

We arrived in Paris in the evening. I had heard that this was the most prosperous place in all of Europe, and I had heard correctly. The houses in town are all six or seven stories high, built of stone, rising vertically. Along the edges of the eaves there are carved people, flowers, and birds in an arabesque

Street scene from Paris

71. Fuchibe, Ōkō nikki, pp. 37–38. A jō is approximately 10 feet; a li is 2.44 miles.

design. The doors and windows are all of glass. The larger
streets are thirty *ken* wide, and lined with trees on both
sides. The alleys are seven or eight *ken* wide, and all have
glass-covered lantern stands placed on both sides at five *ken*
intervals. In the evenings gas lamps are placed inside the
stands and lit. We arrived at our inn. Here, in order to see
clearly at night, dozens of gas lights are placed inside the
glass doors of the shop fronts. Gold and silver jewelry is displayed under lights that make it sparkle. It is a nightless
city—so that one imagines being in the fabled "palace in the
moon." The travelers' inn is located in front of the palace
gates and is the best inn in the entire city. The guest rooms
number six hundred and fifty, and all measure between three
or four *jō* to seven or eight *jō*. The table cloths and curtains
are embroidered brocade, and at each seat are hung great
mirrors, sometimes on two sides, sometimes on three or four
sides. Nothing was left unprepared for us; we had bedding,
a chronometer, a wash basin, and more.[72]

Fuchibe's prose reflects a breathless reaction to Europe; suddenly
there was so much new and impressive before him that he barely had
enough time to record it, much less reflect upon it. Up until his arrival
in France, he had composed much poetry, both in Chinese and Japanese, but in the days immediately after seeing Marseilles, Paris, and
London there are only a few scant poems. Europe was a wonderland,
a paradise of sorts, where the city streets were illuminated at all
hours, transportation was convenient and readily available, and city
centers rose high above the street level. All of these things, unknown
in Japan, would have been hard to imagine without the benefit of firsthand experience. Fuchibe rarely comments on Europeans' behavior;
in his diary they appear only to show him about new locales, to host
dinners or parties, or to provide transportation. Thus, they are visible
but not integral to the narrative. One imagines that Fuchibe would
have been just as pleased with Europe had all the countries been suddenly depopulated and he left to roam abandoned streets, for he

---

72. Fuchibe, *Ōkō nikki*, p. 39. A *ken* is approximately 6 feet. Fuchibe uses the word "chronometer" (*jishinbyō*) here instead of "clock" (*tokei*). Although the manufacture of "Japanese
clocks" (*wadokei*) based on the lunar time system had been active throughout the Tokugawa period, the manufacture of Western clocks based on the Western time system did
not begin in Japan until 1875. Thus, a clock such as the one Fuchibe found in his hotel
room would be unusual to the Japanese.

would still have had the opportunity to see the architecture that he so admired. Fuchibe retained a reverence for all he saw, and this, mixed with a persistent curiosity about things, is shown in his description of the Paris Zoo:

> We went to the zoological garden, which is half a square mile in area. The trees, verdant green fragrant grasses, ponds, streams, and rocks are all suitably arranged. Amongst them are scattered about hundreds of little pavilions, each of which has a grass or tile roof and lacquered pillars. They are built using the natural trees, and are thus extremely taste-ful. In each pavilion are kept first lions, tigers, leopards, rhi-noceros, wolves, foxes, and badgers; next are birds, including peacocks, parrots, ostrich, eagles, hawks, and other small birds; reptiles and fish include snakes, scorpions, carp, loaches, and an exhaustive collection of other small animals. The thing that above all held the interest of the observing crowds was a beast from Africa [sic] called a kangaroo. It is about six feet long, its front legs being short and its hind legs long. It stands and walks as a man does. It has a nat-ural pouch below its chest, where it keeps and raises its young. They also have a white peacock; both the male and female are snow white, their eyes being the only black thing on their bodies. Marine animals are kept in a glass box that is filled with either sea water or fresh water, as is appropri-ate. The bird of paradise and other animals from India are in a small room through which steam passes. There is a ther-mometer within and the temperature is set at a normal of ninety degrees. I have not the time to record each and every of the other strange beasts in the zoo. In the case of ani-mals such as whales and large fish that cannot be kept, a skeleton is gathered and arranged to display the general size of the body. I believe that if a museum curator could see these things they would surely elicit a gasp.[73]

Fuchibe's description lies somewhere between the dispassionate description of the zoo provided by Nomura and the humorous com-ments of Shibusawa. He is impressed with the layout of the zoological park and with the collection of animals therein, but he avoids mock-ing any of the strange beasts he sees. As in many of his descriptions,

73. Fuchibe, Ōkō nikki, pp. 41–42.

Fuchibe appears excited in the above passage; the run-on sentence, which I endeavored to keep whole and that describes the different species in the zoo, reads as a breathless litany of wonders, as if once he began naming the animals, he did not know how to stop. His description of the summer palace at Versailles displays an equal excitement, as he enthusiastically describes the elegance and sumptuous furnishings therein: the ceilings are painted with images that "exhaust all beauty," the crests were polished until they "shone like sparkling mirrors," the oil paintings of animals were so accurate as to "seem alive," and the paintings of ladies and children were "exquisite and subtle."[74] More than once Fuchibe notes that he cannot record all he sees, either for lack of time or an imperfect memory, implying that the wonders he beheld were greater than depicted on the page.

Fuchibe is at his best describing the gardens of Europe, such as those at Versailles:

> There are ponds scattered about, and there are groves and hillocks. Each garden is clean and refined. There are various pavilions built, and they are elegant. I had previously thought that Westerners loved nothing more than beautiful things, but I was surprised at how fond they seemed to be of refinement. About the ponds were placed assorted bronze figures of dragons, snakes, tortoises, turtles, and geese, from the mouths of which spouted water to a height of seven or eight feet, sometimes exceeding the height of the tree tops.[75]

The botanical displays, both indoor and outdoor, at the Crystal Palace in London also caught his eye:

> They have placed earth inside of the palace, and have made cultivation ponds for trees and flowers, that are filled with water and in which there are grown lotus-like plants. It is not only the lower storey that is like this; the second and third stories, too, all have gardens and ponds. Everywhere there are fragrant grasses, flowers, trees, streams, rocks, and pavilions. There are also cultivated plants that are shaped like strange birds and beasts, and whose leaves are pruned to look like real feathers and fur. . . . The ponds and marshes

74. Fuchibe, Ōkō nikki, p. 43.
75. Fuchibe, Ōkō nikki, pp. 43–44.

Crystal Palace engraving

are clear, and the manmade hills are elegant; one never tires of looking at it all, especially the thousands of mechanical streams that shoot up in the sky many yards for the guests' entertainment. I was quite surprised by the spectacle of it all. Those who come to this country to see this spectacle cannot but tour about once they arrive. There are even some from my own country who, if they have the leisure to do so, tour about for a few days. Whether one calls this an enchanted land, or perhaps a paradise, it occurred to me as I returned home at dusk by steam train that there was certainly no comparison for it in this world.[76]

Compared to those passages in the travelogue that describe technological advancements, such as the displays he saw at the Exhibition in London, these garden passages exude the aesthetic sensibility one might expect of a traditional Japanese travelogue, minus the pathos. The latter passage also clearly demonstrates his fond attachment to the West, a fondness that precluded nostalgic or preferential passages about Japan. After experiencing *ryojō* on the leg out to Europe, Fuchibe has no time for it on the continent. *Ryojō* necessitates an

76. Fuchibe, *Ōkō nikki*, pp. 53–54. Fuchibe's reference to "those from my own country" probably refers to other members of the mission, some of whom were guided about famous tourist sites by their French hosts.

ennui with one's surroundings, and Fuchibe could not feign such an indifference.

Throughout the travelogue, Fuchibe introduces places in a formal manner by giving the name of a locale and then beginning his explanation with either the phrase "this place is . . ." or "this area is. . . ." He is consistent in this method, more so than Nomura, Nakai, Shibusawa, or Muragaki, and although he usually tells his audience the same things that his French hosts probably told him—that a place is famous for having such-and-such a building or such-and-such a garden—it is still striking that many of the things he mentions later became stock references when other Japanese travelers wrote of the locale. Fuchibe assumes little previous knowledge on his readers' part in this respect, and does them a great service by providing necessary information on the famous places of Europe.

If one were interested in the important people of Europe, however, this would have been one of the last things to read; Fuchibe avoids giving names to the royalty he meets and usually only cursorily describes people, if at all. His penchant for nature is evident in the numerous visits to zoological parks (four in all), greenhouses, and gardens, and palace grounds. It was not that he disliked people but rather that he generously afforded them a position beyond criticism. Whereas Muragaki seemed perplexed by the throwing of bouquets as a celebratory gesture, Fuchibe blithely describes a similar event as one full of pleasing scents that made him wonder if he had entered a fairyland in a dream.[77] The language and imagery he uses (the term *senkyō* [fairyland] in particular) evokes both Chinese poetry and Noh theater, and speaks to his fascination and pleasure. No one crosses Fuchibe, no one is rude; all go about their business to the delight of this Japanese observer.[78]

After touring in France and England, the party headed for Russia, where they had audiences with dignitaries and toured famous places. As one might expect, the latter captured more of the author's attention than the former. Many visits were made to the summer

77. Fuchibe, *Ōkō nikki*, p. 84.
78. Fuchibe's apparent happiness among foreigners may have been enhanced by his inability to understand what they were saying. Although any training he may have had in foreign languages is undocumented, he gives no indication of being able to speak any Western languages, and also mentions that, when he met someone with a little proficiency in Japanese, he was able to ask questions. Fuchibe, *Ōkō nikki*, p. 89.

palace outside of St. Petersburg, a place of which Fuchibe was particularly enamored. On the third visit he writes:

> Groups of gentlewomen enjoying themselves made it seem like a marketplace. I walked for a bit in the garden, and climbed up the tower. The evening was cool, and the moon shone as bright as broad daylight. Along the shore are more than twenty court minstrels playing flutes and drums; the pure sound echoes off the river and is pleasurable. Several princes came to greet us, and we followed the river for four or five blocks, to a place where there were moored various colorful ships and the gentlewomen had gathered together. On each ship were dozens of five-colored round lamps lit, making it look like a collection of stars. Away from the river, the lamps made fifteen or sixteen wild, ceaseless streams of light, hanging in mid-air. On land, the assorted shapes of the towers, tall pavilions, rooftops and long boats appeared in the light. As one figure disappeared in the five colors of light, another would appear, creating an endless show. For more than one hour, it was a splendid sight.[79]

The Russians at the palace remain nameless, faceless figures who inhabit the spectacular landscape. Fuchibe never divulges conversations he may have had with his hosts, although this may be attributed as much to the language barrier as to his disinterest in conversation.

Shortly after this thoroughly enjoyable evening, the party left Russia to begin the journey home to Japan. The narrative becomes rushed as Fuchibe and his companions travel through Berlin and Paris, along the Spanish coast, through Lisbon, Gibraltar, Algeria, and to points beyond. The voyage is miserable, and Fuchibe, who dedicated pages upon pages to the journey out, abbreviates the journey home dramatically, giving it little consideration. There is no poetry to celebrate his return, and he expresses no nostalgia and relief at the thought of seeing his homeland again. The final entry leaves him at sea, somewhere in the eastern Mediterranean, with the unremarkable comment, "Clear and humid. We are headed south. Have gone one hundred and forty-eight miles."[80]

79. Fuchibe, Ōkō nikki, p. 107.
80. Fuchibe, Ōkō nikki, p. 124. This entry is for November 15, 1862.

Fuchibe's travelogue has more lyricism in it than all the other early Meiji travelogues combined. He included not only his own compositions but occasionally those of his companions, in the same way that Bashō includes poems by his traveling companion Sora, or Ki no Tsurayuki records the poems composed by his fellow travelers. And unlike Nakai, Fuchibe continued to compose poems in Europe, mostly about sights that moved him. The poems retain a distinct Japanese flavor to them, for they celebrate nature and emotion, all the while capturing the essence of the sights that affected the author. Fuchibe's attempt to capture his emotions in verse exhibits his own willingness to see and feel the beauty of the West; the other travelogues present a passionless, tepid tone, but Fuchibe throws caution to the wind in his excitement at this adventure.

NARUSHIMA RYŪHOKU AND POST-RESTORATION TRAVELOGUES

After the Restoration of 1868, travel to the West continued on a larger scale. Prior to this time, the overwhelming majority of travelers were students or diplomats, with only an occasional exception, such as Niijima Jō (1843–90), the founder of Dōshisha University in Kyōto, who spent ten years in the United States (but who did not write a travelogue of his experience), and traveling artisans, such as Sumidagawa Namigorō (dates unknown), and his son, Sumidagawa Matsugorō (dates unknown), who went to the Paris Exposition in 1866 to peddle their wares.[81] In the early Meiji period, however, persons of different professions took the opportunity to travel, and among those early travelers were professional writers, including newspaper journalists, playwrights, novelists, and poets. Travel after the Restoration was still an adventure, but perhaps not such a dangerous one. This was not only because transportation had improved slightly, but also because the threat of being arrested or attacked upon repatriation for sympathetic

---

81. There are two indices of Japanese travelers to the West, Tomita Hitoshi, ed., *Umi o koeta Nihon jinmei jiten* (Tokyo: Nichigai asoshieetsu, 1985) and Tezuka Hikaru, ed., *Bakumatsu Meiji kaigai tokōsha sōran* (Tokyo: Kashiwa shobō, 1992). The former predates the latter, but neither one is comprehensive. Some persons are listed in both, some one or the other, and still others in neither. This is partly due to a different scope—Tomita's index covers the years 1551–1897 and Tezuka's covers 1861–1912—but not entirely.

views toward the West was virtually eliminated. Of those early Meiji travelers, Narushima Ryūhoku (1837–84), wrote one of the most literarily refined travelogues, *Diary of a Journey Westward*.

Ryūhoku began studying *waka* with his grandfather at the age of seven, and soon progressed to reading such classics as *The Tale of Genji* and gaining knowledge of the elementary attainments of both Chinese and Japanese literature. In 1854, at the age of seventeen, he was appointed tutor to the *shōgun*, a post his father had held until his death that same year. In August of 1854, he joined the editing staff of the *True Record of the Tokugawa*, and in September he accompanied the *shōgun* Tokugawa Iemochi (1846–66) on a martial arts inspection where he recited Chinese poetry, a sign of his accomplishment in the literary arts. In 1859, he completed *New Poems of Willow Bridge*, one of his first poetic publications.

Well established as a scholar of Chinese literature, Ryūhoku then made an error, one that would help change the direction of his studies and his life: he wrote a comic poem that was satirical of the *bakufu*'s vacillation at the time, and thus he was prohibited from further tutoring and confined to house arrest. During this time, he acquired a copy of a Dutch grammar book and proceeded to teach himself Dutch; he also invited the likes of Western Learning scholars Yanagawa Shunsan (1832–70), Kanda Takahira (1830–98) and Mizukuri Shūhei (1826–86) to his home and through them pursued his study of Britain. In 1865, he was appointed as a cavalry chief and directed Western-style cavalry drills at the Yokohama military barracks.

Later, despite his previous ill-favor with the shogunate, his skills in things Western helped him obtain the shogunal posts of Cavalry Administrator, Foreign Affairs Administrator, and Vice Governor of Accounting. He quit his government position mere months before the fall of the Tokugawa *bakufu*, refusing offers of employment from the new Meiji government. After a brief time making his livelihood assisting in a pharmacy, he was taken on to accompany the Buddhist abbot Gennyo (aka Ōtani Kōei 1852–1923) of the Nishihonganji Temple on a journey to France, Italy, England, and America in 1872.

Ryūhoku kept his diary of the journey in Chinese and then later translated it in to Japanese. It was published serially from 1881–84

82. Some of these poems may be found in *Bakumatsu Meiji kaigai taiken shishū*, pp. 524–26.

in the magazine that Ryūhoku chaired, *The New Journal of the Poetic Arts*, appearing in almost every issue during that period. Unfortunately, Ryūhoku died before the entire work was completed, and the narrative ends while he is still in America. The editors of Ryūhoku's complete work tried to find the untranslated portion among his papers, but it had been scattered and lost, leaving *Diary of a Journey Westward* a permanently unfinished work. Because Ryūhoku waited ten years before publishing his work in Japan, it is possible that the literary influences of the mid-Meiji flavored his prose; on the other hand, the work is ostensibly a straight translation of what he wrote in 1871. But because the Chinese manuscript has been lost, confirmation one way or the other is impossible. The only remaining fragments of the original journal are a collection of Chinese poems written while in America, insufficient to determine the nature of the lost text.[82]

Ryūhoku had, in addition to Gennyo, three companions on this journey: Ishikawa Shuntai (1842–1931), a Buddhist monk, Matsumoto Byakuka (1839–1926), also a Buddhist monk, and Seki Shinzō (1843–80), an educator. Of these three, only Seki excelled at languages, although his command of English at the outset of the trip is unclear. Ryūhoku and Gennyo left Tokyo on a clear autumn day in 1872, with no well-wishers present. They met the rest of their party in Yokohama, where they boarded a French postal ship. On the eve of their departure for the West, Ryūhoku composed the following two poems:

> Who knows of my splendid spirit, about to harness giants,
> As we sing parting songs, liquor permeates my being
> As if gay, the bright autumn moon shines over Yokohama harbor
> The ship heads for France under one sail.

> I gaze at the moon, shining in the Paris sky to my right
> And I see the clouds over the London quay to my left
> How pleasing, to cross leagues of wind and waves!
> I shall surely compose poems that celebrate man's life.[83]

83. Narushima Ryūhoku, *Kōsai nichijō*, in *Meiji bunka zenshū*, vol. 16, Yoshino Sakuzō, ed. (Tokyo: Nihon hyōronsha, 1928), p. 405. See also Kawaguchi, *Bakumatsu Meiji kaigai taiken shishū*, p. 474.

Ryūhoku was excited about what lay ahead, and imagined the sky over Europe. This parting is felicitous, and offers no portents of danger or peril. Nostalgia for a homeland soon to be left behind is notably absent. Once at sea, however, this elated state soon gives way to a voice reminiscent of its homeland. The ship had barely left Japanese waters before Ryūhoku began to dream of his homeland and feel anxious about the sea. He writes:

> A chicken clucks outside of the cabin; the remnants of dusk
> A servant brings water in a white porcelain basin—
> I am suddenly woken from my sleep, and a dream of my home town.
> And then feel a cold dread at the sound of the waves, rocking my pillow.[84]

A crew member told Ryūhoku the next day that they were passing Taiwan, but it was not visible from deck. The endless horizon was disturbing to Ryūhoku and gave him no recourse but to imagine land— not surprisingly, he envisioned the mountains of Japan.

> I wonder if the mountains of my hometown keep watch over me,
> day and night?
> Truly I have been gloomy since leaving home.
> Who at home knows of these evenings, tossed about by the sea?
> The autumn flowers bloom in my dreams.[85]

The ship arrived in Hong Kong two days later [October 21, 1872], and the party went ashore to stroll about in the parks and take a drink at the European Hotel. The respite was brief, but Ryūhoku recorded that Hong Kong was very prosperous, if not raucous. They set sail again in two days, headed for Saigon, then on to Singapore, Sri Lanka, and Aden. In each place, Ryūhoku went ashore to see the sights, and was generally in favor of what greeted him. The architecture, natural bounty, and cuisine of each place pleased him greatly, and his only

---

84. Narushima, *Kōsai nichijō*, p. 406. See also Kawaguchi, *Bakumatsu Meiji kaigai taiken shishū*, p. 476.
85. Narushima, *Kōsai nichijō*, p. 406. See also Kawaguchi, *Bakumatsu Meiji kaigai taiken shishū*, p. 477.

disdain was directed at noisy natives who crowded him. The party passed through the Suez Canal and into the Mediterranean Sea. The mountains of Naples, spotted in the distance off the starboard bow one sunny day in late November, inspired him to write of his leisure and the change of seasons:

> I climbed up on the poop deck after my bath, yawning happily
> I am a man of leisure among these travelers
> The waters are quiet, the clouds warm
> I know now that Indian summer has come to the western sea[86]

The next day the ship passed Elba and Corsica, causing Ryūhoku to compose a poem about Napoleon I, who was born in the capital, Ajaccio:

> I think of you, accompanying the fishermen as a child
> And it was here, at the end of your life [sic] and chased from the
>   Empire, that you came
> The evening sun sinks in the shadow of the islands, the clouds
>   trail in the distance
> The islands stand in the blue ocean, cliffs on either side.[87]

Here Ryūhoku alludes to a place-associated event in verse. Although in the preceding passage, he does tell his reader that the poem is about Napoleon the poem itself omits his name. The reader is certainly expected to know Napoleon's history, and why Corsica, the site of his childhood, and Elba, where he goes to govern after abdicating in 1814, are significant landmarks. By composing a poem on the subject and forgoing an historical explanation, Ryūhoku's work has more allusive depth than the objective reportage of the earlier travelogues, and is evocative of earlier *uta makura*-laden domestic travelogues. Such poems are rare in *Diary of a Journey Westward*, however; most of the poetry tells of the remarkable but not unique characteristics of various locales, with little or no allusion to a profound significance of place.

86. Narushima, *Kōsai nichijō*, p. 412. See also Kawaguchi, *Bakumatsu Meiji kaigai taiken shishū*, p. 494.
87. Narushima, *Kōsai nichijō*, p. 413. See also Kawaguchi, *Bakumatsu Meiji kaigai taiken shishū*, p. 495.

The party landed for one day in Marseilles, where Ryūhoku saw the buildings "soar into the sky" and was surprised by the prosperity of the city and her denizen. Like so many Japanese, Ryūhoku comments on the gas lamps used to light the city streets. This particular observation is ubiquitous in the early travelogues. Even in travelogues written decades later, Japanese travelers note the use of gas lighting and marvel at the triumph Westerners had over the night; these lights were certainly brighter than the kerosene lamps prevalent in Tokyo until 1874, when gas lighting first came to the Ginza.[88] After Marseilles they went to Lyons, where once again Ryūhoku admired the street lamps. When Japanese travel writers referred to these lamps, they evoked an image of a place both literally and figuratively bright. The lit streets and store fronts were a sort of *uta makura* for the West, in that they represented progress, the special characteristic for which the West was best known in Japan. Furthermore, this was one of those rare images created and perpetuated by Japanese writers, not an image taken from Westerners or Western literature.

Ryūhoku's impressions of France were favorable. While there, he visited parks, viewed oil paintings in a gallery, went to museums, toured churches, went to the theater, toured a prison, and, like all good tourists, went to a zoo. He enjoyed French cuisine and said nothing disdainful about the French or their culture. His was a leisurely trip, and he spent most of his time enjoying the sights and visiting other Japanese travelers. He meticulously records the occasions of these meetings, but he tells the reader nothing of what transpired in the many conversations. He refrains from much introspective reflection, instead focusing on recounting sights. His descriptions are reminiscent of Fuchibe's: full of admiration and exuberance for the splendor of Europe. His entry for the day he visited Versailles exemplifies this:

> We went to visit the Grand Trianon. The palace was the home of Louis XVI, and Napoleon I also lived in this palace. Inside, there are portraits of Louis XIV and Louis XV. The most grand items of all are a large water basin and flower vase made of malachite, which were a gift from Russia to

---

88. The first gas lights were installed on the Ginza in 1874 and were extended in the following two years to reach Asakusa, and the Imperial Palace. Edward Seidensticker, *Low City, High City: Tokyo from Edo to the Earthquake* (New York: A. A. Knopf, 1983), p. 81.

Grand Trianon, Chamber of Napoleon

the emperor Napoleon. There is also the emperor's library. His bed, chair, desk and table are there, just as he left them. In the room in which the emperor received his empress, there are brilliant brocades drapes, embroidery, and cushions. One is taken back to that time in thought. The clocks in the palace are all made of gemstones, as are the tables. One cannot but be surprised at their beauty. There is also a storage place for carriages. All sorts of items are there, from Napoleon I's carriage and the carriage used for the wedding of Napoleon III to the carriages and equestrian tack of Louis XV and Louis XVI. It is all quite splendid. The inner garden of this palace is very much like that of the Fukiage garden of the old shogunate of Japan. It inspired in me a feeling of melancholy. In the center of the garden is a greenhouse. It is constructed in a rustic manner, and it is said that the queen of Louis XVI herself went milking there.[89]

More than Fuchibe, however, Ryūhoku associates Versailles with the prominent individuals of the French monarchy and empire. It is not

89. Narushima, *Kōsai nichijō*, p. 415. The Fukiage garden was an inner garden in the imperial palace in Edo. This entry is dated December 12, 1872.

The dairy, Versailles

the opulence of the items he sees that impresses him but rather the fact that they were possessions of famous people. He makes a deep connection in his mind between the place, as delineated by the items that occupy it, and the men, and it is the thought of the latter that conjures his poetic pathos:

> I wonder how many times the carriages passed by here.
> Gaily the empress sang her songs.
> Although the drapes are as they were, the people are gone.
> The evening sun shines brightly outside the glass windows.[90]

The days become a blur of similar entries after a few weeks in France. The sentences are terse and uninformative: "Visited so-and-so," "Went to the park for a walk," "So-and-so came calling," "Went to such-and-such a place," "Ate a delicious meal." Ryūhoku appears bored in a way, until he visits the St. Germain district where the landscape causes him

90. Narushima, *Kōsai nichijō*, p. 415. See also Kawaguchi, *Bakumatsu Meiji kaigai taiken shishū*, p. 500.

to experience the melancholy of travel and a longing for his homeland. He writes three poems:

> Half this hillock resembles Hong Tower, and half resembles
>   Wuyixiang
> The scenery call to mind the autumn mountains of my hometown.
> Today I climb the hills, and partake in wine at stops along the way,
> Cleansing my bosom of its copious sorrows.[91]

> I lived alone in a grass dwelling on the River Sumida
> And then set off forlorn like a cloud
> Now I am living on the Seine, myriad miles away
> And have suddenly met the familiar spirit of spring.

> Greeting the New Year as a guest abroad is quite strange
> I do not know these barbarians whom I face
> I drank up a bottle of champagne
> Yet the song I sang was an old tune of Tokyo[92]

The first poem is written about the vista he sees from the top of a
cafe. The two places he invokes are not Japanese but rather Chinese,
and they are historical references, not contemporary ones. Why mix
China into a poem that celebrates the memory of Ryūhoku's hometown? I would suggest that he felt the need for an urban allusion to
match his own urban setting. Unfortunately for Ryūhoku, *waka* is virtually void of urban imagery, the exception being a few early poems
from the *Man'yōshū*, which are modeled on Chinese precedents. This
leaves him to choose the Hong Tower, built by the first Qin Emperor
in the third century B.C., and Wuyixiang, a neighborhood in what is
now Jiangsu province, known as the home of the aristocracy during
the third and fourth centuries A.D. and a popular image in later Chinese poetry. The equation of the ancient Chinese landscape, which
Ryūhoku had never seen, with modern-day Paris is strained but shows
how difficult it was to leave behind the poetic tradition in which
Ryūhoku had been trained.

91. The original poem refers to a place called 鳥邱, the first character of which is probably a
    typographical error. It is thought to refer to Wuyixiang. Narushima, *Kōsai nichijō*, p. 416.
    See also Kawaguchi, *Bakumatsu Meiji kaigai taiken shishū*, p. 501.
92. The second and third poems appear together: Narushima, *Kōsai nichijō*, p. 417. See also
    Kawaguchi, *Bakumatsu Meiji kaigai taiken shishū*, p. 502.

The second poem equates the early springtime of Paris with that of Tokyo along the Sumida River. It lacks specific mention of the features of the landscape, but the evocation of springtime has a deeper meaning in both contexts: Paris, of course, is famous for its verdant spring, and the eastern banks of the Sumida are known for their cherry blossoms. Whether Ryūhoku was familiar with the Parisian seasonal significance is unclear, but even without it, the poem has all the elements we have come to expect from *kikōbungaku*: the longing for home, the image of the forlorn traveler, suffering in impoverished circumstances at the mercy of the elements, and the importance of seasonal ritual. What also is striking about this poem is that the seasonal referent is strained; Ryūhoku is evoking springtime, as one would traditionally with the beginning of the lunar year. However, the beginning of the lunar year would not come for another month. The New Year holiday in this passage is according to the solar calendar, to which Japan had switched just a month earlier.

Immediately following comes the poem on the New Year's festivities. Once again, Ryūhoku is nostalgic for Japan (specifically his hometown) and unsure of the company of Westerners. The foreign rituals hold no significance for him; he cannot enjoy them nor savor their cultural milieu. He is hopelessly attached to Tokyo, the only place where "New Year's" can have meaning.

The sagas of Napoleon I and Napoleon III catch his fancy, and many of the historical locales he visits are associated with them. He visits the catacombs in Paris, only to describe them in a rather dispassionate manner, concluding with "the foreigners who see [the catacombs] all say that there is no place as strange as this in any other country."[93] Yet he remains unable to make any such statement on his own. The plight of the early Christians in the Roman Empire fails to capture his imagination, and he refrains from commenting further, his silence implying disinterest in the subject, if not disagreement on it. Later however, in Italy, he becomes uncharacteristically loquacious on the topic of burial rights, describing coffins and memorials, and he likens the wreaths placed at grave sides to the Japanese *shikimi*, a tree whose branches are placed as memorials on Buddhist graves. But verbose or

93. Narushima, *Kōsai nichijō*, pp. 420–21.
94. Narushima, *Kōsai nichijō*, p. 426. See also Kawaguchi, *Bakumatsu Meiji kaigai taiken shishū*, p. 510.

laconic, Ryūhoku cannot muster the poetic muse in response, or rather in reference, to these foreign surroundings. His travelogue maintains a dual voice: one that reports on the things seen and heard and one that delves into the poet's heart to find his deepest longings. This leads one to believe that Ryūhoku's terseness or verbosity is quixotically dependent on his mood from day to day, and not on the topic at hand.

After three and a half months in France, Ryūhoku and his traveling companions boarded a train for Italy. They went through the pass at Mt. Cenis and stopped in Torino, where Ryūhoku commented that the Italian houses with their red tile roofs were remarkably like those of Japan. He spent less than a month touring Italy but managed to see Milan, Venice, Florence, Rome and Naples, all of which left favorable impressions upon him. Italy was prosperous, like France, and was an extremely elegant place where the cathedral bells rang through the streets. He composed a poem on Milan in mid-March:

> Upon reflection, she is more prosperous than all other regions,
> The ladies and gentlewomen who fill the streets are naturally
>   tranquil
> The bells of the cathedral ring endlessly, announcing the arrival
>   of dusk
> A light rainfall on the stone towers, the chill of spring.[94]

Venice too inspired a poem:

> Hundreds of canals flow towards the inlet
> The image of beautiful ships reflects in the dredged canals'
>   waters
> Women sell flowers; men play the flute
> It is like the gentle spring breeze in a land of gods.[95]

These poems are unremarkable in their description and absent of emotion. The images of the light rain and the gentle spring breeze are perfunctory and reveal nothing of the author's state of mind. From this point forward, Ryūhoku pulls away from the narrative, perhaps out of

95. Narushima, *Kōsai nichijō*, p. 428. See also Kawaguchi, *Bakumatsu Meiji kaigai taiken shishū*, pp. 510–11. The reference to a "land of the gods" is actually Yingshu, one of the three fairylands of Chinese legend. The legend holds that sages live in this place, somewhere in the eastern sea.

a realization that the imposition of *kikōbungaku* conceits on his experience in Europe was a literary strain. He continues to see beauty and magnificence in the landscape, but he removes himself from it, leaving it to stand a slightly dehumanized scene.

Ryūhoku's description of Italy differs little from his description of France, except that he had no business to conduct in Italy, and so was occupied even more by tourist activities. Each day brought a new itinerary, and he was able to see a large number of sights in a short period of time. Most of his objectives were architectural, and he was disappointed in no building he saw. The building materials (marble and stone in particular) are commonly noted, as is the height of the building and its furnishings, if any. Qualitative adjectives are all positive: a soaring tower, a grand hall, beautiful gardens. As if watching a Japanese version of *Lifestyles of the Rich and Famous*, the reader learns much about the opulence of the surroundings without more than a snippet or two of information about the people who inhabit them. Ryūhoku is only interested in people of the past; contemporary Italians are invisible, or vague figures, as in the poem on Venice. Consequently, one reads of the Napoleons, Caesar, and Brutus, but not the people with whom the author interacted.

After Italy, Ryūhoku returned to Paris briefly before crossing the English Channel to London. The passage was characteristically rough, and in a poem Ryūhoku noted that even Napoleon had failed to cross over to take England. He was as pleased with England as he had been with France and Italy, and his activities there were similar. He visited the zoological gardens, Windsor Castle, and other points of cultural interest. As other travelers of the time, he found the air thick with industrial smoke, but being the eternal optimist he depicted in a poem the smoke clearing away to reveal a beautiful sunset over London Bridge. After two weeks in London, the party boarded a ship bound for New York. It is here that the travelogue ends, with the following three poems written under way on the Atlantic Ocean on June 1:

> We have traveled across the eastern hemisphere and three
> continents,
> And now muster our remaining courage to head westward.
> I am made well aware that this was the route of Columbus,
> As our ship passes through the giant waves like a single, frail leaf.

The broad sky and endless waves spread azure far and wide,
Alone I stand at the rail and feel the coolness of the salt air,
The solitary moon shines above the infinite billows,
The passenger ship passes through the night, across the Atlantic.

A large whale surfaces between the azure waves,
The northerly spring breeze is cool, and is brisk on my face.
We have come two thousand miles from London,
And not seen even the wisp of an island.[96]

CONCLUSION

The traditional imagery and *uta makura* of Japanese travel writing had been established for centuries by the time the Tokugawa shogunate weakened, fell, and made way for the modern era. However, the art of creating this imagery—going to a new locale, recognizing the *hon'i* or essential character of that place, and recording it in poetry—was one long out of practice. Domestic travel writers had branched out into writing a variety of guidebooks, but all of those focused on the previously set imagery of place. This made overseas travel writing for early Meiji writers a difficult feat, for they faced the daunting task of venturing into an unknown world, bereft of familiar poetic images. If a writer were to employ *uta makura*-style imagery in this new type of travelogue, he would have to make it or borrowed it from the Western tradition.

Initially, the shocking differences from Japan in the West prevented most writers from employing much in the way of lyrical or poetic language; assimilation took all their energy. Exemplified by Nomura, their response to the West was to practice reportage, describing the appearance of what they saw without assigning special characteristics of place. Furthermore, they virtually ignored nature in the West, despite the fact that it was precisely that which played a dominant role in domestic travel writing. Instead, they focused on the technological and cultural developments that differed from Japan.

There were, however, travelogues that broke out of the mold of reportage and incorporated some of the characteristics of domestic

96. Narushima, *Kōsai nichijō*, p. 441. See also Kawaguchi, *Bakumatsu Meiji kaigai taiken shishū*, pp. 522–23. The first line of the third poem is probably inspired by a similar line in Herman Melville's (1819–91) novel *Moby Dick*.

kikōbungaku. In both the poetry and prose of these travelogues, images are overwhelmingly related to human history; locales are noted for what events took place there, and what role those events played in the development of civilization. These images are often reworked versions of Western origin, such as Ryūhoku's comments on Corsica and Elba, and Nakai's comments on Peter the Great. But as we have seen, Ryūhoku and Nakai also evoked canonical imagery from Japan and China in an effort to conflate East and West. What they did *not* do was to find the natural elements in the West that could hold their own in competition with the fabled cherry blossoms and fall foliage of Japan. In Fuchibe's observations, nature and man alike merit attention. Fuchibe also attempted to establish famous places in the West by regularly explaining their significance in a much more informative way than his contemporaries did.

Most writers narrate with a cautious tone, passing judgement on the West only in rare situations. Unlike their Western counterparts who traveled to Japan both to observe and criticize, they refrain from normative comment. Perhaps it was due to the overwhelming nature of the experience, or the thought that the West was more advanced than Japan and thus beyond much criticism, or a natural reticence toward expressing an opinion, but no matter the cause, cultural assessment is notably absent in these travelogues.

CHAPTER THREE

༺ཡཤ༻

Transitions: Mid-Meiji Travelogues, 1880–1900

We have seen how new surroundings presented problems for travel writers overseas in the early Meiji period. Their successors still faced novelty in the West, but they had the advantage of access to materials on foreign lands before departure. Works such as Fukuzawa Yukichi's (1835–1901) *Conditions in the West* (1867), which covered social and political structures, class division, education, and economics, were widely circulated and provided the potential traveler with sound background knowledge on Europe and the United States. Furthermore, translations of Western works, both fiction and nonfiction, were produced at a surprisingly fast pace, thus giving Japanese a Western view of the West. Popular titles included nonfiction, such as Samuel Smiles' *Self Help*, and fiction, such as Jules Verne's *Around the World in Eighty Days*. As a consequence, travel writers could focus on finer points of interest instead of being distracted by each and every sight: they could expect to see the Champs-Élysées in Paris, they could expect to see extensive gardens at Versailles, they knew that their hotel rooms would most likely be furnished with gas lighting and other such luxurious amenities. The journey West was still an adventure, but one that now held some anticipated events.

In the mid-1880s, travelogues of the West appeared at an incrementally rapid rate. These included Hosokawa Junjirō's (1834–1923) *Travels in New Countries*, Sawa Tadashi's (dates unknown) *Journal of a Westward Voyage*, Imamura Seinosuke's (1844–1924) *Miscellany from Abroad*, Akiyama Tokusaburō's (dates unknown) *Diary of a Voyage Around the World*, Arisugawa no Miya Taruhito's (1835–95) *Diary of a*

Tour of Europe and America, Yano Ryūkei's (1850–1931) *Miscellany of a Tour*, Nozu Michitsura's (1842–1908) *Diary of a Tour of Europe and America*, Yamashita Yūtarō's (b. 1859) *Things Seen and Heard Overseas*, Kamata Eikichi's (1857–1934) *Miscellany from a Tour of Europe and America*, and Kuroda Kiyotaka's (1840–1900) *Diary of a Tour*.

Travelers in the mid-Meiji period journeyed for a wider range of objectives than the students and diplomats of the previous two decades. Hosokawa Junjirō, a legal and literary scholar who worked for a division of the Ministry of Finance, went to the United States in 1871 to "observe Western civilization"; Itagaki Taisuke, a prominent politician, went to Europe in 1882 to study constitutional government; Yano Ryūkei, a politician and novelist, went to Europe and the United States in 1884 as part of a privately funded tour group. So although many trips were made to accomplish some specific goal, the travelers did not have the strict guidelines that the early mission members had. Ryūkei and others like him were part of the new breed of travelers who could afford the journey overseas without government assistance and who were willing to finance the undertaking for the simple goal of satisfying curiosity. This lack of official capacity, and along with it such hindrances as the *metsuke*, gave travelers more freedom in planning their itinerary.

ARISUGAWA NO MIYA TARUHITO

Arisugawa, a prince in the imperial family, traveled to Europe and the United States June 1882 through February 1883, visiting famous sights, factories, libraries, museums, and the like, and wrote a record of the experience, titled *Diary of a Tour of Europe and America*. The preface shows that his primary intent was not to create a literary work but rather to report on the state of the West. It states that all the scenic spots, historic ruins, factories, museums, and the like that Arisugawa visited on his trip had been recorded in detail in Kume Kunitake's record of the first mission sent abroad by the Meiji government, *True Account of a Tour of America and Europe*. Therefore, the author says that he will refrain from repeating this information and instead will write a narrative chiefly of each country's government and the reception given to ruling families. This does not hold much promise as entertaining reading, but the preface adds that it will also include a detailed description of the "two or three" strange sights.[1]

Diary of a Tour of Europe and America is written in a diary format, with entries for each day. It has no poetry, only prose. It covers the party's departure from Japan, the journey through Southeast Asia and the Indian Ocean, ports and cities visited in Europe and America; it ends abruptly, giving the return journey to Japan across the Pacific Ocean no more than four lines of comment. As promised, most of the travelogue describes the reception Arisugawa and his party received in each locale. There is an afterword by three of Arisugawa's entourage on the protocol involved in royal visits. Overall, the narrative is objective and dispassionate. The following entry for part of a day spent in Italy is typical:

> Ninth Day. We arrived in Milan in the morning. The Duke of Genoa came to greet us at the station in plain clothes. An honor guard lined up at the head of the platform and played our national anthem. [I] boarded the same car as the Prince and we went straight away to the royal palace. The Duke of Genoa is also staying at the palace. Imperial body guards are regularly stationed at the entryway, and every time one leaves or enters they line up all along the front gate and play music. At three in the afternoon the King of Italy paid a visit dressed in his everyday clothes. [I] came out and greeted him; we met in the Duke of Genoa's room.[2]

Descriptions of diplomatic meetings, awards ceremonies, and dinners of state follow one after the other. Passages of note occur when Arisugawa interjects historical commentary. Near Naples he writes the following entry:

> The ship arrived in the village of Pozzuoli, where there is an old bridge pier. It is made of layered bricks, and the furthest point of it is a platform hundreds of feet out in the middle of the sea, separated from the shore. This is said to be the

---

1. Arisugawa no Miya Taruhito Ōbei jun'yū nikki (Kyōto: Tokudaiji ku'naikyō, 1883; reprint, vol. 2. *Meiji Ōbei kenbunroku shūsei*, Tokyo: Yumani shobō, 1987), p. 7. Page numbers are those in the Yumani reprint.
2. Arisugawa, *Ōbei jun'yū nikki*, pp. 22–23. The personal pronoun "I" has been put in square brackets because in the text the author refers to himself in the third person as His Highness. The Duke of Genoa was Tommaso di Savoia (1854–1931).

ruins of a bridge that the Roman Emperor Nero tried to build to reach the islands in the middle of the bay. There are also many old pillars and walls made of stone in the village. One could see that they were all eroded from the sea water, for they were relics from two thousand years ago, and had been sunk at the bottom of the sea, then exposed to the expanding crust of the earth in an earthquake, leaving them as they appear today. . . . On the way home we passed along a covered road that was built by the Romans long ago. It was about six and half meters tall and half as wide. The length was many city blocks, and we went along giving and taking with the mountain. We left the road, headed for Naples. On our left was the grave site of Virgil.[3]

Here Arisugawa combines a visually descriptive passage of the scenery and connects the significance of it with European history. His style is smooth, evoking the times past while simultaneously depicting the texture and beauty of the present ruins. His sensitivity to the stone pillars and walls shows an appreciation of the events of antiquity, and he is clearly moved by the scene, which graphically displays the passage of time. This sort of writing, in which the author expresses an awareness of place but refrains from composing a poem, is in part what I imagine modern critics mean when they speak of travelogues "influenced by Western writing." The absence of poetry is certainly untraditional, but Arisugawa proves himself quite capable of rousing the reader's sensibility and sympathy. He writes a similarly perceptive passage while visiting Peterhof, the summer palace outside of St. Petersburg:

Tonight the entire sky is the color of the sea. The distant autumn breeze is especially clear. Looking around one sees the layers of trees surrounding the palace, green and floating like billows of smoke. In the front garden countless streams spurt into the air. Colored lamps burn one by one, some red, some violet, some green, some white, each mixing with the other. The landscape is elegant, the likes of which a painting could not capture.[4]

3. Arisugawa, Ōbei jun'yū nikki, pp. 19–20.
4. Arisugawa, Ōbei jun'yū nikki, p. 38.

The passage recalls Fuchibe's description of Russia, in which he tells of "colorful ships" moored on the river and multicolored lamps looking "like a collection of stars," but Arisugawa surpasses Fuchibe in his choice of language and imagery. In his vision, the diaphanous tree tops float in the distance, punctuated by the colored lights and fountains in the foreground. It is not surprising that some critics might have felt the need for a poem to express this chimerical scene, and were dissatisfied with Arisugawa's decision to follow a nontraditional (for travelogues) prose style. Being a member of the imperial family, Arisugawa must have had the necessary schooling to compose at least a passable *waka*, and so his choice not to is worth note. His decision was probably not a conscious effort, however, to ape Western travelogues. Rather, his obsession with royal protocol and not lyricism bespeaks of his political interests. Arisugawa, a staunch supporter of the imperial family, had agitated before the Meiji Restoration for the overthrow of the shogunate. He fought against the shogunate in the Boshin Civil War (1868–69) and again against Saigō Takamori (1827–77) in the Satsuma Rebellion (1877). In sum, when he traveled about Europe, he made great efforts to focus on his interaction with other families of royalty and/or nobility, legitimizing his own title and theirs at the same time.

After touring Europe, the party sailed for the United States, arriving in New York. There they were welcomed and lodged in the Windsor Hotel. Ulysses S. Grant, who was living in New York at the time, was one of their hosts; he held a reception for them at the Union Club, which was attended by more than twenty high-ranking and wealthy Americans. This is all the information Arisugawa provides. The next two entries say simply, "Left New York and went sight-seeing at Niagara Falls" and "Arrived in Washington, D.C."[5] President Arthur greeted the group in Washington and arranged for them to tour a navy steamship and Mt. Vernon. There was yet another reception that involved a gun salute and a band, and the tour of Washington was over. One line mentions visiting San Francisco, but no information is given on how the group arrived there. Suddenly, they are on a postal ship, the *Peking*, headed for home, and the diary ends. This conclusion is

5. Arisugawa, *Ōbei jun'yū nikki*, pp. 58–59.

even hastier than Nakai's in *Setting Off on a Tour* or Fuchibe's in *Diary of a Trip to Europe*; we learn nothing about what transpired at sea.

Arisugawa's travelogue defies easy categorization. It is at once a political, historical, and personal document. He was not a particularly skilled writer—his cadence and diction are unremarkable—but he was certainly competent to write this record. Moreover, the work shows an instinctive response to the act of keeping a travel diary: that there is merit in doing so, and that personal impressions are a legitimate element therein. Indeed, the fact that Arisugawa saw the need to supplement Kume Kunitake's detailed account shows a feeling of incompletion without a personal (and imperial) element. Perhaps he was emulating, albeit unconsciously, his ancestors whose poems establishing imperial dominion appear in the *Collection of Myriad Leaves*. Of course, he could not expect that naming and celebrating foreign lands would give him power over them as it had earlier imperial poets. But the role of the imperial family in writing travel poetry was nonetheless continued through Arisugawa's efforts.

KURIHARA RYŌICHI

At the same time that Arisugawa was touring Europe, the influential politician Itagaki Taisuke (1837–1919) was there also, studying constitutional government. Itagaki had formed Japan's first political party, the Liberal Party, in 1881, and was the object of an assassination attempt in 1882. The Liberal Party did not have the Meiji government's good favor, and it was perhaps for this reason that Itagaki was encouraged to leave the country for a stint overseas. He traveled with an entourage, among whom was a translator and fellow politician, Kurihara Ryōichi (1855–92). As a young man, Kurihara had traveled widely in Japan on oratorical campaigns for the Freedom Rights Movement, an early Meiji political movement that touted the expansion of liberty and rights for citizens and sought to participate in the national government. During the Second Opium War (1858–60), he traveled to China as a newspaper reporter. The trip to Europe and the United States in 1882 was his first and only journey to the West.

Kurihara's travelogue, *A Diary of Itagaki's Tour of Europe and America*, describes the voyage to Europe.[6] The work is written in a diary format, with entries for almost each day.[7] Kurihara writes in a mix of prose and Chinese poetry. The travelogue is exclusively about the journey to Europe; the record ends once Kurihara arrives, telling us almost nothing about his impressions of his destination. Indeed, despite the title, we never see the party arrive in the United States. *A Diary of Itagaki's Tour of Europe and America* differs from works like Ryūhoku's *Diary of a Journey Westward* in that it ignores most of the itinerary of the group. We are given just enough information to know where the action takes place, but Kurihara's companions are rarely mentioned, and, because Kurihara omits the activities in Europe and the United States, we are spared the monotonous accounts of meetings and receptions.

The party departed Tokyo on November 11, 1882, boarded the French postal ship *Volga* in Yokohama, and set sail. Still in Japanese waters, Kurihara waxes nostalgic on the scenery:

November 12. Gloomy at dawn.

We have already passed the Toba offing. Toba is my hometown, but due to bustle of work I had not returned to the province for what was already many years. Now I gazed toward it, a mere speck in the misty vastness. I could not see the silhouette of my hometown, and could not but feel a slight regret at parting from it.[8]

After spending years in Tokyo, he felt sad to be so close to home, yet so far away. Further down the coast he passes Tosa off the coast of Shikoku and, recalling the many friends whom he made while traveling there in 1877, he gazes at the mountains with the same thoughts (he tells us) as he had when gazing at his own hometown.

6. This work has been reprinted: Kurihara Ryōichi, *Itagaki-kun Ōbei man'yū nikki*, Morooka Kuni, ed. in *Meiji Ōbei kenbunroku shūsei*, vol. 2 (Tokyo: Yumani shobō, 1883, 1987).
   Another record of Itagaki's journey is Shimizu Masujirō's *Itagaki-kun Ōbei man'yūroku*, reprinted in the same volume as Kurihara's work. This work is also written in diary format but ends upon arrival in France and records nothing further on Europe.
7. Although there are discreet entries, they are grouped together and labeled for the place from which the entire group was sent. Thus, for example, the letters about the Middle East are part of the fourth section labeled "From Paris."
8. Kurihara, *Itagaki-kun Ōbei man'yū nikki*, p. 70. Page numbers refer to those in the Yumani shobō reprint, not those in the original.

The following day they pass the cape of Sata on the southern tip of Kyūshū, and Kurihara recalls that it was the site of an imperial battleship's defeat during the rebellions that led to the fall of the Tokugawa shogunate.

These entries show Kurihara's sense of place, which he expresses through both nostalgia and historical reference. Even when the place is one about which he can feel no personal nostalgia, he is quick to associate it with important human events to give the reader a deeper appreciation and understanding. In the South China Sea, the ship passes Fuzhou. Kurihara comments that Fujian province was one of five ports, along with Ninbo, Xiamen, Guangdong, and Shanghai, to be opened after the Opium Wars. In Hong Kong, he tells us that the island was taken by the British in 1842 after the Chinese lost the first Opium War, and that the Kowloon peninsula was ceded to the British in 1858. In Palawan, he explains that the Philippines was where the first Spanish and Portuguese arrived in the East, that King Philip II colonized them, and that because he was the one to open these islands to foreign contact, they were named after him in 1580.[9] In Saigon, he tells us that the Mekong is a superlatively large river that originates in the Koulkun mountains of Tibet, flows in a southerly direction, and eventually empties into the sea. Almost every locale is given some historical background, so the travelogue reads as much like a history primer as it does a diary of one person's experience.

Kurihara's writing is not dry, however. When he is not providing the reader with objective geographical information, he expresses his opinion readily. Whereas the earlier writers such as Nomura withheld subjective statements, Kurihara is quick to compliment and criticize. Furthermore, his descriptive passages are laced with beautiful language and imagery. Consequently, *A Diary of Itagaki's Tour of Europe and America* is a pastiche of historical explications, political commentary, and poetic reflections. It is more like Western travelogues than its predecessors, but it still maintains some similarities to the traditional Japanese travelogue in that it places some emphasis on the significance of place.

Kurihara's political commentary finds the Western treatment of Asians unsatisfactory, if not appalling. He looks favorably on most

9. Kurihara was mistaken; the Philippines were named in 1571.

things Asian, and unfavorably on things Western. In both Hong Kong and Singapore, he notes that the Westerners treat the natives "practically as if they were slaves."[10] In describing the long history of India, he says that two millennia ago the Indians had already become a civilized nation while the Westerners were still "barbarians." In Sri Lanka, he recounts having a conversation with a Sri Lankan leader—the leaders spoke English, as did Kurihara—about British rule:

> The members of the native leadership understood English very well, and I wanted to try to delve into the natives' feelings. Pointing to the Sri Lankan Governor's house, I asked, "Do you natives venerate the British governor, and do you love the British expatriates?" The leader's countenance changed to one of terror and he replied, "No, no, we natives hate this very much. However, we have not the power to oppose them. No matter what, we are all devout Buddhists, and among us is a particular dislike of Western teachings. Consequently, although we hate the Westerners, we cannot but obey them."[11]

When Kurihara is denied a drink of water at a roadside shop, he is told it is because he wears Western clothing and eats Western food. Because he has not undergone the Buddhist Purification of the Six Roots of Perception, the shop owner fears defilement if he gives but even one drop of water to him. His Western-style hat and shoes, plus his lack of purification, are also given as reasons why he was not permitted to enter a temple. Kurihara's reaction is to say that he bore the incident and became accustomed to such attitudes, showing not only his sympathetic dislike for Western imperialism but also his respect for religious beliefs. (He gives pages of descriptive commentary on the development and dissemination of Buddhism on the Indian subcontinent.) He goes on to say that he could not possibly be a judge of the Sri Lankans' feeling, given the short period of time he spent observing them, but that he sees religious similarities between the Indians and the Japanese. The political commentary is abruptly ended with a beautiful description of the evening:

10. Kurihara, *Itagaki-kun Ōbei man'yū nikki*, p. 77 and p. 91, respectively.
11. Kurihara, *Itagaki-kun Ōbei man'yū nikki*, pp. 99–100.

I walked along the alleyways, and dusk had fallen by the time I had gone a distance from the ship. The lights from the ships in the crowded harbor were like clustered stars, blinking and twinkling, their reflections falling on the water. The sound of what seemed like the natives singing chanteys and reciting *sūtra* made it quite a strange sight.[12]

From Colombo the party sailed to Aden, which was then under British control and being administered as part of India. Dark clouds half obscured the sight of the tall mountains, but Kurihara finds the landscape impressive:

The African continent faced the port of Aden. Inland there is a great desert, and along that are mountains, all of which are barren and tower over one. Angry waves pound the shore, sending up a fierce thunder and blowing snow; it is a most magnificent sight.[13]

Camel hitched to water dealer's cart in Aden

12. Kurihara, *Itagaki-kun Ōbei man'yū nikki*, p. 102.
13. Kurihara, *Itagaki-kun Ōbei man'yū nikki*, pp. 104–5.

Native boys on the boat at Aden

He finds the natives of the Arabian Peninsula less impressive, and, in comparing them to the Indians, says that there are some who "resemble apes" and look quite like "barbarians."[14] This despite the fact that he did not land, and thus was left to muse about the landscape without the direct interruption of interaction with the shore. Still, he gives a cursory and nonjudgmental history of Mohammed and Islam. Kurihara's activities in the Red Sea were limited to gazing at the scenery to both sides of the ship and taking comfort in the music performed every evening on board. Kurihara mentions nothing about other passengers on the ship, which sets him apart from most other travel writers who, even if they were prevented by a language barrier from freely communicating with them, saw fit to describe their fellow travelers.

14. Kurihara, *Itagaki-kun Ōbei man'yū nikki*, p. 106.

In the Gulf of Suez, Kurihara gives a history of the Suez Canal, providing the sort of information and detail one might expect of a writer describing a foreign place to his home-bound compatriots. It is curious that earlier writers did not provide this information; it seems more likely that this was because they did not have access to it rather than because they assumed audience familiarity with the topic. Once through the canal, Kurihara lands briefly at Port Said, which he describes as a small, prosperous city, and then continues on into the Mediterranean Sea.

The ship passes through the Ionian Sea, where the seas were rough enough to concern some of the passengers. They passed between Italy and Sicily, and Kurihara comments that it is a very ancient locale, one that has gone through many changes through the ages. He says that he is deeply impressed as they pass by. They land in Naples, over which looms Mt. Vesuvius. Naples is but briefly described; we are told that there are hillocks in the roads, that there is an old stone wall, and there was a large armored ship docked in the harbor. The latter brings rise to the comment that Italy has an appearance of might, and that, since the rise of Giuseppe Garibaldi (1807–82) and his Liberal Party, it had unified the many small states and suffered many battles, "throwing off her Austrian shackles to become a strong nation."[15] His final comment is that this unification was not one of chance (implying that intent and effort were key). As the boat sets sail for Marseilles, Kurihara writes:

> Gazing out at the southern shore of the harbor, I saw houses on the mountainsides, some sparsely scattered, some clustered together, joined together and facing the sea. The day

Bay of Naples

15. Kurihara, *Itagaki-kun Ōbei man'yū nikki*, p. 118.

was clear and due to the exceptional seasonal warmth and
atmospheric clarity of Italy, the sky was a dyed a solid azure,
like the sea in springtime.[16]

Kurihara's sensitivity to nature is noteworthy, and even though he is
equally concerned with the history of locales, his ability to depict the
landscape sets him apart from his predecessors. In Marseilles, dark-
ness prevented any clear view of the harbor, but he comments that
the reflection of the lighthouse was like "chaotic stars." He is equally
sensitive to emotion; when the ship is held at anchor for a day in the
harbor at Marseilles, waiting for quarantine clearance, he notes how
eager the Western passengers must be to return to their hometowns
and be united with their families. Being on the outbound leg of his
journey, Kurihara could not express his own nostalgia for place, but
the idea of a homecoming is so central to Japanese travel imagery that

The harbor at Marseilles

16. Kurihara, *Itagaki-kun Ōbei man'yū nikki*, p. 118.

he borrows it from his fellow passengers and thus gives the travelogue more resonance.

Kurihara went sightseeing for one day in Marseilles, and gives a simple, unremarkable account of it. The next day in Lyons, he was impressed with the city, especially the sericulture, and likened it to the city of Kobe in Japan. In Paris on the following day, he says the fountains at his inn on the Champs-Élysées are particularly nice in the summer. The remainder of the travelogue—a sparse four pages— is dedicated to discussing the negotiations for which Itagaki Taisuke had gone to France. Kurihara does not chronicle the journey to the United States or the return journey to Japan.

Although *A Diary of Itagaki's Tour of Europe and America* ends abruptly, Kurihara did not stop writing altogether; a collection of twelve Chinese poems, titled *Twelve Selected Poems from Paris*, gives his impressions of the French capital.[17]

The Seine

The shadows of the trees link together the bridges, the blue
    water flows willfully
A deep mist imprisons the stately mansions
The water tinged with the rouge of many beauties
Pushes aside the sorrow of parting and flows to the world

l'Arc de Triomphe

The machine of war spread north and south
Conquering the world, flaunting its military power
But his exploits caused so many deaths
How many men have returned to the Arc de Triomphe?[18]

Land of Immortal Happiness

With royal horse clad in beautiful bridle and golden saddle,
A beauty's carriage runs with crimson wheels and pretty axles.
But the Parisiens cannot yet be proud of their prosperity
For those of lesser provenance gather in the town[19]

---

17. These poems are reprinted in Kawaguchi Hisao, comp. *Bakumatsu Meiji kaigai taiken shishū* (Tokyo: Daitō bunka daigaku tōyō kenkyūjo, 1984), pp. 282–94.
18. It is thought that the third and fourth lines refer to Napoleon I's failed campaign in Russia in 1812.
19. The first two lines are thought to depict events on the Champs-Élysées.

L'Arc de Triomphe

Place de la Concorde
A dragon spouts raindrops in the bronze basin of the fountain
Reaching to the clouds, the tip of the stone tower sharply thrusts
This is where, long ago, blood dripped from necks
But now people come here to relax[20]

The Tuileries
The hedges are gone, but the stone walls of the palace remain
Countless generations of royalty have passed, but now it is
    burned empty
The garden of flowers and trees has returned to a place for all to
    come
Now there is no one to lord over the spring breezes[21]

20. The tower in the second line refers to the Egyptian obelisk still in place today in the Place
    de la Concorde. The dripping blood in the third line refers to the death of Louis XVI, who
    was guillotined in the then Place de la Révolution on January 21, 1793.
21. The Palace of the Tuileries was begun in 1564 for Catherine de Médicis, after which time
    it was occupied intermittently by French royalty. It was destroyed in 1792 in the popular
    uprising. Napoleon I renovated the palace, which underwent further renovation under
    Napoleon II. In 1871, ten years before Kurihara saw it, it was burned during the Com-
    mune of Paris uprising.

Place de la Concorde

The Tuileries

The Louvre
I cannot hear the royal bells or jewels
But only see the remaining pillars
Touring within the palace is not forbidden
Now there is a museum on these old palace grounds[22]

Colonne Vendôme
Triumphal voices shatter the heavens and split the earth
As if maddened in battle they took the old city
The heroic spirits of those who protected the country will never
    fade away
The soaring metal tower shows his great achievement[23]

The Louvre

22. Construction of the Louvre was begun in the twelfth century and completed in 1850. Originally a fortress and royal palace, it was expanded over the century by various rulers and
came to house an enormous art collection. It began being used as the National Art
Museum in 1791. The "royal bells and jewels" in the first line refer to the bells worn by
the horses of the French king and gems attached to the king's clothing, which tinkled as
they swung together.
23. This poem is about the Colonne Vendôme, a monument built in 1806 in the Place Vendôme
by Napoleon I, destroyed in 1871, then rebuilt in 1874. The monument commemorates
Napoleon's victories against Austria and Russia in the Battle of Austerlitz in 1805.

Napoleon's Tomb
He used all his great power, but conquest was in vain
One cannot but be moved when recalling that era
Grudges may remain for his heroic eternal achievements,
Napoleon lies dejected, entombed in his coffin

Napoleon's Tomb

The Luxembourg Palace

Deep in the grove it is quiet; have I died and gone to another
    world?
A stone horse dances in a pool, spouting mist
The roses bloom and scatter, covering the ground with their
    fragrance
The spring breezes blow as they did then[24]

Reminiscing on Paris

The waters of the Seine; the city of Paris
This is the first name in great lands
The Eastern traveler who has traveled far on his raft
Has no one to whom to express his nostalgic feelings of Paris
I think of Louis XIV
Whose brutal government oppressed the people with a tiger's
    strength
With an iron will and no quarter for the disheartened
The people were felled and punished by cauldron and sword[25]

The Luxembourg Palace

24. The fountain in the second line is probably Fountaine de Médicis, installed on the grounds
    in the nineteenth century.
25. A "cauldron" (*teikaku*) was used to boil prisoners alive.

Thus the Bourbon King's multifariously evil rule caused his
    subjects' pain
But ominous portents left admonitions undone
And in July a sorrowful wind blew[26]
A ferocity roiled the heavens and rose in the city
Men broke boughs and soldiered forth, raising the sticks as
    banners[27]
In one action, the ad hoc troops felled the monarch[28]
Execution by guillotine is like cutting grass; the machine
    replaces the sword
The corpse falls into a mound, and the blood flows away
"All autocracies are our enemies!"
Said the manifesto sent out to the world
Their eternal indignation came from the Social Contract[29]
The Montagnards carried out the exploits of the day
But then the country fell to violence and chaos
Why did the hero grow old amongst the people?[30]
Fierce battles broke out, and there was no end to the chaos.
Nothing remains of the master plans or the empire.
The people laud freedom, and peace reigns over the land.
In the Republic rich and poor stand alike
Do Confucianists really know the ways of the family and state?
When chaos peaks the result is good government![31]
As now, the flower of European civilization
Has grown entirely from rank wind and putrid rains.

In these poems, Kurihara's chief concern is not nature but man; he
dwells on French history in a manner more reflective than in his prose.
He seems torn between admiration and contempt for Napoleon, for
the ideal of liberty associated with the French Revolution appeals to
him, but the brutality of the guillotine is dreadful. In any case, he

26. "July" here refers to the events of July 14, 1789, when the Louis XVI and the royal family
    were forced to leave Versailles for Paris.
27. This line refers to the storming of the Bastille prison.
28. This refers to the guillotining of Louis XVI in January 1793.
29. This refers to Rousseau's *The Social Contract* (French: *Du Contrat social ou Principes du droit
    politique*).
30. "The hero" refers to Napoleon I. "The people" (*sōmō*) could also be construed as "the grasses."
31. This line implies that good government resulting from chaos goes against the expectations
    of the Confucianists, who hold that order results in good governance. The author seems
    to be referring not only to Confucianists but also to the Japanese people.

clearly feels that the Japanese (Neo-Confucian) predilection for stability and order is misguided, because, according to him, modern advanced European civilization was the result not of order but of bloody battles and political turmoil. The oblique allusions, which require explanatory footnotes even for the Western reader, may be about French history, but their presence is reminiscent of traditional *waka* and *kanshi* allusions.

Kurihara laments that he has "no one to whom to express his nostalgic feelings of Paris." Apparently the French were uninterested in reflecting on the Napoleonic empire of the Revolution (by then it had been rendered passé?), or perhaps discussing such deep issues with a Japanese in English was not an enticing proposition. And Kurihara discounts having a conversation with the Japanese, although, traveling with Itagaki's entourage, he certainly had the opportunity to do so. No, his problem was that in order to properly express nostalgia and experience *ryojō* he needed the company of other poets, men who could appreciate the historical poignancy and gravity of his verse. Those men were apparently not on hand, and without an outlet for these emotions, Kurihara's travel experience was diminished.

YAMASHITA YŪTARŌ

In October 1880, Yamashita Yūtarō set sail for England on a self-financed, three-and-one-half year trip. A student at one of the imperial universities in Japan, he went to Europe to study law, which he continued to teach once he was repatriated. His return journey was via the United States, where he visited New York, Washington, D.C., Niagara Falls, Chicago, and San Francisco. His travelogue, *Things Seen and Heard Overseas*, was published in 1886.

Yamashita's trip followed the standard route through Asia, with stops in Hong Kong, Singapore, Penang, Colombo, Aden, and Alexandria, and across the Mediterranean to Brindisi, Italy. In Hong Kong, he described the island as an "extremely unhealthy place" where the British nonetheless had built roads and developed a bustling trading port. People rushed about day and night there, and a veritable "little England" was established. He reports that the favored form of transportation was a sort of palanquin, although *jinrikisha* were also in use.

It is a dispassionate description, very much anchored in the present. Singapore, like Hong Kong, was heavily flavored with British imperialism. Yamashita comments that "the streets are modeled in a Western style and are very clean, however, the natives' houses are painful to see, being little more than thatched cottages."[32] The natives' appearance was no better: "like women they wear earrings and nose rings, and their clothing carefully covers half their bodies; I cannot stand to see their ugly state."[33] He was much more pleased with the natives in Sri Lanka, where he described the port of Galle, to the south of Colombo:

> Pointe de Galle is located on the southwestern coast of Ceylon. The harbor is large and shallow, and if the seas become rough ships can safely anchor there. This is the main reason why British and French postal steamships changed the location of where they land. In the port perfect rows of houses extend in all directions like city streets. It is lush with strange trees, such as banana and other such tropical plants. Of all the ports we have passed through since leaving Japan, I like Point de Galle the best. The people of India are, for the most part, of the same race as Europeans and therefore the people I have met—even of the lower classes—have a very attractive facial bone structure.[34]

When he went ashore the next day, he saw beggars in the streets but spared them the sort of caustic remarks he made in Singapore. It is hard to imagine that Sri Lankan beggars with their "naked bodies" chasing vehicles in the streets presented a more pleasant picture than the average person in Singapore or Hong Kong; Yamashita's bias was apparently caused by both racist conceptions and the thrill of seeing something totally unfamiliar.

In Aden—which, when Yamashita arrived, had not seen rain for three years and was desert-like in appearance—the one thing that "one must see" was the large reservoir that had been built by the Romans in ancient times and recently discovered after many years. The reservoir impressed him, but the natives did not:

32. Yamashita Yūtarō, *Kaigai kenbunroku*, in *Meiji Ōbei kenbunroku shūsei*, vol. 2 (Tokyo: Yumani shobō, 1886, 1987), p. 208.
33. Yamashita, *Kaigai kenbunroku*, p. 208.
34. Yamashita, *Kaigai kenbunroku*, p. 209.

The natives of this place are from a more westerly place than those in Hong Kong, and the ones I observed were from the middle and lower classes. The color of their bodies is like black lacquer, and their hair is straw colored. When swimming, they are like otters. On land, they scurry about the hot sand in bare feet. Geography texts tell of these people, but I found these true barbarians to be shameful.[35]

Yamashita was a snob of sorts; he was only interested in the famous and advanced sights of the Western world. When his party was delayed six or seven hours on their way to Alexandria by a break in the railroad tracks, there was much grumbling at the unfairness of it all, for they were stranded in a deserted area with nothing but an "army of mosquitos" to keep them company. The natural landscape is not featured sympathetically or affectionately, and it is not until he reaches Alexandria that Yamashita changes his tone, for it is a "famous ancient" city that "one really should observe intently," apparently for its place in human history and not for its present state. Sadly for Yamashita, he did not have time to do the city justice. While at sea, he does not see fit to reflect on the view or on the nature of his journey. Longing for home is not expressed, nor is any reaction to his psychological state. He is so enamored of the West and her civilization that the rest of the world remains beneath his notice.

Beyond the Suez Canal and into the Mediterranean, Yamashita continues to focus on cultural advancements and refinements. He goes to Brindisi and Verona, and then on to Leipzig, Munich, and Hamburg. None of these places gets more than a sentence or two of passing surface observations, however. In Copenhagen, he goes to the theater and here begins to give his reader more detail:

> I went to the Royal Theater [in Copenhagen]. This was the first theater I saw in Europe. Afterwards, every other theater I went to I compared to this one. The origins of today's Western theater lie in the courts of ancient kings, where performances were held. Eventually the masses were also permitted to view performances, so the actors held positions of high esteem in society. Indeed, if we translate the name "Royal Theater" it means a "theater connected to the

---

35. Yamashita, *Kaigai kenbunroku*, p. 211.

Royal Theater in Copenhagen

emperor." In England, too, there are two or three large theaters that are directly under the control of the royal palace.
In such high-class theaters they usually perform refined
works, such as those by Shakespeare or Goethe. In the Royal
Theater, everything is grandly gilt with gold and silver, and
both inside and out is decorated. Performance times do not
exceed three or four hours. Performances begin in the
evening, and end halfway through the night. The actors are
not in the least bit indecent—they try to imitate everyday
behavior. The audience always dresses nicely for the performance. There are rooms outside the theater for food and
beverages and for smoking. Inside the theater quiet order is
maintained; there is never any boisterousness. It is quite like
a temple or a palace inside. Of course, there is applause and
cheering when a performance ends. It is said that for Europeans the theater is a place in which to study human nature.
There are, after all, some actors who have a noble spirit.[36]

Shortly after attending the theater, Yamashita met a Mr. Paulsen, who
was a lead actor in the Royal Theater. He notes that Paulsen "studied literature at university and upon graduation entered the theater

36. Yamashita, *Kaigai kenbunroku*, pp. 218–19.

where he became an actor. He eventually rose to the position he has today, and commands much respect."[37] Clearly Yamashita is impressed with the social status of performing artists in Europe; it was far and away above the respect afforded actors in Japan at the time. He was one of many Japanese of the time who were fascinated with the social status of artists—literary, theatrical, visual, etc.—and came to the realization that powerful and admired personages in the West enhanced rather than detracted from their status by participating in the creation of art. In particular, it came as a revelation to the Meiji Japanese that one could be both an artist and a leader, as was demonstrated by Benjamin Disraeli (1804–81), who published novels, histories, and political essays and was elected as British Prime Minister in 1868. Such a mixing of art and government was unheard of in Japan, where artists were usually considered a debauched group of undesirables. And although Yamashita did not meet anyone particularly skilled at both diplomacy and art, he was clearly struck by the respectability of the actors in the theater.

On occasion, Yamashita depicts things Japanese in a positive light, as when he tells us that upon a visit to a museum he taught a curator the proper way to don a Japanese theatrical wig—after the curator had initially donned it backwards. Yamashita stifles a laugh at the sight but does not poke further fun at the confused Westerner.

Also while in London, Yamashita writes about the natural landscape and in particular mentions an aspect of the city that surprisingly had not been noted by previous travel writers: the fog. He introduces it in his travelogue almost apologetically, prefacing his remarks with the note that the fog has nothing to do with trade, politics, society, religion, or any other such thing, as if only those were expected topics in such a work. But with his observations, he echoes the contents of the premodern travelogues:

> The weather in [London] is rarely settled. Barely thirty days of the over three-hundred and sixty some in the year have clear skies. Otherwise, it is cloudy or rainy. During the change from spring to summer it is rare to have half a day of clear skies. Thick fog rolls in during early winter and during November, December, January and February it is par-

37. Yamashita, *Kaigai kenbunroku*, p. 220.

ticularly heavy. At such times one cannot distinguish daylight from night; candles are lit in order to conduct daily
business, as one would normally do at night. Trains come to
a stop in all directions, and it is rare to hear the sound of
carriages. The light from thousands of street lamps becomes
dim. It is truly a gloomy sight. The fog of London has been,
after all, famous since ancient times; Julius Caesar declared
this country "The Island of Mist." The source of this dense
fog is the nearby sea, in which southerly warm currents
meet the cold current of the North Sea.[38]

Indeed, Yamashita has considered all aspects of the fog in London.
But what is of particular note here is that he is perpetuating established *hon'i* (if we can say that Westerners coin their own *hon'i*). London was known for its fog long before Yamashita arrived, and although
he brings a slightly different perspective to it, he is ultimately simply
mentioning what his readers would expect of any travel writer: allusive variations on a theme. Just as Bashō mentions the harvest moon
at Kashima Shrine, Yamashita mentions the fog in London. We can
see by the lack of similar passages, though, that Yamashita was not
inclined to follow this formula. He is primarily concerned with the
here and now, and is an astute political observer. He sees his role in
writing *Things Seen and Heard Overseas* as ambassador of information
on the West. Consequently, interspersed in the personal account of
his journey he includes a translations of William Kingston's (1814–80)
biography of William I (1797–1888), king of Prussia and the first German emperor, Margaret Oliphant's (1828–97) biography of Queen
Victoria of England (1819–1901), and an 1883 article in the London
Daily News on how to help the poor.[39] He also gives a long explanation of holidays' meanings and how they are celebrated. It is a shame
that Yamashita dedicated so much time to these translations, for
when he writes about his own observations, he is more entertaining
and thoughtful. When in the royal palace in Berlin, his description
displays a greater sensitivity than that of Muragaki in Hawai'i or
Nakai in Russia:

38. Yamashita, *Kaigai kenbunroku*, p. 227.
39. It is not clear from the text, but the probably original sources were as follows: William Henry
    Giles Kingston, *Count Ulrich of Lindburg: A Truthful Story of the Reformation in Germany*
    (New York: Carlton & Lanahan, 1868); Margaret Oliphant, *The Queen* (New York: Harper
    & Bros., 1878).

When the Emperor or the Prince are not in residence, the
Royal Palace and the Prince's palace are open for inspection
by commoners. They are thus able to have a peek into both
the interior and exterior decorations—above all, they may
see the Emperor's study, in which books and an old desk lay
in disarray. Truly they are afforded a view into the details of
imperial decisions of state affairs of the royal family. There
are a number of statues of Bismarck about, and in the private room of the prince there is a chair in the shape of a
saddle, which is the strangest sight indeed. Various ceremonies are conducted within the palace, and the meeting
halls prepared for such activities are really quite beautiful.
A room called the "Silver Room" is entirely painted in silver,
and another large ballroom has tens of large portraits hung
on the walls, including one of Napoleon I, a landscape of
the Alps in which the mountains soar, and a portrait of the
present emperor William. The portrait of the coronation
held in Versailles in France is strikingly similar. However,
every room is not necessarily prepared; there are some
strange things to be seen, such as the statues of the goddess
of victory, which were presented to the emperor by army
commanders or local citizens as an expression of congratu-
lations whenever Prussia clashed militarily with other countries and was victorious. The shape of each statue is different,
and some of them are quite skillfully done. Clearly they are
of high craftsmanship, and by them one can tell that this
country's military spirit is thriving. There are also gorgeous
worship halls. On Sundays the emperor and the royal family worship here. These halls are also used for royal weddings,
christenings, funerals, and the like.[40]

Muragaki and Nakai saw palaces as strange but beautiful structures,
separate from the mundane. They did not imagine the everyday activities within, nor were portraits any more than pieces of art—they did
not recognize the personages portrayed, much less the significance
of said person in history. In short, everything they saw was so unfamiliar that it defied categorization. Yamashita is able to make those
categorizations: he calls some things "strange," and others "beautiful,"
differentiations that seem simple enough but were often beyond the
earliest travelers. He is familiar with Western architecture, enough so

40. Yamashita, *Kaigai kenbunroku*, pp. 292–93.

Lyons

that he does not tell us the size of the palace or the layout of the building but rather focuses on the decorations and other fine points.

He is also able to be critical. Although is it true that some of the early diplomats found Western customs inscrutable and thus unpalatable, that distaste never went beyond gross observations. Yamashita takes his criticisms further, and as a result, whether purposely or not, he leaves the reader chuckling, as when he describes the Germans:

> Although the Germans are good at the careful practice of profound reticence, they are lacking in sagacity, and are actually close to being a bit stupid in some things, particularly in regard to three penchants of theirs: sausage, tobacco, and beer. Sausage is a dish made of finely crushed meat stuffed in pigs' intestines. It tastes quite good; it is round and fat and not expensive in price, but some have bad things mixed into them. However, the Germans' fondness for them is like a monkey's fondness for persimmons. It is as if they are mad with drink. Tobacco, too, is widely smoked before women and children. The British and the Americans are not

strict in censuring them, nor is the German government yet
taking authority to tax tobacco. The price is extremely low,
but they do not want to increase the people's taxes. The best
beer is that produced in the state of Bavaria, especially that
from the city of Munich—I myself am confident of this. They
have few wants, and are endowed with great perseverance.
Thus, there are many who go to England or America, who
establish their own company or work for others and make
their own livelihood. Truly in London the society of lower
class merchants is composed of this sort of German immigrant who is diligent and intently envies the profits others
make. They are known as the Chinese of Europe.[41]

Earlier travelers found the food unpalatable but never described it in
detail. Yamashita not only describes it but criticizes it, ridiculing the
Germans simultaneously. Indeed, Yamashita was quick to make stereo-
typed distinctions about the races (the Japanese excepted) and often
wrote about the Chinese immigrants he encountered with the same
contempt and disdain he expressed while describing the native residents of Hong Kong. On his voyage home across the Pacific, he states
that Chinese laborers are lazy and only do one-tenth of the work of
a European.[42] He goes on to describe his fellow passengers:

The lower class cabins are filled with hundreds of Chinese.
They are all repatriating after having gone to various locales
in America—especially to San Francisco—working for a
number of years and saving a bit of money. So, there is one
group that is composed of an entire family traveling together.
Old and young, men and women are all mixed in together.
Over half the men and women in this group spend their time
together betting on dice—the arguments are tremendous.
Those who do not participate in these activities spend their
days and nights lying about smoking opium. Their color is
that of one half alive, half dead. When I look at their state
I see that they are poor excuses for humans. One can only
regret the diminished strength of the Chinese empire. Three
of the Chinese died at sea. Immediately the ship's doctor
was beckoned and he disemboweled the corpses, removing

41. Yamashita, *Kaigai kenbunroku*, pp. 296–97.
42. Yamashita, *Kaigai kenbunroku*, p. 411.

the vital organs. The flesh was preserved and placed in a prepared coffin, which was taken back to Hong Kong. Because
the Chinese have a custom that one's bones must be
returned to one's motherland there has sprung up in Hong
Kong and San Francisco a company that ships corpses.
Agents from said company travel on ships between the two
ports. When someone dies at sea, they take care of each and
every detail. Like the ship's doctor, they disembowel the
body, for which they receive five dollars a head. They have
thus made a business for themselves.[43]

Yamashita seems a bit disgusted with it all—these indolent Chinese,
either gambling or drugged lifeless are representative of their failed
empire. Worse, a rather sordid enterprise sprang up to capitalize on
their misery. Yamashita is representative of most Japanese here in that
he finds China a pale shadow of her former self and dismisses it as a
lesser neighbor. As Joshua Fogel notes, ". . . the China of the classics, whence [Japanese travelers] sought cultural referents, and the real
contemporary China were not the same."[44]

By the end of his journey, Yamashita had become a true malcontent. Like Tobias Smollett (1721–71), the lovable British grouch who
hated every aspect of travel and whose travel writing was popular precisely because of that, Yamashita is dependably grumpy and disgusted. His vocabulary is rich with variations on "vulgar," "crude," and
"unsophisticated" in a way that amuses, whether intentional or not.
The disdain and contempt that early on had been reserved for other
Asians is later aimed at Westerners, too. In Queenstown (modern-day
Cobh), Ireland, he writes:

> The environs here are desolate fields with a few sparse trees.
> The condition of the fishing boats within the harbor is
> extremely crude. The peasant women who come to sell fruit
> and the like are pure Hibernians and can only speak in vul-
> garities. It isn't a particularly thriving trading port, either.
> There are no more than two or three large ships at anchor.[45]

43. Yamashita, *Kaigai kenbunroku*, pp. 413–14.
44. Joshua A. Fogel, *The Literature of Travel in the Japanese Rediscovery of China: 1862–1945* (Stan-
    ford: Stanford University Press, 1996), p. 46.
45. Yamashita, *Kaigai kenbunroku*, p. 395.

It was an unpleasant, if not rotten, time at port. Admittedly, late nine-teenth century Ireland was not the center of the European industrial revolution or culture, but even in larger, more prosperous ports, Yamashita rarely finds things in which to delight. He finds the human condition disheartening and miserable. Uncharacteristically he turns to Nature for solace while crossing the American West by train. There he is struck by the number of cattle he sees dead and frozen along the tracks, and is surprised by the sound of the passing train echoing between the mountains. For a moment, the reader sees a sensitive side to this narrative as Yamashita says that he is comforted by the strange sight of prairie dog "villages" on the Great Plains, perhaps because they were a source of life and not death on the bleak winter landscape.[46] But the American West was too young to have a *hon'i*, and so Yamashita refrains from saying much more.

The return voyage across the Pacific Ocean is afforded little con-sideration, as with most travelogues. No stops along the way are recorded, only rough seas. The ship arrived in Yokohama on March 15, 1884, three and one-half years after the author's departure from Japan. The resulting travelogue was written, the author tells us, not as a lofty treatise but rather as an attempt to record two or three things that touched his spirit while traveling abroad. This it does, as it dis-plays the slowly evolving Japanese view of the West.

YANO RYŪKEI

Yano Ryūkei (1850–1931) was a politician, novelist, and journalist from northern Kyūshū. He made his first trip abroad in 1884, when he traveled to Paris and London to observe the constitutional polity, then continued on to tour all of Europe and return to Japan via Amer-ica in 1886. He recorded his impressions both in *Report from Yano Fumio* and *Letter from London*, which appeared in the *Postal Dispatch News* in 1884–85, and in *Miscellany of a Tour*, which was published in July 1886. *Miscellany of a Tour*, written after the fact, presents infor-mation about the West in a more formal, analytical fashion. In his intro-duction to *Miscellany of a Tour*, Ryūkei says that he originally planned

---

46. Yamashita, *Kaigai kenbunroku*, pp. 408–9.

a much larger work, one that would contain a total of thirteen sections; however, work obligations called him away to Europe again, and he was forced to leave the work with a mere six sections, something he greatly regretted. The sections are topical and cover Western customs regarding men and women, the military and weaponry, foreign relations and the state of world nations, commerce and manufacturing, Western political systems, and the nature of Eastern and Western civilizations and their differences. It is a work designed to inform the reader, not to express the emotions of the author.

Report from Yano Fumio and *Letter from London*, on the other hand, capture the author's immediate reactions to his surroundings and the political events of the time. Like many of the early Meiji travelers, Ryūkei begins by describing the sea voyage through Asia and the Middle East. In Singapore, he is fascinated with the physical appearance of the natives, whom he says, look like the Bodhidharma with "slightly longer faces." He also describes modes of transportation (horse cart versus *jinrikisha*), provides verbatim a *hitsudan* conversation he had with a journalist Hong Shiwei, and comments on the sartorial customs of the Singaporeans. He does not mention the natural landscape or associate the locale with historical events (save his mention of the Bodhidharma, which seems anachronistic in this case). Instead, he seems in a rush to move on to his next destination.

In Colombo, he visits the place where Māyā, the Buddha's mother, was supposedly buried. He does so not for religious reasons, apparently, but rather to see a famous historical spot. His comments are limited to the quality of the paintings he saw there and musings on whether his guide's information was correct. Ultimately Ryūkei is not classically or historically oriented; he is a reporter, and remains focused on the contemporary world. This sets him far apart from the likes of Kurihara Ryōichi and Arisugawa no Miya Taruhito, whose romantic take on the Western landscape we have already seen. His comments are not superficial, but they pale in contrast to Kurihara's allusive poetry.

Ryūkei is rarely nostalgic, but on occasion he reveals some personal sentiment. When he reaches France he says:

> Like those people who traveled from Kyōto to Azuma and
> who yearned for the capital while on the banks of the Sumida River, I have shrunk distances with the help of steamboats,

trains, and telegraphs and landed here in Marseilles. Upon
reflection on my departure from Japan and the journey here,
I feel like it has been a year since I bade farewell to my close
friends and boarded the *Volga*. The time seems extended by
the circumstances of this journey; I am cooped up in my
room, busy with my affairs that normally would take me more
than two or three days to finish, but in this case are completed.
My sense of how long those two or three days are is dramatically changed. And so it is natural that the mere forty-six days
we have been aboard from April 20 to June 4 seem like a year.
It must be because we have encountered so many unusual
things in these foreign lands during these forty-six days.[47]

Here Ryūkei likens himself to the earliest Japanese travelers who ventured to the distant Azuma (to the east of Kyōto) and the Sumida River
(that runs through modern Tokyo), all the while pining for the life and
society they left behind in the capital (Kyōto, or in some earlier cases,
a nearby city). But unlike those "people who traveled from Kyōto to
Azuma," Ryūkei does not wish he were home. He may have traveled
far from home, but it is there that the similarity with premodern travelers ends. His journey is not arduous, it is not punishment, it does
not separate him from all that he holds dear. We see from the commentary in this travelogue that Ryūkei is partial to Japan and her ways,
and is often critical of European political events, but that dissatisfac-
tion never escalates into a lament. Ryūkei was first a reporter and second a travel writer. Much of *Report from Yano Fumio* and *Letter from
London* contains synopsis of political events in Europe during the
week, in keeping with the venue (a newspaper) of the works.

Ryūkei loves Paris, with her boulevards, parks, and colorful urban
settings. He mentions a few sights by name, such as the Champs-
Élysées and the Bois de Boulogne, but he is not name-dropping in
the style of Nakai. Besides, his interest is in how these places appear
to him in the present, not their historical significance. In contrast, he
is disappointed with London and finds it a sorry place in comparison
with Paris, contrary to his expectations. It is filthy with soot, the area
around the train station is desolate, and the streets are disorganized.
Ryūkei suffers from a respiratory illness (that he attributes to the air

47. Yano Ryūkei, *Yano Fumio tsūbō*, in *Yano Ryūkei shū*, in *Meiji bungaku zenshū*, vol. 15 (Tokyo:
Chikuma shobō, 1969), p. 291.

The lake at Bois du Boulougne

The Medici fountains in Bois du Boulougne

pollution in London) and goes to Kensington Park for some fresh air,
only to find that the park is also filled with smog. Nonetheless, he
stays in London to report on the events of the day. And after his ini-
tial shock, he refrains from commenting on the cityscape. Perhaps
most importantly, he does not wish to return to his homeland, or long
for her environment. Old Japan and old Europe have no place in his
mind. He focuses solely on the contemporary.

He may have strongly disliked London, but he was equally critical of the Japanese who inhabited its "Japanese Village," a sort of exhibition community established to introduce the British to Japanese
customs. According to Ryūkei, the village had an average of three
thousand visitors a day, and this only added to his fears that this disgrace of a display would have adverse affects on the Japanese as a
whole. In his brief summary of what was wrong with the Japanese village, he says that although the "inhabitants'" clothing was not dirty,
it was slovenly and discordant—everyday attire mixed with dancing
clothes—and an embarrassment to be seen. Ryūkei was appalled and
wrote, "Usually such things don't bother me, but it was all so pitiful
that I felt like I wanted to crawl into a hole somewhere."[48] He fears
that the Japanese are equated in the British eye with the "barbarian"
tribes of native North Americans. Later on he enthuses about introducing Japanese cuisine to the West, and how such a feat could help
Westerners understand Japan. Although he concedes that Westerners need forks and knives to eat, he makes few concessions to the
Western palate. One can only read this as his response to the spectacle he saw at the "Japanese Village," where his own culture was so
incredibly misrepresented as to cause him personal embarrassment.
Surely crosscultural exchanges could be done right, he thought, and
perhaps cuisine was a good place to start. That he did not choose some
other venue, the visual arts or literature, for example, for the introduction of Japanese culture to the West shows his disregard for his
own premodern heritage.

The underlying theme throughout Ryūkei's work is his desire to
establish Japan as a sophisticated, civilized country on the same level
as Western Europe. Whereas the earliest travelers seem disinterested

48. Yano, *Yano Fumio tsūhō*, p. 324.

at best in what their hosts thought of Japan, Ryūkei worries about it constantly. He states:

> As far as [our appearance to] foreigners is concerned, it is human nature to want to stretch the truth a bit. However, in these days of easy travel, stretching the truth too far beyond reality into a false representation is, of course, not a good thing. It is enough if one is simply able to represent the truth as is. In Japan's case, unskilled, crude music, dance, and other arts that no one would give consideration, are viewed as high-class art admired by the true Japanese. They are the laughing stock of all Europe. It is imitated in the theaters and vaudeville and billed as a real copy of the Japanese original. One cannot but think it unpleasant that Japan has come to be known as a crude, low-class country.[49]

Curiously, Ryūkei does not discuss what arts *should* be exported to the West, perhaps because he himself was not well versed enough in them. He alludes to greater art but fails to show why or how it is superior. In his own writing he omits *waka* and other traditional *kikōbungaku* sensibilities. He thus promotes a Japan that did not exist yet, one that had fully incorporated modernization but held on firmly to her artistic traditions.

Ryūkei is at once proud and ashamed of his heritage. He tells us that the vaudeville performers in Europe were an embarrassment, not "high-class art," but fails to recognize that they were simply responding to Western elements—in a word, modernizing—and incorporating them into older theatrical forms. In other words, he tries to have his cake and eat it, too. He wants Japan to be viewed as modern, but he also wants her to maintain her premodern traditions.

MORI ŌGAI

In the same year as Ryūkei went to Europe, the young Mori Ōgai (1862–1922) set sail for a four-year stay in Germany. A doctor in the Japanese army, his journey was by military order. Nonetheless, he

49. Yano, *Yano Fumio tsūhō*, p. 328.

enjoyed himself during his time abroad and found the leisure to make many friends and acquaintances. Unlike many of the Japanese travelers to Europe, Ōgai spoke the local language and was thus quite capable of communicating with the Germans and fending for himself without the aid of a translator or tour itinerary. Ōgai was also keen on Western medical studies, and expected to learn much during his journey that he could bring back to Japan and implement. His assigned topic was hygiene, and he hoped to promote good hygiene in Japan. Despite the rather staid image portrayed of him by scholars, the young Ōgai was intrepid and participated fully in every cultural and educational opportunity presented to him.

After his stay overseas, Ōgai returned to Japan not only to continue his work for the military but also to pursue a long and prestigious writing career. To this day, he is considered one of the fathers of modern Japanese literature, and it is for this reason that one might expect great things of his travel diaries, *Diary of a Voyage West*, *German Diary*, *Army Diary*, and *Daily Record of a Return to the East*. Scholars of Ōgai have meticulously studied *German Diary* to trace Ōgai's steps in Europe, and as an historical source, it supplies many details.[50] But what it supplies in biographical information, it lacks in lyricism. Likewise, *Army Diary* is the duty record of the Second Infantry Regiment of the Imperial Army, and, as the name implies, lacks in artistic flourish. *Daily Record of a Return to the East* is the dispassionate diary Ōgai kept on his journey back to Japan. All three diaries were originally written in Chinese, and some scholars characterize the works as stiff, although terse may be a more accurate description.[51] It has been suggested that Ōgai recorded his emotional responses to his journey in his fiction, such as his short stories "Dancing Girl" (1890), "The Courier" (1891), and "A Record of Foam on the Waters" (1890), instead of in his travelogues. Indeed, it is important to note that Ōgai and some of his contemporaries, such as the painter Kuroda

---

50. Two examples of studies of *German Diary* are Takimoto Kazunari's "Mori Ōgai to Doitsu," in Ashiya Nobukazu, Ueda Hiroshi, and Kimura Kazuaki, eds., *Sakka no sekai taiken: Kindai Nihon bungaku no dōkei to mosaku* (Tokyo: Sekai shisōsha, 1994), pp. 13–32; and Ueda Toshirō's *Mori Ōgai no "Doitsu nikki": Ōgai bungaku no fuchi* (Tokyo: Dai Nihon tosho, 1993).

51. A Japanese (*yomikudashi*) version of *Diary of a Voyage West* and *Daily Record of a Return to the East* can be found in Kawaguchi, *Bakumatsu Meiji kaigai taiken shishū*, pp. 801–66. *German Diary* was published in an edited *yomikudashi* form; the original was never published.

Seiki (1866–1924) and the writer Nagai Kafū (discussed in the next chapter), responded to their experiences abroad by expressing their emotions through visual representation or fiction, not through a traditional travelogue. However, because these are not travelogues by my definition, I have omitted them here.[52]

Diary of a Voyage West, published in installments between April and December 1892 in *The New Hygienics Magazine*, is aesthetically pleasing and literarily styled, despite the vehicle in which it appeared. *Diary of a Voyage West* contains over two dozen poems, in addition to the diary-format prose. Ōgai begins the journey with many of the traditional sentiments expressed in premodern travelogues—sadness at leaving familiar shores and trepidation at the long journey ahead. On May 25, 1884, he writes:

> The ship is tossed and turned in the rough seas
> As the setting sun across the distant ocean gives rise to a
>   traveler's melancholy
> The sky is the color of a lotus flower[53]
> Fellow travelers join in calling this vessel home.[54]

Ōgai uses the word *ryoshū* in the second line, which I have translated as "melancholy," although the meaning runs much deeper. It is alternatively translated as "loneliness on a journey" or "sadness felt while on a journey" and specifically refers to the feelings of isolation and longing associated with separation from one's hometown. The longing in *Tosa Diary*, for example, is closely related to the emotion of *ryoshū*. *Ryoshū* also goes hand in hand with *ryojō* (see chapter 1).

Ōgai quickly became seasick, as did most of the other passengers on board, and all lay prostrate and silent in their misery. The only sound to be heard among the nauseated travelers was the slap of waves against the hull. As the boat was tossed in the waves, glimpses

---

52. The interested reader is encouraged to refer to these works, all available in English translation in the journal *Monumenta Nipponica*: "Dancing Girl" is in vol. 30, no. 2 (summer 1975): 151–76; "The Courier" is in vol. 26, no. 1/2 (1971): 77–100; "A Record of Foam on the Waters" is in vol. 29, no. 3 (autumn 1974): 247–61. My thanks go to an anonymous reader of my manuscript who pointed out the "bifurcation" of art and life in Ōgai's works.
53. This is probably a reference to the sight of Mt. Fuji, rising like a lotus flower above the Kantō plain in the distance.
54. Kawaguchi, *Bakumatsu Meiji kaigai taiken shishū*, pp. 805–6.

of the Japanese coast came and went until finally land disappeared from sight. Ōgai sounds terribly sad, almost regretful, but it appears to be a mere affectation, for the next day he writes that the seas are calm, and the following day a poem describes the ten other Japanese passengers on board in a cheery tone: Mr. Tanaka provides interesting conversation, Mr. Iimori drinks sake in great quantities, Mr. Miyazaki is always in deep thought, and Mr. Sumikawa is hard at work on his French conversation. "Who could but regret how quickly the days pass?" Ōgai asks us.

Ōgai's education included both Western and Chinese studies, so when the ship passed by Fujian and Taiwan, it was not surprising that he immediately recalled a poem by the Tang poet Li Bo. Off the coast of Xiamen (Amoy), he was moved by the sight of two islands together and wrote:

> I left my home and traversed the great sea
> In the mouth of Xiamen's harbor I feel pained
> The sight of two islands among the waves saddens me
> The sailors call them siblings.[55]

The ship landed in Hong Kong on May 31. At first blush, Ōgai thought it looked like the city of Kobe, and he composed a few poems while gazing across the water, but that was while he was still on board. Once ashore, he busied himself with visits to a botanical garden and a hospital, where he made careful observations of the facilities, detailed and dispassionate enough to rival Nomura Fumio's in *A Record of Things Seen and Heard in the West*. After Hong Kong, the ship continued on along the Vietnamese (Annamese) coast to Saigon, then through the Straits of Malacca. Ōgai is laconic but not trivial in his comments, alluding to literary sources and historical events where possible. Of particular interest is his comment in Sumatra that he had read Hayashi Ki's (1844–82) travelogue of his experiences with the Dutch army in Sumatra, titled *Travels in Sumatra*, and that being there made him reflect on Hayashi's experiences. No other travel writer examined here mentioned such works—they were too late in the scheme of literary history, and they were too foreign to be the objects

---

55. Kawaguchi, *Bakumatsu Meiji kaigai taiken shishū*, p. 811.

of allusion. Because Hayashi's work was not the sort of travelogue to inspire a lyrical response, Ōgai cannot use it as a precedent for new *uta makura*, but reference to it shows a reflection on the significance of place that is much more recent than other travelogue to date.

The ship continued on into the Sea of Bengal, landing at Colombo June 18. Ōgai comments briefly on architecture ("the people's houses are of red brick, and do not differ from those in Saigon"), clothing ("the same as in Singapore"), transportation ("one cannot but despise the pitiful state of the oxen pulling carts in the street"), and a museum ("there was all manner of birds and beasts on display, including the bones of an elephant that were as big as a house"). He notes that this was the land where Buddhism originated, and visited a Buddhist temple in which there was an image of Shakyamuni and a priest clad in yellow robes and leather shoes. Ōgai refrains from making any normative remarks here, but he clearly sees the contradiction of a Buddhist cleric donning leather. He mentions that India is the "land of the moon," as described in the *Record of a Journey from the Great Tang to the Western Regions,* the account of the Chinese monk Xuan Zang's (596–664) journey to India in 645. It is not surprising that Ōgai would recall this work as he passed through the subcontinent, for he was well educated and this work figured prominently in the classical literary canon. Rather, it is perhaps surprising that other travelers (contemporaries of Ōgai) almost never mention it. Once outside of Japan, other travel writers focus on the state of colonized Asia, consequently, the landscape between Japan and Europe becomes deracinated from any tradition. Ōgai seems at ease connecting the historical world with the present, and even though Xuan Zang's work and its popular descendent *Journey to the West* by Wu Cheng-en (ca. 1506–82) were set in a time far separated from the Meiji period, Ōgai brings them together in a smooth, flowing fashion.

On June 19, the ship entered the Arabian Sea. Ōgai's entries for the next seven days are extremely short, less than a dozen characters each, perhaps reflecting the high winds and rough seas they encountered. Once away from India, he continues to tie in locale with historical significance by mentioning historical events, both ancient and recent. In the port of Aden, he says that he heard there was a reservoir for collecting rainwater nearby, and that it was built by King Solomon. At the Suez Canal, he expressed admiration for Lesseps'

accomplishment that had been completed only fifteen years earlier.
At the same time, he mentions that it was Napoleon who first
dreamed of digging the canal, and that now that it was a reality, the
former shipping routes around the Cape of Good Hope would
become forlorn. Within one short paragraph, Ōgai encompasses past,
present, and future in his attempt to contextualize his experience.

Once in the Mediterranean, the ship passed by Sardinia and Corsica, where, as one might expect, Ōgai feels inspired to write a poem
on Napoleon:

> The past, like clouds, cannot be chased
> The hometown of a hero passes before my eyes
> He subdued all of Europe
> With a will held close since childhood
>
> His brilliant military power held sway as far as America
> His common battles disposed of his enemies
> "Liberté" is stronger than steel
> Heroes have many schemes[56]

The ship arrived in Marseilles on July 7; Ōgai went to stay at a hotel
after clearing customs. Here he admits to having been bored on the
ship for forty days, but now he was excited about being in Europe
and wrote in a verse that his "traveler's melancholy" had been completely washed away by the light rain that fell on Marseilles. Here people jostled in the streets and thousands of gas lights lit the roads—he
was thrilled by the very sight of it all. The following day, accompanied by seven Japanese companions, he boarded a train for Paris.

The group spent only one day in Paris. Ōgai mentions that he ran
into Satō Tasuku (1857–1919), who had been studying in Berlin for
a long while and who was now headed for Marseilles.[57] In the evening,
he and Satō went to the theater, where the audience numbered six
thousand and was seated in four levels, a much larger production than
anything Ōgai would have seen in Japan. There were both actors and
actresses on stage, which was also different from the male-only *kabuki*,

56. Kawaguchi, *Bakumatsu Meiji kaigai taiken shishū*, p. 845.
57. Satō was an exchange student from 1882–86 in Germany and Austria, where he studied
medicine.

nō, or *jōruri* performances back home. The sets were extremely fine, and used mirrors and colored lights. Ōgai felt that it was all terribly lifelike. After Paris, he went to Berlin, and it is here that the travelogue ends.

The last paragraph in the Kawaguchi edition, written by Shizuishi Nagase, an acquaintance of Ōgai's, reads in part:

> In recent times, people who have gone to the West have all written accounts. They write in the manner of politicians and students, recording minute details about flora and fauna, but they leave no record of the *West,* one in which we could see the conditions of all countries. However, [Mori Ōgai's] travelogue of his voyage west is written in verse, and although it is perhaps too indignant and tragic in tone, this stormy spirit spills across the page and should cause the reader to feel driven by the gods—it is a truly superior work.[58]

Shizuishi may not mention Murata by name, but it is travelogues such as Murata's that he criticizes here. He commends Ōgai for blending traditional travel writing form, verse with prose, and presenting a work that he feels conveys they *real* West. His point is well taken, although one may argue that even Ōgai falls to dry description on occasion and this is less than a perfectly lyrical work whose "stormy spirit spills across the page." Still, even compared to Ōgai's other diaries, *Diary of a Voyage West* is certainly closer in tone to early domestic Japanese travel literature than most other travelogues of the West.

German Diary is a much more complex work than *Diary of a Voyage West.* This is in part due to meticulous editing of the text before it was published. In fact, the work languished in Ōgai's possession until 1899, when he began to rewrite it in earnest. It picks up where *Diary of a Voyage West* leaves off: he gets settled in Berlin and decides to study hygiene at the suggestion of a Japanese colleague, Hashimoto Tsunatsune (1845–1909). At first, he appears both nervous and excited about his mission, wanting both to learn as much as possible and also to fit in to German society as best he can. He moves to Leipzig to study under a German named Franz Hoffmann who taught

---

58. Kawaguchi, *Bakumatsu Meiji kaigai taiken shishū,* pp. 852–53. Shizuishi refers to Ōgai by his given name, Mori Rintarō.

at Leipzig University, and remained there for about a year. In 1885, he moved to Dresden, where he remained for five months and attended medical lectures at the university. In March 1886, he moved to Munich, where he spend more time with Japanese expatriates than he had in Leipzig or Dresden. At the university, he studied hygiene under Max von Pettenkofer (1818–1901); most of his experiments at the time dealt with diet and its effect on health. In April 1887, he moved to Berlin, where he studied hygiene under Robert Koch (1843–1910) at the Hygienisches Institut of Berlin University. He left Berlin to return to Japan in July 1888.

The diary covers his entire stay in Germany, but there are many days for which there is no entry, and likewise many days for which the entry is short and uninformative ("visited with so-and-so today"). In a way, Ōgai's stay in Germany was too long to produce a poignant travelogue. He became familiar with German customs and way of life quickly, and ceased to note the different within a matter of months. Also, he did not pine for his homeland—the closest he comes is mentioning a letter from a friend that contained a poem and a brightly colored autumn leaf to remind him of Japan—nor did he feel much nostalgia for the historical significance of places he visited in Europe. One rare exception to the rule is an entry written shortly after his arrival in Berlin:

> But suddenly here I was, standing in the middle of this most modern of European capitals. My eyes were dazzled by its brilliance, my mind was dazed by the riot of color. To translate Unter den Linden as "under the Bodhi tree" would suggest a quiet secluded spot. But just come and see the groups of men and women sauntering along the pavements that line each side of that great thoroughfare as it runs, straight as a die, through the city. It was still in the days when Wilhelm I would come to his window and gaze down upon his capital. The tall, broad-shouldered officers in their colorful dress uniform, and the attractive girls, their hair made up in the parisian style, were everywhere a delight to the eye. Carriages ran silently on asphalt roads. Just visible in the clear sky between the towering buildings were fountains cascading with the sound of heavy rain. Looking into the distance, one could see the statue of the goddess on the victory column. She seemed to be floating halfway to heaven from the

midst of the green trees on the other side of the Branden-
burg Gate. All these myriad sights were gathered so close
at hand that it was quite bewildering for the newcomer.[59]

But even here he is reveling in the present, not the past. Later, during Ōgai's stay in Munich, Ludwig II (1845–86) drowned in the Starn-
bergersee, and Ōgai used the event as material for his short story
"Utakata no ki" ("A Record of Foam on the Waters," 1890) but did
not speculate in his diary as to what historical significance might be
attached to the tragedy, or what role Ludwig played in German history except hasty mention of the large number of buildings he commissioned near the end of his life.

Ōgai's diary is really a record of his movements and what he
learned about contemporary Europe during his stay; verse plays no
role in this work, and there are few passages that could be described
as lyrical. Ōgai was trying to appropriate the foreign and make it familiar; for example, when he went to see a dance at the Schlosskeller, he
was pleased by the performance "even though" it was an unusual and
experimental work. He rarely mentions places without giving a cursory explanation of them, indicating that he does not expect his audience to be familiar with them, as perhaps he himself was not.

But allusive mention of famous people and places is rare, and often
followed by some form of explanation. Whereas many of his contemporaries headed for museums and other cultural centers, Ōgai was
more interested in socializing with the Germans than in exploring German history. Ostensibly he was studying hygiene, but that part of his
trip is rarely recorded. Most of what he felt merited note involved the
many events and gatherings he attended, and the people he met
there. He appears at ease among both expatriates and natives, apparently suffering no language barrier problems with the Germans and
thus smoothly conversing with all whom he met. None of his contemporary travelers approached their journey with quite such enthusiasm. He is tireless in his endeavor to absorb German culture; for
example, after a long day of study, the entry for October 24, 1884,
reads, "I decided to do extensive reading in the evenings of a collection

---

59. Translation by Richard Bowring in *Mori Ōgai and the Modernization of Japanese Culture* (Cambridge: Cambridge University Press, 1979), p. 10.

of German poets' works." But, disappointingly, he tells us nothing in his travelogue of what thoughts such reading inspired.

Informative as it is on Ōgai's life abroad, *German Diary* ultimately proves a poor travelogue. One tires quickly of the brief daily entries and the terse sentences that, as Donald Keene notes, intimate the diary was first composed in Chinese and later translated into Japanese.[60] They reveal little of the author's inner thoughts, nor do they convey deep reflections on his experiences. This may perhaps be partly due to editing of the diary after its original composition, but because the original manuscript has been lost, nothing may be said conclusively. Many scholars postulate that Ōgai's experiences with one or more women in Germany may have been eliminated from the diary in order to preserve his dignity. There certainly is ample evidence that at least one such love affair existed (shortly after Ōgai's repatriation a German woman who claimed to have followed him out of love also arrived in Japan). But even if such diary entries were omitted they would likely not contain the sort of emotive response to the landscape nor the nostalgia for home typical of traditional travel works.

Daily Record of a Return to the East is a very brief work that, like *Diary of a Voyage West*, was published in *The New Hygienics Magazine*. It begins with Ōgai's departure from Berlin on July 5, 1888. His return trip took him through Amsterdam, Uttrecht, Queensborough, London, Calais, and Paris. The entire work is but a few pages long, and includes some Chinese poems. Ōgai seemed melancholy at the prospect of returning to Japan; in Germany, he had been afforded a freedom and status that he would lose at home, and the job of transmitting the knowledge he had gained in Europe to Japan was a daunting task. He knew that he would face skepticism and doubt, and that it would be a difficult repatriation. Unlike most travelers, Ōgai did not miss Japan, did not long to return to her shores, did not write nostalgically of his hometown. The few times he did write of Japan in his travelogues and diaries, it was to defend her against criticism as an undeveloped, barbarian land, in other words, to emphasize Japan's modernity, not her past.[61]

---

60. Donald Keene, *Modern Japanese Diaries: The Japanese at Home and Abroad as Revealed Through Their Diaries* (New York: Henry Holt & Co., 1995), p. 196.

61. The most notable case is when Ōgai responded to a sharply critical speech given on March 6, 1886 by Edmund Naumann, a German who had taught in Japan for two years but then

SUEHIRO TETCHŌ

Quite different from Kurihara's *A Diary of Itagaki's Tour of Europe and America* and Ōgai's *Diary of a Voyage West* and *German Diary*, but still anchored in the Japanese literary tradition, is Suehiro Tetchō's (1849–96) *Journey of a Deaf Mute*, published in 1891.[62] Suehiro was a political novelist and a politician. Along with Narushima Ryūhoku he was jailed for his opposition to the government and its restrictions on liberty. Suehiro produced a number of popular works, including *A Plum in the Snow* (*Setchūbai*, 1886), which combined the genres of political novel and novel of manners.

Suehiro left Japan in April 1888, heading for Europe and the United States, ostensibly to observe the political situation in those places. He returned in February of the following year and published his travelogue two years later. *Journey of a Deaf Mute* is a comic romp through various misadventures, all caused by the author's inability to understand Western languages and culture. Suehiro's work borders on the edge of my earlier definition of *travelogue* (see Introduction); it is rather more like a Tokugawa period *meishoki*, such as Asai Ryōi's *A Record of Famous Places on the Tōkaidō* and Jippensha Ikku's *Shank's Mare*. However, one distinction that *Journey of a Deaf Mute* has is that the author based the narrative on real experiences, whereas Asai Ryōi never visited all the famous places on the Tōkaidō of which he wrote, and Jippensha Ikku did not travel about Japan with a companion as is depicted in his novel. Surely some of Suehiro's narrative is fabricated, and in this sense it resembles some Western travelogues, such as Richard Halliburton's *The Flying Carpet*, in which Halliburton tells of a real journey he took to the Middle East but colors the narrative with occasional untruths that the audience is meant to recognize as such.

Journey of a Deaf Mute is a travel novel in which the protagonist encounters a preposterous number of silly situations in his travels

---

lost his job and returned to Europe. Naumann was also the author of an article in *Allgemeine Zeitung* on June 26 and 29, 1886, which reiterated what he had said in his talk. Naumann found the Japanese backward and incapable of efficiently adapting Western technology. Ōgai took offense at Naumann's talk, and responded in *Allgemeine Zeitung* on December 29, 1886 with an article titled "Die Wahrheit über Nipon" (The Truth About Japan). For more details, see both Bowring, *Mori Ōgai and the Modernization of Japanese Culture*, pp. 16–19 and Keene, *Modern Japanese Diaries*, pp. 207–8. The passage of *German Diary* that covers this is in *Mori Ōgai zenshū*, vol. 20, pp. 106–11.

62. This work has been reprinted in *Meiji Ōbei kenbunroku shūsei*, vol. 19 (Tokyo: Yumani shobō, 1891, 1987).

abroad. Suehiro writes as if the stories are autobiographical, but the sheer absurdity of the dilemmas portrayed and the author's confession to embellishments in the preface indicate the fictionalization of his real experiences. His motive for writing the story was not to represent the West in poetic form, nor to inform the reader of the state of the West. In his preface, he describes his *bon voyage* party, which gave him the impetus for the work:

> Most of my guests were people who had traveled overseas before. As we talked about being in Europe the previous year, we convulsed with laughter at the strange tales of what had transpired then. And so I took the initiative and said, "If we put the stories of your blunders together with my experiences, we could write a book!"
>
> A few days later I had an audience with a certain gentleman, who asked, "Do you have a traveling companion?" to which I replied, "No."
>
> "Do you speak English well?" he asked.
>
> "I can't speak English," I said.
>
> The gentleman replied, "In that case, this trip is sure to be a failure."
>
> "It is my hope that I will make as many mistakes as possible," I said.
>
> The gentleman found this suspicious and asked, "For what reason?"
>
> I replied, "Because when I travel, I travel with the aim to drink in the world."
>
> The gentleman smiled and said, "I cannot but be shocked at your obstinacy." Nonetheless, at the time I did not have the intention of writing down my experiences. Aboard a boat in the Pacific Ocean, with no one to speak to and faced with endless tedium, I thought of our jesting before my departure and thus it came about that I began to write. I wrote in my hotel in San Francisco, and on board a train on the trans-continental railroad. The entries written between my departure from Yokohama to my departure from San Francisco became the first chapter of *Journey of a Deaf Mute*. In any case, this book is a mixture of truths and falsehoods; it is not a travelogue, nor is it a novel. Truly it is an unworthy comedy.[63]

63. Suehiro Tetchō, *Oshi no ryokō*, in *Meiji Ōbei kenbunroku shūsei*, vol. 19 (Tokyo: Yumani shobō, 1891, 1987), pp. 7–9. Page numbers refer to those in the Yumani reprint, not those in the original.

So it comes as no surprise to the reader that *Journey of a Deaf Mute* is full of farcical tales and bereft of poetic sensibilities. The humor is less bawdy than that of *Shank's Mare* but equally silly. The preface also elucidates the meaning of the title: without any English skills, Suehiro is no better than a deaf-mute. Indeed, most of his problems originate from language-barrier misunderstandings. Suehiro is not interested in local histories or any significance of place. He rarely sees the beauty of the landscape, for he is perpetually distracted by his own confusion, and spends most of his time bumbling through difficult situations of his own causing. Still, he is a lovable protagonist quite capable of laughing at himself. The work is not only entertaining but also informative, and provides the potential traveler abroad with anecdotes about possible pitfalls, much in the same way the *dōchūki* of the Tokugawa did. Thus it is a hybrid style, somewhere between the *meishoki* and *dōchūki* of the Tokugawa period.

The preface and opening pages of *Journey of a Deaf Mute* indicate a significant change in overseas travel by Japanese: by the 1890s, travel to the West had become popular and was not longer solely done with work, study, or governmental business in mind. Suehiro's protagonist, referred to only as "the Gentleman" (*shinshi*), has no more knowledge of the West than is absorbed through browsing a few pages of Peter Parley's *Universal History* (the Japanese translation of which was published in 1870), but because travel to the West had become fashionable, he decided that he, too, should hasten to journey abroad. Thus, equipped with little wisdom and no English, he embarks on the *Belgique*, bound for San Francisco. At first there is some confusion about his cabin, and lost in a sea of other passengers and concerned lest his luggage be stolen by the many thieves about whom he had been warned, he sits down upon his bag and searches the crowd for a fellow Japanese to help him. He finds one, and prattles at him in Japanese. The young man looks askance at the Gentleman, and replies in broken Japanese that he is Filipino.[64] Thus a portent of the comedy of errors that awaits the Gentleman.

The Filipino man speaks broken Japanese and is vaguely familiar with things Western, so thus he becomes the Gentleman's companion

64. The Filipino character is modeled on Dr. José Rizal (1861–96), a physician and political activist. Rizal and Suehiro did meet on the boat across the Pacific, and traveled together. Later in life Rizal returned to the Philippines and was publicly executed by the military on grounds of sedition.

Panorama of San Francisco, 1919

and assistant in the journey across the United States. Despite his help, the Gentleman still manages to find himself in many crises; most of his problems involve the need to urinate. In San Francisco, he inadvertently becomes locked out of his hotel room with a full bladder. Desperation pushes him to try crawling through the open transom, only to be found halfway through by a hotel staff person who mistakes him for a burglar. Later on a train, the Gentleman, unaware that there are toilets on board, shows such discomfort on his face that his companion finally asks him what the matter is. The ensuing exchange displays the slapstick-style humor employed throughout the work:

> The Gentleman furrowed his brow and said, "I'm not ill, just a little . . ."
>
> "But your color is not at all good."
>
> "Since we left Oakland we've only stopped for two or three minutes at each station. Won't there be somewhere where we'll stop for more than ten minutes?!" the Gentleman cried out with a voice of discomfort.
>
> The Manilan thought that the Gentleman was hungry, and hoping to hasten the arrival of food he brought the timetable out of his pocket and perused it. "Once we get to Sacramento there should be bread . . . you can have a meal."
>
> "How long until we arrive at that station?"
>
> "About an hour."
>
> The Gentleman became more troubled at hearing this. "There's no way I can wait until then." He had drunk quite a lot of beer the night before, and this morning he needed to urinate badly. At the Oakland station, he had been too busy and had leapt onto the train. But now the need had become unbearable. In Japan he had only ridden a train between Tokyo and Yokohama—now he was on a cross-continental train in America. He never dreamed that there would be a toilet on the train, so he bore down and wondered when the train would stop. His lower abdomen felt

like it would burst as he turned toward the Manilan and said, "*shōben . . . shōben . . .*" in a low voice. The Manilan seemed not to understand, so the Gentleman pulled out his English-Japanese dictionary, but he was flustered and couldn't find the word. In desperation, he extended his left index finger above his trousers and with his right hand gestured a stream of water coming out of it. The Manilan laughed dryly and said, "Didn't you know there's a W.C. on the train . . . ?"[65]

Similar language-barrier problems occur repeatedly: after being sick for a spell, the Gentleman is terribly hungry and thirsty, but when he asks for "water," the steward mistakes his mumbled English for "water closet," leaving our protagonist with no relief. In another episode, the Gentleman mistakes a steward for a burglar and strikes him. In retaliation, the steward neglects to empty the Gentleman's chamber pot, which is later accidentally overturned, creating a mess. This bawdy humor leaves little room for more serious observations, but on a few occasions even the bumbling Gentleman notices the breathtaking scenery of the American West outside his train window, and (as might be expected) composes poetry in Chinese on it.

Suehiro assumes little knowledge of the West and blends practical information with personal observation in this work. In New York, he describes the buildings briefly but does not focus on any particular one, nor does he associate historical events with specific sites. In England, where he goes after leaving North America, he describes London in a similar voice:

> The four square miles of London have rows of four and five-story houses, and the population is over four million. Thousands of ships carrying cargo from all the countries of the world sail up and dock on the Thames River. Railroads bring goods from all quarters here, as if weaving a spider's web across the whole country. Distribution begins with continental Europe, and extends to the countries of the Far East. This is truly the greatest land of commerce in the world. The goods of all nations are stockpiled in London's stores. Sparkling gems dazzle the eye. The sidewalks are polished, the streets spread with chaff. The buildings that soar to the

65. Suehiro, *Oshi no ryokō*, pp. 65–66.

sky from between the other dazzling structures are Westminster, where the parliament meets, and St. Paul's Cathedral. Large and small public parks are nestled in between
bustling market streets. These are thick with foliage and
recall being in the mountains.[66]

The Gentleman is excited by the liveliness of London, which ostensibly could be considered the greatest city in the world at the time.
Suehiro does not dwell on the past—what happened in St. Paul's, the
baroque style of the architecture and the role the building, both the
version he saw and its predecessor, are irrelevant here—but rather
focuses on the present and future. For the Gentleman, the West is
still a confusing place full of unknown hazards, but there is a major
difference between his approach and that of the shogunal and early
Meiji diplomats. Suehiro consistently uses the word "blunder"
(*shissaku*) to describe the Gentleman's follies, a word that implies cul-
pability of committing an error. The Gentleman is expected to conform to the West, to eat the food, to wear the clothes, to understand
where the bathroom is, to get from point A to point B without special dispensation in the form of official assistants or guides. The earlier diplomats, in comparison, were suspicious of their surroundings
and uneager to conform. Misunderstandings, when they occurred,
were often described with an air of contempt toward the different.

The Gentleman maintains his jovial disposition throughout the
work. In the final scene, he is happy to have returned to Japan, but
sees his experience abroad as an enriching one. As his companion
(another Japanese) says, "Now that I've been bathed in a Western
breeze and returned to Japan, I, too, have become a formidable gentleman." The men are proud of their country but also see Western
experience and learning as an important component in modern Japan.

KAMATA EIKICHI

Whereas the West is a fanciful place full of unknown hazards to Suehiro's Gentleman, it is a civilized and dynamic place to Kamata Eikichi
(1857–1934), a scholar who traveled to Europe and the United States

---

66. Suehiro, *Oshi no ryokō*, p. 211.

in 1897–99. Kamata had no specific agenda for his journey; he was a private traveler primarily interested in the modern aspects, both artistic and technological, of the Western world. His travelogue, *Miscellany from a Tour of Europe and America* (1899), is organized chronologically, but instead of diurnal entries, it presents sections topically. Kamata covers assorted items of interest to him, including "The Train Between Marseilles and Paris," "Hospitals," "The Eiffel Tower," "The French Like to Change Names," "Cafés," "Germans in London," "Judicature in the Schools," "English Newspapers," "Japanese Goods in the Hague," "The People of Spain," and "Bullfights in Spain and Portugal." On occasion, Kamata reflects on the historical aspects of a place, but his focus quickly returns to the present. His travelogue is not lyrical, and only rarely does the author's opinion speak out from between the lines of objective observation. Still, it is impossible to miss the excitement that he felt; this journey was taken two years after Japan's victory in the Sino-Japanese War, a conflict that promoted Japan globally and brought her, at least in the eyes of the Japanese, a new legitimacy as a serious player in world politics. Kamata was thrilled with his country's newly found status, but he also marvelled at the advancements he saw in the West, and was a constant advocate of technological progress. He never depicts himself as a bumbling fool, struggling to understand the West, nor does he dwell on other Japanese doing so.[67] Like the Gentleman, he is traveling on his own, without the guidance (or hindrance) of *metsuke*. He clearly spends more time paying attention to his surroundings and conveys a host of information about everyday life that either eluded or never impressed his predecessors. In the section titled, "The Conveniences of Daily Life" he describes a host of amenities that, although later commonplace in both the West and Japan, were exciting innovations of the time:

> Civilized society has countless conveniences, and if one but dispenses a bit of money one can be at perfect freedom to have what one wants. Transportation is like a spider's web,

67. There is one point in the narrative at which he mentions some Japanese misunderstanding the purpose of an emergency stop on a train: "There is a story that some Japanese mistook this for the regular service bell and caused quite a disturbance." See Kamata Eikichi, *Ōbei man'yū zakki* (Tokyo: Hakubunkan, 1899; reprint, vol. 20. *Meiji Ōbei kenbunroku shūsei*, Tokyo: Yumani shobō, 1987), p. 32. Page numbers refer to those in the Yumani reprint, not those in the original.

as it were, spreading out in all four directions, and for a modest fare one can travel from any point on the compass to another. I cannot mention each and every such convenience, but for example, if a tourist who is a stranger to London goes sightseeing in the city and enters a bookstore whilst out on a walk, buys one volume and doesn't want to carry it home, he can write his address on a card and hand it to the clerk, who will quietly take his leave. When the tourist returns to his lodging, the book will be waiting for him on top of the table. The cost for this service may be paid at the shop, or paid in exchange for the book after one returns home—whichever one prefers. Also, if one wants to send parcels to a far away place, one writes the two letters "CP" on a piece of paper about eight inches square and hangs it outside the window. The initials "CP" stand for "Cutter Patterson," the name of the company that delivers from door to door. There are many horse-drawn carriages that travel back and forth within the city, and this sign signals them to stop. When the driver, who spurs on his horses with a harsh yell, sees the "CP" sign outside a window, he will immediately stop the carriage and pick up the parcel. There are transport companies that deliver within the city, within the country, and abroad. Their methods and convenience are the same, regardless of the type of company. There are also many amenities for travelers. For example, if one buys a round-trip ticket and takes the train to the destination but wants to take a different route home, one would of course be bothered by the fact that the return ticket was wasted. But if one sends off a detailed letter explaining the circumstances, the company will refund half the ticket price without incident. If one reserves seats at the theater and does not use one of the seats, the price of the seat will be refunded upon explanation of the situation. Of course, one must recognize that a proper excuse for any such situation is necessary. When laying in goods, if one purchases coal the company will pile it into a carriage and bring it to one's front gate upon request. [The company men] then remove an iron lid that sits over a large hole dug into the center of the sidewalk and overturn the opened coal sacks. The coal pours into the hole like water over a waterfall, and fills the coal storage area for the kitchen. Houses are generally built with an underground room, which is used as a pantry or storage area. So, the hole on the right is for moving goods from ground level to the storage area. Before the residents know it, it is filled

with the ordered coal. The public stores are all extremely
large structures, and there are no daily necessities that are
not prepared there. There are restaurants and barber shops
that are like the bazaars in our country, and not like public
meeting houses.[68]

One of the most notable things about Kamata's travelogue is his acu-
ity. This may be attributable to the advantage of writing almost forty
years after Japan opened her doors to the West, or it may be simply
keen observation on the author's part, but in any event, Kamata
records details that escaped earlier writers. When reading Fuchibe or
Ryūhoku, one occasionally feels that the landscape is strangely unpop-
ulated and that contemporaneous life pales in comparison to historical significance. But while reading Kamata, one imagines the author
blending in with the Parisian crowd and savoring the pleasantries of
everyday life in France. For the early travelers, everything was so unfamiliar and strange that nuances were lost in the effort to assimilate.
They did not notice the fine differences of cuisines, customs, and
architecture. For them, it was simply all foreign, all Western. Indeed,
it is the sharp and refined criticisms of the British in Hastings Berkeley's farcical book *Japanese Letters: Eastern Impressions of Western Men
and Manners* (1891) that belie its true British origins (as mentioned
in the introduction, Hastings wrote the book as a criticism of British
culture but claims in the preface that it is a translation of actual letters written by a Japanese traveler). No genuine Japanese travelogues
from that time note the differences, for example, between the Church
of England and the Roman Catholic Church, as Berkeley does.[69]
Although Kamata was not quite as keen an observer as Berkeley, he
does break new ground with his comments. On the subject of cafés
in Paris, he writes:

Cafés are the specialty of Paris—their numbers are enough
to truly surprise one. If a tourist really wants to know Paris,

---

68. Kamata, *Ōbei man'yū zakki*, pp. 101–3.
69. Berkeley writes, "the Roman Catholic Church, wherever established in those Western lands,
   occupies a more independent and dignified position than do the Reformed Churches, it
   lies less at the mercy both of popular whim and of independent thought, it preserves
   unchanged the even tenor, the steady persistency of its way." See Hastings Berkeley, *Japanese Letters: Eastern Impressions of Western Men and Manners* (London: John Murray, 1891),
   p. 73.

he should go to one of these numerous shops and sit down
at any of the rows of tables, order coffee or wine or some
such beverage, and while sipping observe the other cus-
tomers for at least an hour or two. These shops have seat-
ing not only inside, but also outside, where countless round
tables and chairs are lined up on flagstones in front of the
store. There are cloth awnings spread out overhead, and
Parisians enjoy stopping in front of these cafés to watch the
people walking by while they enjoy a meal.[70]

Kamata's predecessors may have mentioned the beverage "coffee," but
they never recorded the traditions associated with drinking it, traditions that are deeply rooted in European culture and thus reveal
much more than dietary preferences.

Kamata's travelogue is primarily a mix of political and social commentary, and in this sense it shows the Western influence mentioned
by Takasu Yoshijirō; *Miscellany from a Tour of Europe and America*
reads very much like Anthony Trollope's (1815–82) *North America*
(1862), in which Trollope travels about the United States and holds
forth on the political situation (most notably, events surrounding the
Civil War), the economic infrastructure, and various social phenomena. As a point of comparison, let us look at what both men say about
the postal systems in their respective locales. Kamata says:

The postal system [in Turkey] is imperfect, thus England,
France, Germany, Russia, Austria, et al. maintain their own
postal offices in Constantinople because they cannot trust
the Turkish postal deliveries. Each nation issues their own
special postal stamps, which are used not only by foreigners but also by the Turks themselves. However, the Turkish
postal system is not necessarily untrustworthy; I have pur-
chased Turkish stamps a number of times in my hotel and
had my packages delivered without mishap. When I inquired
how it had come to be that there was no post office in Constantinople, I was told that once there had been one, but it
had catered to the sultan and was involved in such disrep-
utable work as delivering intimidating decrees and love letters to the rear palace. Thus, it was abolished. Such being
the case, letters sent within the city are usually delivered by

70. Kamata, *Ōbei man'yū zakki*, pp. 57–58.

black menservants who travel about the streets carrying envelopes. This method seems to be quite tedious, albeit interesting. Inwardly I feel that the restrictions of such a system are hard to tolerate.

The sources of such problems lie not only in the Turkish government's lack of revenue, but also, as I mentioned in the previous paragraph, in that there is no Turkish post office in the city of Constantinople. A good case in point is that other nations freely take in the postal profit there to be had. The Turkish government truly cannot understand why one would want to run one's own domestic postal system (as other countries do). When I asked why this was the case, I was told that the Turkish government had not been terribly negligent; rather, they often tried diplomatically to get other countries to discontinue their postal business, but those countries had used the excuse that they could not trust the Turkish post. This could not be easily denied, and when the Turks asked if the other countries would not entrust their letters to the Turkish post, they replied curtly, "It is self-contradictory for you to discontinue your own post within Constantinople because you are discontent with deliveries and also depend on we foreign countries' post for your domestic deliveries. If you complete your own postal system, then we'll talk." Although one cannot but hate Western countries' subjugation, the Turks' weakness makes it impossible to avert and thus such is the way of things internationally; it cannot be helped.[71]

Trollope is also critical of the postal system:

> Any Englishman or Frenchman residing in the American States cannot fail to be struck with the inferiority of the Post-office arrangements in that country to those by which they are accommodated in their own country. . . . Letters also in the States are subject to great delays by irregularities on railways. One train does not hit the town of its destination before another train, to which it is nominally fitted, has been started on its journey. The mail trains are not bound to wait; and thus, in the large cities, far distant from New York, great irregularity prevails. It is owing to this,—at any rate partly to this,—that the system of telegraphing has

71. Kamata, Ōbei man'yū zakki, pp. 297–99.

become so prevalent. It is natural that this should be so between towns which are in the due course of post perhaps forty-eight hours asunder; but the uncertainty of the post increases the habit, to the profit, of course, of the companies which own the wires,—but to the manifest loss of the Post-office.[72]

Inefficiency bothered both men, and they could not but make comparisons to other countries. They saw their role as objective mediator, one who is called in from the outside for a fresh view. The underlying assumption, of course, is that they have privileged knowledge heretofore unknown to the natives, and are thus in some way superior. If we substitute knowledge for wealth, it is not a far step to find the *plutocrat pro tem* traveler described by Paul Fussell.[73] Indeed, for Kamata and his peers, being a member of a "civilized" society was tantamount to having great wealth; the two went hand in hand. Japan, having won the war with China in 1894–95, had begun to see herself as a member of the "civilized" club, and this confidence is evident in Kamata's writing. Westerners have faults, he tells us, and in order to say this with confidence, Kamata must assume a superior position. In addition to his contempt for the Turkish postal system, he tells of the "laziness of the Austrians," the fall of Vienna from a position of grace,[74] the disregard that Turks have for timeliness,[75] and their corrupt officials and dishonest merchants.[76]

Kamata is representative of many of his peers. These men were primarily something besides writers: Kamata was a scholar, Arisugawa was nobility, and Kurihara and Ryūkei were politicians. Even Mori Ōgai could be construed as a nonwriter for our purposes, for he traveled abroad in his capacity as a medical doctor and military officer, not as a writer. Kamata, Ōgai, and Suehiro all took pride in their ability to function abroad. They saw themselves as members of the new,

72. Anthony Trollope, *North America*, vol. 2, (New York: Hippocrene Books, 1987 [first published in 1862]), pp. 367–69. Trollope began working for the post office as a clerk at the age of nineteen. He remained in their employ and was eventually promoted to Postal Surveyor in Ireland in 1841. As a result of his experiences with the post office, he was a particularly astute and critical observer of other postal systems.
73. Paul Fussell, "Travel and Literary Imagination," in *The Norton Book of Travel* (New York: W. W. Norton & Co., 1987), p. 86.
74. Kamata, *Ōbei man'yū zakki*, pp. 251–54.
75. Kamata, *Ōbei man'yū zakki*, pp. 292–93.
76. Kamata, *Ōbei man'yū zakki*, pp. 306–7.

up-and-coming class of educated leaders, familiar with the latest developments in the modernized world. They journeyed to gain knowledge of new lands, and because modern technology made it possible for them to do so. Such was the primary incentive for most Japanese travelers before the turn of the century, and their writing reflects that; it is written to convey hard facts and information about the locale, not to muse on the poetic qualities of the scenery or delve into the emotional state of the author. The nostalgia so prevalent in the medieval travelogues has no place in these works; of course, Japanese writers had difficulty feeling nostalgia for foreign events in foreign lands. Moreover, there seemed great hesitation to express nostalgia about the motherland, as if Japan, being behind in technological advancements, should not be pined for by the generation of "modernizers." A fondness for the new Japan, the one that won the Sino-Japanese War (1894–95), was acceptable, but a fondness for the old Japan would be a sign of feudalistic, and therefore outmoded, preferences. This left writers such as Ryūkei in a literary limbo, not yet comfortable enough with the West to have internalized her cultural milieu but obligated to abandon traditional Japan.

CHAPTER FOUR

❦

Assimilation: Late Meiji Travelogues, 1900–1912

In the early twentieth century, Western travel literature, specifically in English, was still not taken seriously as a legitimate genre by the critics, but it flourished nonetheless. A number of well-known and widely read authors—Henry James, Mark Twain, D.H. Lawrence, Rudyard Kipling, and Sir Richard Burton among them—published travel accounts. Popular periodicals such as *Harper's Magazine* and *The Atlantic Monthly* regularly printed short accounts of journeys abroad. A similar trend appeared in the Japanese press, where periodicals such as *New Novels* and *Reconstruction* sent correspondents abroad. Although these travelogues were not afforded the serious academic consideration given the novels and short stories by the same writers, they were eagerly read by a general audience.

In Japan, the arrival of the twentieth century brought forth a new wave of literary travelers. These men, such as Nagai Kafū (1879–1959), Shimamura Hōgetsu (1871–1918), Tokutomi Roka (1868–1927), and Anezaki Chōfū (1873–1949), had different incentives for traveling to the West but they had one thing in common: they were all professional writers, and most of them were literary scholars. This is not to say that the travelogues of the early twentieth century were uniformly lyrical and captivating—there were plenty of dispassionate records of the West. However, the era did see the emergence of travelogues marked by a familiarity with both the Eastern and Western traditions, and that expressed an aesthetic appreciation for both. It is not the simple matter of Japanese travelogues becoming more Westernized, as some critics would have us believe. Rather, we see in these late Meiji works elements that hearken to earlier domestic works: nostalgia for both the place visited and home, the journey as religious pilgrimage, and attention to the natural landscape and its inherent beauty. These writers were establishing a new, hybrid form of travelogue, one that mixed traditional and Western sensibilities. The result was often a work that transcended its time, as is evidenced by their continued popularity.[1]

What caused such a change? Of course, for each author there were myriad influences and inspirations, but in general the catalyst was a comfortable familiarity with the West brought on by readily available information in Japanese. Japan's activities in the global community also encouraged this familiarity; her victory in the Russo-Japanese war in 1905 was a psychological boost to the average citizen, making him feel a part of the first world instead of an outsider, peering in (as Yano Ryūkei often seems to do). Finally, the comforts of travel in the new millennium made it a qualitatively different experience than it had been a few decades earlier. Travel was affected by a number of technological and engineering advancements: the Trans-Siberian railway, which gave Japanese an over land route to Europe, was completed in 1904; railroads in the United States increased in length seven-fold between 1865 and 1916; improvements in shipbuilding and an increase in passenger ships made the journey across the Atlantic ocean from Europe to the United States faster and more comfortable. The decade preceding World War I also saw the rapid increase in travel by private car: by 1914 the number of private cars in use in England reached 132,015, an increase of 1,460 percent from 1904.[2] For the first time ever, people were traveling overseas in great numbers for the fun of it. A. Norval notes that, "At the close of the [19th century] and up to the outbreak of the World War in 1914, the tourist movement had assumed considerable dimensions and surpassed anything of its kind ever known in the history of the human race."[3]

Tourism grew at a tremendous rate as a result of the industrial revolution, giving birth to an industry led by such entrepreneurs as

1. A number of these works have been reprinted by present-day publishing houses. For example, Tokutomi Roka's travelogue, *Record of a Pilgrimage*, was reprinted in 1989 by Chūō kōronsha in a trade paperback version, despite the fact that it is written in classical Japanese with numerous arcane Christian references that would make it difficult reading for most modern Japanese.
2. L.J. Lickorish and A.G. Kershaw, *The Travel Trade* (London: Practical Press, Ltd., 1958), p. 36.
3. Lickorish and Kershaw, *The Travel Trade*, p. 38.

Thomas Cook and Karl Baedeker, who arranged tours and published detailed tour guides in many languages respectively. Japanese travelers overseas also increased in number as they gradually gained the wealth necessary to join the crowds of tourists; like their Western counterparts, they traveled with Baedeker guides in hand, eager to see the famous sights. The conveniences of the modern world, however, caused a dilemma for the Japanese travel writer. Much of the traditional convention of *kikōbungaku* depended on evoking the loneliness experiences by the traveler, but as communications improved, that loneliness became harder to engender. Togawa Shūkotsu (1870–1939), a literary scholar and critic, a translator, and an essayist who traveled to the United States and Europe in 1906 wrote:

> Travel today is absolutely not a melancholy thing. In today's convenient world one can converse with those underway by telegram, or in urgent cases by wireless. And thus the poetics of travel have been lost. First and foremost, travel requires severing one's contact with one's home. [Oliver] Goldsmith said that as his journey progressed along its itinerary, the chain that linked him to his hometown grew longer; that chain is a chain of the soul, and as it is a chain of the soul, it is poetic. But the conveniences of today's world construct a real chain between the traveler and his hometown. The post is the chain. The telegraph is the chain. These two are forbidden objects on a journey. But as poetics are lost to the benefits of today's convenient world, the melancholy of travel has also been left behind. Today's traveler no longer has any worries about privations. This makes me wonder, upon reflection, whether this journey should have no melancholy at all; here I am in the unusual tropical air, gazing at the moon, enjoying meals with the same delectability as those of home, sleeping on a proper Western style bed—I have no privations in dress, food or accommodations. But I am most thankful that I have entirely severed all communications with home. Indeed, I have received not one telegram from anywhere on this trip, which leaves me like a traveler through a deserted land. It is this that makes this an unsurpassedly enjoyable journey.[4]

4. Togawa Shūkotsu, *Ōbei kiyū niman-sanzenri*, in *Meiji Ōbei kenbunroku shūsei*, vol. 29 (Tokyo: Yumani shobō, 1908, 1989), p. 65.

Togawa is puzzled: he has indeed severed connections with Japan, but instead of feeling sad about it, as he thinks precedent would indicate he should, he feels happy. Indeed, the modern age presents a new challenge for the travel writer: surrounded by every comfort, it is difficult to yearn for less. Togawa's main problem, as he confesses in the beginning of his travelogue, is that he has not a patriotic bone in his body. All his adult life he wanted to travel to the West, and so he jumps at the opportunity without hesitation or later regret. Japan is not of interest to him, and he cannot feel nostalgia for her. However, there were a number of travelers who suffered longing as a result of their "severed chain." Most importantly, they were travelers who were willing to explore their loneliness in writing, to find beauty in the pathos. They maintained an emotional balance that allowed them to simultaneously suffer from and savor the loneliness of their journey. It was this characteristic that Togawa misunderstood (and, it would seem, Goldsmith understood); the chain should not be severed cleanly and completely. Rather, it should be weakened but left enough intact such that the traveler cannot forget his origins.

The late Meiji period brings with it a much larger collection of travel writing than the previous years. Travelers abroad increased in number, as did their diaries. Whereas in chapters two and three I could be relatively inclusive, here I have had to be exclusive. The reader familiar with Japanese literary history may look askance at my purposeful omission in this chapter of such luminaries as Natsume Sōseki (1867–1916), who lived in England 1900–1903 as a student. However, it is not my purpose to cover *all* travelogues and diaries of abroad—indeed the sheer number of them would make such a study unfeasible—and Sōseki's diaries are sadly unremarkable. He was unhappy during most of his stay in England, and that malcontent shows in his diary, in which he petulantly records his daily activities. Despite his strong training in Japanese and Chinese literature, Sōseki showed no interest in creating travelogues in those veins. The closest he comes to doing so is seen in twelve *kanshi* composed before his departure from Japan, most of which express a reticence and melancholy towards the upcoming journey.[5]

5. In Kawaguchi Hisao, comp., *Bakumatsu Meiji kaigai taiken shishū* (Tokyo: Daitō bunka daigaku tōyō kenkyūjo, 1984), pp. 875–85.

Likewise, there are other travelogues that, by merit of their author(s), promise more than they deliver, such as Sugimura Sojinkan's (1872–1945) *Grand Record of Travels in England* (1907) and *Halfway Around the Globe* (1908), two accounts of similar journeys to England as a special news correspondent. These works recount Sojinkan's movements and activities in a tedious fashion but tell us little of anything else, despite the fact that the author was writing to entertain a wide audience. (Sōseki did not intend his diary for public consumption, but Sojinkan wrote with an understanding that his diary would be published.) Finally, works that report on the state of the West without much contribution of the author's emotional state, such as Togawa Shūkotsu's *23,000 Miles Through America and Europe* (1908), are hesitantly given little attention here. Of the three types mentioned above, this type seems the most worthy of attention, although it is not within the scope of this study. Togawa's observations are clear and witty, and the reader is encouraged to seek out this work for its sheer entertainment value.

SHIMAMURA HŌGETSU

Shimamura Hōgetsu was a literary critic, rhetorician, and dramatist who traveled to England and Germany in 1902–5 as a student. In England, he attended Oxford University where he studied psychology, aesthetics, and English literature. In Germany, he studied the same subjects at the University of Berlin. An avid fan of the theater, he attended regularly, often more than once a week. After his return to Japan, he took a job teaching aesthetics and art at Waseda University and also helped found a *shingeki* drama troupe, the *Geijutsuza*, under the tutelage of distinguished writer Tsubouchi Shōyō (1859–1935). Shimamura became one of the canonical artists of his day, and he also gained notoriety as the lover of the tempestuous actress Matsui Sumako (1886–1919). This love affair was publicized and scandalous—Shimamura was a married man, and Matsui was notorious for "corrupting" him—and sadly overshadowed Shimamura's artistic accomplishments, which were not few. Shimamura has thus been remembered as a tormented man, the sort of quintessential Japanese literary and cultural hero who was crushed in the end by his artistic sensibilities. It is no surprise, then, that he incorporated many of the traditional travelogue characteristics in his work.

While engaged in his studies in Europe, he wrote and published articles in the Japanese periodical *New Novels* on his experiences. These articles were clearly meant for public consumption, and they served two purposes: first, they informed Shimamura's audience of customs and life abroad, like so many travelogues before. Second, they incorporated both domestic and foreign travel aesthetics into a coherent whole by focusing both on the nostalgia and loneliness ("homesickness") experienced by the traveler and on the excitement of adventure in a new, foreign locale. Shimamura's writing is carefully crafted, particularly in the early installments, and it captures emotion in a way unseen in earlier works. Certainly the ship and her passengers presented a new environment for him, but not to the point of distraction. Whereas for some earlier travelers it was all they could do to record what they saw, Shimamura is able to reflect on his experiences with greater profundity. Indeed, his journey is as much a spiritual one as it is a physical one. As the ship leaves Yokohama, he feels inspired:

> Happily the starlight shines gaily in the clear sky, and the fresh water washes me from within as always. The cool water absorbed by my towel touches my warm body and clusters of steam surround me; my spirit flourishes—even my spittle could form a poem! I feel as though I must let my voice expound thousands of volumes of [Buddhist] scripture. Ah, at times like this I wonder if man is divine or human?[6]

As his fellow passengers come on board off the launches, Shimamura watches them and reflects on their appearance. There is a young wife who looks forlorn, an old woman of apparent low standing, a mother who embraces her crying daughter. He guesses that they have come to see off her foreign husband, who must return to his mother country. The pathos of the girl's plight moves him as he asks rhetorically, "Oh, what karma brought you to a life like this my dear?"[7] This sort of sensitivity toward one's fellow passengers, relatively unusual in

6. Shimamura Hōgetsu, *Kaijō nikki*, in *Shin shōsetsu*, vol. 8 (August 1902): 137.
7. Shimamura, *Kaijō nikki*, p. 137.

contemporary travelogues, would not seem out of place in Heian period works such as *Tosa Diary*, in which the author and his/her fellow passengers often join in poetic lamentation of their condition. Indeed, Shimamura focuses on this pathos; almost absent is the excitement of traveling abroad to the fabled West—the futuristic world for the *bakumatsu* travelers—and in its place is a somber, contemplative tone. When the ship raises anchor, he writes:

> Then the steam whistle blew and the bulk of the ship, like a mountain, healed a few yards. Many, lamenting the departure of the launches, waved handkerchiefs and hats in the sea breeze. Gradually, as we drew further away, the white handkerchiefs and hats grew smaller and smaller until they disappeared, and with a sigh there were many who finally came back to their senses.[8]

One cannot help but suspect that Shimamura had the following passage from *Tosa Diary* in mind when he wrote this:

> The boat rowed out from Ōminato shortly before dawn on the Ninth. . . . As the boat moved away, the figures on the seashore shrank, and the passengers became invisible from the land. Those on the shore must have had things they wished to say, and those in the boat felt the same way, but nothing could be done about it. Someone murmured [a poem] to himself before turning his mind to other things.[9]

Moreover, although the classical Japanese grammar he uses was still common enough at the time, as if to emphasize a connection to the Heian travel works, he punctuates his prose with grammatical forms and vocabulary anachronistic to the Meiji period.[10] It is surprising that Shimamura chose not to compose poetry, for that would complete the Heian façade of his travelogue. What he does do, however, is comment on experiencing *ryojō*. As we have seen, the early Meiji travel writers were so overwhelmed by the technological advancements of

8. Shimamura, *Kaijō nikki*, p. 138.
9. Translation by Helen Craig McCullough in Helen Craig McCullough, comp. and ed., *Classical Japanese Prose: An Anthology* (Stanford: Stanford University Press, 1990), p. 81.
10. For example, he uses *kakarimusubi* verbal structures. He also uses the adjective *okashi* to indicate something charming, much as Murasaki Shikibu or Sei Shōnagon might have done in their Heian period diaries.

the West and her apparent superior military force that a longing for Japan would have seemed backward-looking and antiprogressive. Their travelogues had no place for such desires. However, by Shimamura's time, Japan had won an international war and was fast becoming, at least in the eyes of most Japanese, an equal to the developed countries of the West. No longer was the West vastly superior; now it had its strong and weak points, as did Japan. This relative equality gave writers such as Shimamura an opportunity to once again express the feelings of *ryojō* that had been temporarily outmoded.

Time on the boat is passed in idle entertainments, such as chess, cards, quoits, and the like. The route takes them through the South China Sea, where Shimamura describes the seascape:

> March 24. Today they hung a curtain over the Promenade Deck, so it is cool. In the evening I lay on a sofa and watched the moon floating in the Eastern sky. The entire view is covered in haze, and the moon shines its silver rays down on the flowing tides, making the sea look like dark, roiling oil. People gather on deck saying such things as "Japan must be in the distant northeast where the clouds are floating." As evening falls the wind becomes colder but I am wrapped in a blanket and meet the moon.[11]

The text is simultaneously bold and ruminative. The moon over the night sea could just as easily be seen in Japanese territory—it is not locale specific—and indeed its rays illuminate the clouds over what the passengers imagine is their home country. Shimamura is looking back, not looking forward. It is not that he anticipates an unpleasant journey; rather, he savors the past and the familiar. That nostalgia for Japan is imposed on expatriots he sees ashore:

> March 28. We arrived in Singapore. Went ashore. Saw the sights. Ordered Japanese food at some Japanese restaurant. Had cucumbers and some other savory—can't remember what it was now. Passed through typical Malaysian streets. Three or five Japanese women dressed in dreadful Western clothing and sporting French hairstyles occupied a table in the front of the restaurant. Some rested their heads in their

11. Shimamura, *Kaijō nikki*, p. 140.

hands, others sat dozing. A group of people in a car beckoned, scolding them that they were a national disgrace, but others laughed and said they were a national asset. Of course they would not tolerate it, and turned their backs on them. Imagining their lives, one realizes that they do not have love, they do not have lust; their flushed cheeks and charming faces are simply caused by their hot tears of regret. Their smiling eyes, now dried of tears, are colder than death; their home town, for which they surely must weep, is but a clouded vision. Their lives are but odd days and nights spent bobbing on a pillow of tears. It is sad that the girls who have been forced to land in this place in the end seem to be fated to this life.[12]

Shimamura sees these women—presumably prostitutes, but at the very least less than proper ladies—and finds their plight pathetic. Of course they are miserable, he asserts, for they have been taken away from their beloved homeland and put in this horrid place. They may be called a "national disgrace" by some, but that does not take into consideration the apparent involuntary participation in their fate. Shimamura feels deeply sorry for them. Compare this to Yano Ryūkei's response to the shabby appearance of the "Japanese Village" in London (see previous chapter), and the contrast is striking. Ryūkei was embarrassed by the Japanese "representatives" in Europe because they gave very much the wrong impression of his mother country; he was only concerned with what others would think of them. Shimamura cares not a jot for what others think of these hapless Japanese; he sees only their pitiable lives. His underlying concern is always with Japan, and although later on in his journey he proves to be an observant traveler, his point of reference remains his home.

The ship continues along the usual course, stopping in Penang, Colombo, and toward the Suez Canal. Shimamura is stricken with smallpox on his arms that itch tremendously but he is told by others that they are probably insect bites. The discomfort he feels seems to be the catalyst for a long rumination on homesickness:

It will take the ship more than two weeks to go from Colombo to Suez, and along the way will be the hot winds

12. Shimamura, *Kaijō nikki*, pp. 140–41.

of the Red Sea, the most arduous part of the sea route to Europe. We have been on the sea now, bored with the monotony, for forty days; who would not think of the weight of their traveling garb at such a time? Those who have set up their chairs beneath the moon to chat have exhausted all topics of conversation. Silently they gaze at the water rushing by. Occasionally a bustling crew member will pat one of us on the shoulder and exclaim, "Homesick!" There are two watchwords on board: *homesick* and *seasick*. And for some people, the terms are repeated many a time. Moreover, those who utter the words usually have a smile on their lips, while those to whom the words are uttered usually reply, "No." Perhaps it is because they feel they are being reproached for these sicknesses. Seasickness ceases soon enough, but being homesick is implicitly an embarrassment to men accused of it. Yet, because there is such censure, there are none who savor homesickness. On board, there is a woman who is traveling to visit her foreign husband's family. In commenting on others who have been accused of homesickness, she said, "That's simply the way things are. . . . If one did not become homesick, one would not be human." One must admit it was a keen observation. And it is not limited to those who have traveled abroad in the past forty years. Although most travelers have brushed with this keen reality, the rarity of we who publicly admit to homesickness is due solely to others being hypocrites. Those who grit their teeth and hold back their tears, who forsake their wives and children and obey the commands of their country, face the incompatible contradiction of obligation and human emotion in this world. This is the ultimate question of nature, and all of mankind's vicissitudes and interests stem from this one thing. When the strength of an invasion and the memories of one's hometown are enveloped in one's vision, then poets could stand to cry. Be that as it may, in today's world "journeying abroad" is measured solely on the basis of one's reputation and gain, and is an object of envy, but none would want to share in the emotions experienced. Ah, for are not those feelings nothing but homesickness?[13]

In this one entry, Shimamura evokes the values of the Tokugawa period (1600–1868) and the aesthetic of longing so important in

13. Shimamura, *Kaijō nikki*, p. 142.

traditional travel writing. The "incompatible contradiction" of obligation versus human emotion, as any scholar of Japan knows, was at
the center of much Tokugawa fiction. The demands put upon the
samurai class in particular during this period often caused self-sacri-
fice in the name of one's lord; that many of the members of the samurai class went into government service in the Meiji period and
subsequently were sent abroad to further their education is not lost
on Shimamura. These "new warriors" were asked to leave their loved
ones behind, and lamentation on that point was seen as a weakness.
Shimamura finds this distasteful and hypocritical, for, as the woman
he meets observes, homesickness is a natural response to long-distance
travel. What he prefers, it would seem, is a return to the aesthetic of
Heian travelogues, in which homesickness, under the name of *ryoshū*,
is a necessary element.

This work is a striking contrast to the earlier works in its willingness to address these emotions. The absence of *ryoshū* or *ryojō* can
in part be attributed to the excitement experienced by the early travelers, but Shimamura here accuses them of dishonesty. Loneliness is
part of the human experience, an emotion to be "savored," not
shunned. One may conjecture that Shimamura is writing for a more
intimate audience and thus is more willing to expose his own weak-
nesses. But we cannot attribute Shimamura's candidness to his anticipated reader; he wrote these travelogues for a widely distributed
periodical, so any shame associated with their contents would be
exposed for all the world to see. Moreover, the earlier travelogues,
such as Ōgai's diary, were apparently meant to be private manuscripts, not for public consumption. Yet, Ōgai and his contemporaries
certainly are guilty as charged by Shimamura: they are suspiciously
free of loneliness and homesickness. Nine days later, in Suez, Shimamura writes:

> When I think of people living in such a place [as an oasis in
> the desert], I find it lonely and sad. The sad wind blows vio-
> lently, enveloping us like a gray twilight shadow from the foot
> of the distant sand dunes. I feel that the clear loneliness of
> ancient man at the break of dawn must have been like this.[14]

14. Shimamura, *Kaijō nikki*, p. 142.

His sensitivity to loneliness is not reserved, then, for his compatriots. Indeed, Shimamura seems interested in the emotional side of traveling almost to the exclusion of all other aspects. When he goes ashore, he habitually writes "went sightseeing as usual,"[15] despite the fact that he had never been to these locales before and must have had a feast for the senses. What he does notice is the state of the people around him, both fellow travelers and natives. This is a stark contrast to writers such as Fuchibe Tokuzō, who admired the inanimate man-made landscape of Europe to the exclusion of its inhabitants. Shimamura sees them both, but he gives the lion's share of his attention to the denizen of Europe, not the architecture. Although "blasé" may be too strong a term, he certainly is not dazzled by the technological advancements he sees in the West; rather, he sees beyond them to the humanity that created them and lives with their effects.

This difference of focus may have been caused in part by Shimamura's apparent ease with the English language. At no point does he mention problems with a language barrier, and it is clear that he functions well in a foreign tongue. He is a scholar of English literature, and he associates what he sees in England with what he has read in English literature. His reading material on the ship is not Japanese but rather Sir Thomas Henry Hall Caine's (1853–1931) novel *The Eternal City* (1901). When describing his fellow passengers, he compares them to characters in English novels.[16] It would seem he has internalized European culture to a comfortable level.

Once Shimamura settles in England, the format of his travelogue changes. The shipboard travelogue was written in a diurnal form, but the later installments in *New Novels* are topical. The first article has a variety of subjects: ping pong, fads in clothing, and a popular song ("The Honeysuckle and the Bee," with complete lyrics included). What is notable about Shimamura's observations, as in the case of Kamata Eikichi, too, is his specificity. Instead of generalizing about English culture, he focuses on particular trends, but not because he is ignorant of the others. Rather, he is knowledgeable enough to rec-

---

15. Instances of this nonchalance can be found upon his arrival in Penang, when he writes "went ashore for the usual sightseeing" (*jōriku kenbutsu rei no gotoshi*), and upon his arrival in Marseilles, when he writes the same sentence (Shimamura, *Kaijō nikki*, pp. 142, 144, respectively).
16. Shimamura, *Kaijō nikki*, p. 145.

ognize the particular importance of the trends that he *does* mention. For example, his choice of mentioning "The Honeysuckle and the Bee" is explained by the commentary that follows the recitation of the lyrics. He writes:

> This is a love song, and its lightness is difficult to translate. It is the sort of thing that does not permit an easy transportation to Japan, for it has a melody that is neither vulgar nor traditional, and it expresses strong emotions and societies' view of love.[17]

For Shimamura, the popularity of the song spoke of an aspect of English culture that was an enigma to his countrymen. Yet he understands that the English profess their love in such a way and appreciates that it is not an oddity but rather an important characteristic that speaks of deeper cultural levels. Certainly this response is different from that of Muragaki Norimasa in *A Record of the Mission to America*, which expressed dismay at the sight of men and women dancing together in public.

The second article written in England tells of Shimamura's trip to the countryside to escape the summer heat of the city. He is invited, along with eleven others, to a rustic lakeside resort. He briefly describes his traveling partners and the scenery, but the body of the narrative is a conversation he heard among some of the women on the trip. They discuss the engagement of a certain miss, and how she informs her family of her intentions to marry. Shimamura is amused by the headstrong ways of English youth, and it is for this reason that he recounts this otherwise unremarkable conversation. He concludes:

> I know this young lady . . . she is a thoroughly thoughtful person, and thus one can be sure that this is a thoughtful engagement. However, as I think about it a little more, I wonder, will this woman necessarily end up a happy woman? I have doubts that, although thoughtful choice is important, that alone cannot fulfill the relationship between man and wife.[18]

---

17. Shimamura Hōgetsu, *Zasshin*, in *Shin shōsetsu*, vol. 11 (November 1902): 183.
18. Shimamura Hōgetsu, *Ryochū ryokō*, in *Shin shōsetsu*, vol. 12 (December 1902): 178.

This observation gives more consideration to the ramifications of Western marriage customs than previously seen. Hamada Hikozō, for instance, remarks dryly that, "In America, both boys and girls fall in love at the ages of fourteen or fifteen *sai* [*sic*], and when they decide to become husband and wife and to live together for the rest of their lives, the boy and girl, without employing a go-between, pledge themselves directly."[19] More importantly, Shimamura's work shows a sensitivity to human emotion lacking in earlier works. The question of whether the young woman would be happy is revisited later on, when the author asks his hosts about what one should look for in a prospective spouse:

> I wasn't sure if I should broach the subject in front of the ladies, but I asked what objectives young ladies and young gentlemen had in getting married, and the Mrs. answered with ease. But before she did so, she asked how it was in Japan. I answered that, my own thoughts on the matter aside, the way it usually was was that although there were plenty of people who married for money and social position, or who married based on looks alone, the usual objectives were, of course, character and education. The Mrs. said that in addition to character and education there was one thing highly valued, and that was love. Love was first and foremost, above character, education and wealth, she said; I thought to myself that one of these should be enough. Marriages were, after all, "love matches," she explained, using the marriages of various queens and princesses as examples. This is a point on which Eastern and Western thinking differ, but it is worth consideration. If one says that one loves one's husband to an extreme, and there is love for one's spouse, then there can be no thoughtful choice before the marriage. But my true feelings on the matter are not such. We must ask ourselves whether true human happiness is brought about by a marriage that comes after love, or love that grows after the marriage.[20]

In the end, Shimamura seems more sympathetic to the Japanese-style marriage (in keeping with his tendency to keep Japan as his point of reference), but he is willing to ruminate on the subject instead of dismiss things foreign out of hand.

19. Hamada Hikozō (aka Joseph Heco), *Floating on the Pacific Ocean* (Los Angeles: Glen Dawson, 1955), p. 77.
20. Shimamura, *Ryochū ryokō*, p. 184.

Lest the reader think that Shimamura was totally insensitive to his natural surroundings, one should note that in March 1903 he wrote a column titled, "A Survey of the Northern English Landscape," in which he describes said landscape in detail. His point of reference, however, is not himself but rather Wordsworth and his poetry. Of course such a landscape would give birth to the great poetry of Wordsworth, Shimamura tells us. In the end, the piece is more a paean than reportage, and not very informative or reflective. This column is a portent of things to come: Shimamura's stay in England lasted for many months, and he continued to write installments for *New Novels* on a regular basis. The content, however, steered away from his early lyrical voice and focused on literary and cultural criticism. For example, in April of 1903, his column covered the customs surrounding the Christmas holiday, the content of popular periodicals in England, and new publications of the year. November 1903 brought a column on theatrical venues and *The Merchant of Venice*. By this point, Shimamura had drifted out of the realm of travelogue and did not return.

TOKUTOMI ROKA

Tokutomi Roka, aka Tokutomi Kenjirō, was a popular writer of fiction and essays. Among his most successful works are *Footprints in the Snow* (1900–1901), *The Cuckoo* (1898–99), and *Nature and Man* (1900). His literary career, although very successful, was filled with controversial aspects, particularly his stormy relationship with his elder brother, Tokutomi Sohō (1863–1957). Sohō was a successful writer, journalist, political pundit, and historian, but he and Roka clashed on a number of family and literary issues. Generally speaking, Sohō was a less aesthetically sensitive writer than Roka, or so it seemed to the latter, but it can be argued that he was the more successful of the two. In any event, Sohō's journey to Russia in 1896 served as part of Roka's inspiration to go on what he called a "pilgrimage" to the Middle East and Russia in 1906. His travelogue of this trip, *Diary of a Pilgrimage*, blends a number of characteristics of its predecessors.[21]

---

21. Of note, but not within the chronological scope of the present study, Roka made another trip abroad—this time around the world—in 1919–20. He was accompanied by his wife, Aiko; the journey took fourteen months and covered some of the same territory of *Record*

First, as the title suggests, Roka saw his journey as a religious retreat, like Imagawa Ryōshun, Shinshō, Sōkyū, and Gyōe did in the medieval period. Raised in a Confucian household, he had converted to Christianity in 1883 at the same time that many of his family members did, too. By 1905, he had fully internalized Christian doctrine. Then, while climbing Mt. Fuji with his wife and niece, he fainted and remained unconscious for three days. He awoke with apparently no permanent effects, but the experience made him feel "reborn" in a Christian sense and was probably the catalyst for his overseas journey in 1906. The Middle East, of course, held the most holy places of Christianity, and Roka very much wanted to see them for himself, hence his choice of destination. But why continue on to Russia? Russia had Lev Tolstoy (1828–1910), whose ideas, particularly on Christianity, appealed to Roka. This put Roka in an unusual position, for few Meiji travelers could find spiritual solace overseas. Like the medieval Japanese travelers who went on domestic pilgrimages to famous temples and shrines, Roka set off to be closer to the heart of his religion.

Second, Roka's travelogue contains the lyricism and reflection of Heian travelogues. After a hiatus of more than a decade, we see here a new attempt at composing poetry in the travel account. The sights Roka saw moved him for the very same reasons that *meisho* moved domestic travelers: they were knowledgeable of the place's history and the import of past events there. They were also familiar with the physical landscape and appreciated its unique characteristics. When Roka first arrived in the Middle East, he focused on places of religious import, although not to the exclusion of the setting. But once *at* his destination, he was, like his domestic traveling predecessors, interested more in the past of the place than the present.

The outbound leg of Roka's trip took him by sea along the usual route through the Indian Ocean to Port Said in Egypt. He records little of each locale, with the exception of Singapore. What he writes concerns the natural landscape more than the human one. In Singapore he describes the colors:

---

of a Pilgrimage—Egypt and Palestine—and some new places, including Italy, France, England, and the United States. He wrote a voluminous travelogue of the experience, titled *From Japan to Japan*, which was published in 1921.

There are all the colors of the tropics. The flowers on the
rows of pagoda trees burn crimson. The sails—full and close
hauled—are the color of coarse tea. The skin of the Indians
and Malays is roasted in colors from a shiny black ebony to
a bronze red. Their mouths, stained from chewing betelnut
and eating curry, are as red as if they were spitting peonies.
The earth is the color of crushed bricks. Along the road that
borders the green ground are all sorts of black men, their
heads wrapped in white cloth, their waists wrapped colorful
sarongs, leading grey water buffalo who have grand horns
and gentle eyes, and who pull carts piled high with pineap-
ple. The botanical garden has ripe bananas, ripe pineapples,
mango trees, travelers' fans, fern trees, orchids, a bamboo
grove, water lilies, and more. In this season, the scarlets, yel-
lows, crimsons and purples that come after the rains burn
brightly; leaves drip flames of green; squirrels jump from tree
to tree. The sound of dew dropping from the grass—plop,
plop—in this deserted place makes me think that a child
somewhere is pounding on a gong. This nature's hothouse
makes both my brain and eyes tired.[22]

Although the squalid living conditions in Singapore appalled him, this
reaction did not bleed into his response to nature. He marveled at
the variety of the life he saw, both on land and at sea. On the Indian
Ocean, he records seeing flying fish, porpoises, and waterfowl. He ate,
among other things, pineapples, bananas, bread, potatoes, and rice.
His writing can be described as laconic, but what he does choose to
record shows a keen awareness of his surroundings.

Gazing at the sea one evening, he composes a *waka*:

> Without bounds,
> Oh, how I long to go
> Off into the distant
> Lunar wilderness
> That travels across the sky[23]

This poem not only follows the structure of traditional *waka* (a
5–7–5–7–7 syllabic order), it also contains a *makura kotoba*, or "pillow word"—*hisakata*, or "distant"—a close relative of the *uta makura*.

22. Tokutomi Roka, *Junrei kikō* (Tokyo: Chūō kōronsha, 1989), p. 17.
23. Tokutomi, *Junrei kikō*, p. 20.

In this case, *hisakata* alludes to the sky. This poem easily could have been composed on a journey within the borders of Japan, and by composing it here, Roka blurs the boundaries that previously contained much of the Japanese literary tradition. The Japanese idiom, he implies, is not limited to describing things Japanese. Although this seems simple enough, it was precisely what Muragaki Norimasa was unable to comprehend forty-five years previously in *A Record of the Mission to North America*, when he found it difficult to compose poetry in Hawai'i for lack of four distinct seasons.

The ship passed through the Red Sea to the Suez Canal. Roka disembarked in Egypt and visited Cairo and its environs for three days while he waited for the steamer for Palestine. Early on, he makes clear that his objectives on this journey have little to do with the excitement of seeing the industrial revolution brought about by the West— he says he has "no interest" in the new Westernization of the city, as represented by high-class hotels and Parisian-style cafés. Instead, he heads for a bazaar and there, in the narrow alleyways lined with shops, he finds the Egypt he was hoping for. Amid the clamor, he sees people washing potatoes, an old man on a donkey, vendors of every sort; he says that he feels as if he were walking in the market place of the *Arabian Nights*.

Although we can see a return to Japanese literary values in Roka's travel writing, we can also see, whether he would admit it or not, some Western influence: at the time that Roka was traveling and writing, his Western counterparts were engaged in similar activities. By the turn of the twentieth century, Americans and Europeans were inevitably faced with traveling to less-well-off places if they left their own borders, and they thrived on the thrill of seeing the undeveloped world, a kind of preserved past, if you will. Roka benefitted from his country's rapid modernization in that he was acclimated to the technological advancements that had dazzled his predecessors, and thus he was able to disregard those advancements—almost disdain them— and savor the past. Certainly it had not been long since Japan had earned her place among the industrially developed countries, but it was long enough for Roka.

After viewing the Nile from the train, he writes, "It brings convenience, but the aggression of civilization dispossesses us of poetry."[24]

24. Tokutomi, *Junrei kikō*, p. 28.

For the remainder of his journey, Roka waxes poetic only on nature or ancient (Christian) history. When visiting the Sphinx, he muses on how man remains "half-beast" even after six thousand years, and that the time of religious deliverance is soon to come. His apocalyptic vision sees Europe, "proud of her culture," freezing over like northern Siberia, and flowers blooming in the Sahara.[25] This image combines the Christian notion of the second coming of Christ with Roka's implicit antimodern attitude, giving the reader some foreshadowing of what drew him to Tolstoy and his ideas. At the end of his stay in Egypt, he writes, "The charm of Egypt is in the past. Its modern self is unsavory, for its civilization bears only a passing resemblance to Islam, and it is abused by tourists who toss their money about."[26]

Disillusioned with what he had seen so far, Roka went to Jerusalem. His primary objective was to see the important sites of the early days of Christianity.[27] Because he was one of the first Japanese to travel to the Middle East, he had no compatriot precedent to follow. However, the rich history of Christianity filled this lacuna for him. At the time, Palestine was under the rule of the Ottoman empire, which was soon to collapse. It was a cosmopolitan place, as it is today, with a population comprised of Muslims, Jews, and Christians. This was Roka's first trip abroad, too. In retrospect, it is surprising that he could produce such a composed and knowledgeable travelogue, one that avoids the sort of daily observations of the mundane seen in *bakumatsu* travelogues of Europe. His writing is indicative of greater trends in the genre of international *kikōbun*, trends that had been a part of the genre domestically for centuries. Even in the same unfamiliar circumstances as the first governmental mission members to the United States and Europe found themselves, Roka's response is entirely different. He still has the role of outside observer, but he also assumes a world citizenship, perhaps legitimized by his religious adherence to a world religion, that allows him to be a part of the scenery and stand outside of it simultaneously.

25. Tokutomi, *Junrei kikō*, p. 30.
26. Tokutomi, *Junrei kikō*, p. 34.
27. Roka is not very sympathetic to the other religions represented in Jerusalem. He is openly critical of the Jews, questioning their beliefs, and he gives Islam equally short shrift. See in particular *Junrei kikō*, pp. 35–36.

The sensitivity to landscape he displayed in Singapore is evident in Palestine as well. In Jaffa (modern day Tel Aviv), he writes:

> Arrived in Jaffa at 8:00 A.M. A line of red sand dunes shines against the emerald of the sea. From the tops of the dunes down to the harbor the red, yellow and white houses stand unevenly—tall and short . . .[28]

And outside of Jaffa he writes:

> Leaving Jaffa, the train passed briefly through orchards amidst the tall dunes. Surrounded by a hedge of cactus in full yellow bloom were oranges, lemons, figs, pomegranates, apricots, grapes, olives—all were well cultivated and grew lushly. Shortly thereafter were wheat fields, a solid mass of color against the late spring sky. This was the first I had seen the green mountains of Judea. A flock of five or six hundred cranes quietly gathering food struck me as quite a sight.
>
> This area is the so-called Fields of Sharon. The full bloom of March and April flowers has passed, but poppies, holly-hock, cornflowers and the like are mixed in amongst the wheat and adorn the railroad with their verdancy. There are a few sheep in the stone-strewn pastures, and the blooming yellow flowers spread across a white plant that resembles wild carrot are beautiful. In Lydda (as in [the New Testament] Acts 9:32), the village children came selling mulberries. I recalled being seven or eight, my hands and mouth stained purple from the mulberries in the fields of my home town. I bought a basketful, and for the first time in a long while my mouth and hands were stained purple with their sweetness.[29]

Nature clamors at him, calling out in brilliant colors and scenery. In one paragraph, Roka is able to tie in *meisho* from the New Testament with memories of his from childhood in Japan. Objectively the two seem at odds, for Roka grew up halfway across the globe. But here he focuses on a natural element (the mulberry) as the catalyst for the connection. Never mind that the landscape in Lydda is like nothing he has ever seen before—he has appropriated it as his own, and

28. Tokutomi, *Junrei kikō*, p. 37.
29. Tokutomi, *Junrei kikō*, p. 40.

through this proprietary act made it possible to find nostalgia where none should exist.

The valley of Jericho makes him remember the historical events that happened there and the people—all Biblical figures such as Abraham, Lot, and Joshua—involved in them. He remarks that the five thousand years of history of the place certainly have seen enough human suffering as to be unbearable. The area around the Dead Sea impresses him for its barrenness, but it also has a richer historical presence. He looks in all directions and thinks of Moses, glancing back one last time upon Canaan before climbing Mount Nebo, and of Christ, fasting for forty days and forty nights somewhere in the near vicinity. Although the marks left by the vicissitudes of mankind had all but faded there, Roka says that in the fifty years since Holman Hunt (1827–1910) had painted his famous work, *Scapegoat* (1854), the landscape had developed wheel ruts that led to a hut along the shore. But Roka is not interested in who inhabits the hut. He does not speak to the inhabitants, preferring to leave the forlorn image as a testimony to the ongoing activities of man.

On occasion Roka expresses disappointment at what he sees. Like many of the Japanese scholars who traveled to China during the Meiji era only to find less than the paradise they had imagined from their books of Sinology, Roka the Christian expects the Holy Land to radiate in all its glory.[30] It sometimes leaves him wanting. At the river Jordan he writes:

> From the Dead Sea we once again boarded our carriage and went through filthy mud, and after a while grass, then shrubbery, then a grove of trees the name of which I do not know. Having little choice in the matter we rode for about thirty minutes, after which the carriage stopped on (what I thought was) the banks of some ditch.
>
> The driver informed me that this was the crossing for the Jordan River.
>
> The dirty current could not have been more than twenty *ken* wide; it formed a crook, and had foam floating on top. On the opposite bank what seemed like an elderberry tree was covered with pale yellow flowers and drooped over the

---

30. For details on Japanese travelers to China, see Joshua Fogel's *The Literature of Travel in the Japanese Rediscovery of China: 1862–1945* (Stanford: Stanford University Press, 1996).

water. Various sorts of willows and long, tall reeds blew in the wind. The bank on our side, deep with mud, was overgrown with reeds, and tamarisk-like evergreens and poplars grew thickly. The cliffs of the opposite mountains could be seen through openings in the tree tops upstream. Could this be the Jordan River associated with the "Elixir of Life?" Could the water used by John to baptize Christ be the water of this dirty river? When I asked, I was told that the baptism of lore was here, and that pilgrims to Jerusalem also come here to bathe. The driver then pointed to litter scattered about two ramshackle huts nearby.

Abdara [one of those traveling with me] hurriedly shucked his clothing and threw his black spindly body into the river, swam to the other shore, and broke off some reeds. Macky [another fellow traveler] produced a small bottle from his pocket and poured some water from the Jordan into it as a memento. I silently watched the flow of the dirty water.[31]

Roka soon repents his negative response, asking God to help him see the beauty that must lie there within, but it is clear that the Jordan was not what he had expected. Certainly the passages from the New Testament that describe it would lead one to anticipate a vast, clear river, one that would cleanse one's soul. Instead of looking to the present Jordan for such a vision, though, Roka must look to the Jordan of the past. He ends this entry with an appeal to the river to "flow forever."

The journey took him next toward Jerusalem, via Bethany. All along the route, he notices the flora and fauna but rarely the people. He relates what he sees to the past, what the scenery used to look like in Biblical times. In Bethany, he says that the village shows no signs of the purity of Mary and Martha, that dogs sleep on rooftops, chickens wander about, and the natives point at visitors from afar. But Roka wants Bethany to mean more, for he interjects, "Beloved Bethany!" (natsukashiki Betaniya), and later, "Oh, Bethany, your name along with those of Mary and Martha must be spread throughout the world."[32] He never goes so far as to say the natives are cretins, but the intimation is there.

31. Tokutomi, *Junrei kikō*, pp. 51–52.
32. Tokutomi, *Junrei kikō*, p. 55.

It is important to notice a major difference between the disdain and near contempt that Roka feels for the natives and the disdain expressed by the members of early *bakumatsu* and Meiji missions. In the latter's case, the strangeness of the foreign culture and the utter inscrutability of Western civilization put off the Japanese. They were not interested in the deeper culture underneath the strange behavior they witnessed—it was categorically beyond consideration. But in Roka's case, the disdain is based in an intimate knowledge of Western, particularly Christian, civilization and history. Surrounded by such a rich environment, those natives who fail to appreciate it dismay Roka. He glorifies the past in a reverent, indeed religious, way, always granting it priority over the present.

This attitude can be seen throughout his travels in the Holy Land. He is not blind to the present, but his descriptions of it are uniformly dispassionate. One could argue that Roka's choice of destination could hardly be better for someone looking for a rich past—unlike Paris and London, Jerusalem offered little if anything in the realm of modern "tourist destinations." However, when he later went to Russia, he avoided the modern sites and immediately headed for the countryside, where Tolstoy was living at the time. Thus, it seems fair to say that regardless of where he was, Roka would have found the locale's history more engaging than its present.

Roka spent twelve days in and around Jerusalem, visiting such places as the Wailing Wall, Bethlehem, Rachel's Tomb, the Garden of Gethesemane, the Mount of Olives, and Golgotha. He then spent three days traveling from Jerusalem to Nazareth, at first by carriage and then on horseback. The route was the same as Christ's as described in John 4:1-4:6, from Judea to Galilee via Samaria. At Jacob's well, where Christ rested and asked a Samaritan woman for a drink of water, Roka pauses to gaze at the scene and read the fourth chapter of the Gospel According to John. It was certainly not the case that Roka harbored ideas of personal grandeur, associating himself with the Messiah; rather, like Bashō following Saichō's footsteps across the countryside, Roka was trying to relive the events of the past that resounded in his soul. And also like Bashō, who wrote poetry about the lice in his clothing, he faced the trials of the road: in Nablus, where he stopped for the night, he writes, "Couldn't sleep at night for the fleas and the pain in my limbs."[33]

---

33. Tokutomi, *Junrei kikō*, p. 89.

He journeys on, through Sabastiyah, Dothan, Janin, and Nazareth, and to the Sea of Galilee, which he finds most "poetic." In the daylight, Nazareth is pleasant enough, if unremarkable. But upon sunset it takes on a special meaning for Roka:

> As I stared out [over the city from my veranda], the daylight shadows disappeared and suddenly at the edge of the hills a golden bronze basin appeared. The moon appeared without warning above the hills of Nazareth. Counting on my fingers, I realized that it had been a month since I viewed the Indian Ocean, and that tonight the moon was full. When I departed, my father composed a farewell poem with the lines, "It is certain that upon your arrival in the land of the Holy Birth/ the moon that greets you shall be tranquil"—I see now that the words were fortuitously in accordance.
>
> The sunlight sank away, and the moonlight grew in the encroaching night sky, submerging the village of Nazareth like water. It would be difficult not to be distracted by it. I went out, and walked along the harbor in the moonlight. There were shadows in the houses, and from one of those dark shadows hurried a woman with her head covered. I wonder if her name could be Mary? Oh children who play beneath the wild shadows cast by the moon in this square, Oh Jacob, where is our Lord's brother? Listen! The dogs howl. This evening, too, the odd figure will surely go to the mountains to pray. Ah, Nazareth! Nazarene moon!
>
>> I came to Nazareth where you lived,
>>
>> And saw the moon of long ago!
>>
>> Seeing this evening the Nazarene moon that you saw,
>>
>> I feel that I am seeing only you.[34]

The final poem, addressed it would seem to Christ, is in traditional *waka* syllabic form. Its topic, the moon, is a common choice among Japanese poets. Indeed, the passage is reminiscent of section 82 of the *Tales of Ise*:

> When the Prince prepared to retire, somewhat befuddled, the eleven-day-old moon was just ready to disappear behind the hills. The Director of the Stables of the Right recited:

---

34. Tokutomi, *Junrei kikō*, pp. 99–100.

Must the moon vanish
in such great haste, leaving us
still unsatisfied?
Retreat, O rim of the hills,
and refuse to let it set.[35]

In *Ise*, the moon is a metaphor for the imperial prince; in Roka's case, the moon represents Christ. Roka has superimposed much of the traditional Japanese aesthetic on a decidedly un-Japanese situation, but he does not do so to be avant-garde or trite. To a man so accustomed to the foreign world, this pastiche of aesthetics seems natural. Indeed, a Western audience may agree that the poem is moving and appropriate, although nothing like it is found in the Western tradition. Roka also makes a strong connection between Christ and Nature, in essence linking the divine in the Western tradition with the divine in the Japanese Shintō tradition. In Galilee, he describes Christ as a "child of nature, a poet, a rustic . . ." associating him less with the specific world of man than with all of natural creation.[36] From a modern standpoint, this may seem innocuous, but at the time, as Muramatsu Tsuyoshi points out in his commentary on *Diary of a Pilgrimage*, such a stance in the West was deemed blasphemous.[37] The French scholar Ernest Renan (1823–92), author of *Vie de Jésus*, lost his academic position as a result of his study that placed Christ not at the pinnacle of existence but rather as an integral part of a bigger whole. However, from a Japanese standpoint, such a blending of religious ideals had a precedent—the doctrine of *honji suijaku* made the combination of Buddhist and Shintōism acceptable—and was not controversial. Indeed, for Japanese, such a conflation of religious concepts was more common than a strict adherence to one or the other.

Roka sightsees in the Nazareth area for a day, then continues on to Tiberias, where he visits the mountain site of the Sermon on the Mount. Next is Galilee, of which he opines, "Oh, poetic Galilee! Your earth is rich, Your mountains peaceful, Your lake waters pure," becoming hyperbolic to a fault. Here Roka is swept up in religious fervor,

35. Translation by Helen Craig McCullough in *Classical Japanese Prose: An Anthology*, p. 60.
36. Tokutomi, *Junrei kikō*, p. 114.
37. Muramatsu Tsuyoshi, *Kaisetsu*, in *Junrei kikō* (Tokyo: Chūō kōronsha, 1989), pp. 266–67.

and his writing suffers for it. Each sentence speaks of the glory and goodness of God, but it is disengaged from the author's environment. Perhaps these passages are best seen as a final attempt to connect to the historical presence Roka had gone seeking. If so, the last entry from Palestine belies his failure to do so. In it, he wonders if it were foolish for him to go searching for the footsteps of Christ in the present day, for none of the places he has visited, he says, is "holy ground." He sees his efforts as fruitless, and recalls that spiritual gratification is more important than earthly gratification of the flesh. Thus, his search for the "elixir of life" is a vain one.[38]

One cannot help but be reminded of Kamo no Chōmei's final words in his thirteenth century work, *Hōjōki* (*An Account of My Hut*), in which he states that although he has gone on a retreat to escape from desire and evil, he has failed because he has grown fond of his hut. Roka recalls the parting words and poetry of his mother, who told him that the font of eternal life is found in one's heart (and, implicitly, not in a geographical locale). Roka finishes this section by quoting John 20:11-18, in which a resurrected Jesus appears to Mary Magdalene. Perhaps Roka had hoped that Jesus would speak to him on this journey, and provide him with renewed hope and faith, but afterwards, as trite as it sounds, realized that faith can only be found within, not received from others.

Such was the Christian leg of Roka's journey. Next on his itinerary was the second objective of the trip: meeting Lev Tolstoy in Russia. Before he had left Japan, Roka had sent Tolstoy an English translation of his [Roka's] novel, *The Cuckoo*, by way of introduction. Of course, his brother, Sohō, had met Tolstoy in 1896 during a tour of Europe, and that, too, would have made his name familiar to the great Russian writer. As it turned out, Tolstoy did not expect Roka to carry through on his promise to visit but welcomed him nonetheless for a few days' stay at his country home, Yasnaya Polyana. Why visit Tolstoy? Roka was enamored of his ideas, particularly his Christianity-influenced doctrines of nonresistance and nonparticipation—this despite the fact that Roka did not speak or read Russian, and so could only read Tolstoy in translation. What he expected to gain from visiting the master when they shared no language is a mystery, but go he did.

38. Tokutomi, *Junrei kikō*, p. 121.

From Galilee, Roka went through Haifa to Constantinople, where he spent two days. The Turkish capital in the waning days of the Ottoman empire held little charm for him, and he saw it as a place of abandon and neglect. Curiously, his criticisms focus on how backward technology was, a criticism he never leveled at the Holy Land. Why was Constantinople to be a gleaming, cosmopolitan place, whereas Nazareth was to exude history and nothing else? Certainly Constantinople had countless sites of historical significance about which Roka could have written. In the event, he chose a small handful, but his first comments on the city are not about them; rather, he says:

> In this city of one million, there are gas lights but no electric lights; there is no telephone; there are old style rail cars and carriages, but as for electric trains there is only a short-distance underground train to Galata, which is there as a result of the German Kaiser's tactful visit last year. This is because the [Turkish] emperor hates electricity. I had heard of the bumpy cobblestones that made the traveler's head ache, but the thing that surprises me now is the dogs. Dogs are what are numerous in Constantinople; if one asks how many inhabitants there are in Constantinople, the answer is that there are one million people but the number of dogs is still under investigation.[39]

Roka goes on at great length about the dog population in the city, and at the end of his diatribe he concludes that the Turks see the dogs as filthy, thus they neglect the dogs, thus Turkey is, as a whole, a place of "abandonism."

After a quick tour of Sancta Sophia (The Church of the Divine Wisdom), described in a rather disengaged fashion, Roka tours the Bosphorus. There are plenty of myths involving this strait between the Black Sea and the Sea of Marmara, but Roka seems oblivious to them. Instead of mentioning Greek legends of Zeus, Hera, and Io, or Ulysses' supposed journey across the strait, he uncharacteristically describes the scenery and the contemporary people he meets in the simplest of terms. Perhaps the most remarkable portion of this entry records that on a side trip to the mountains he met a Turkish man in

39. Tokutomi, *Junrei kikō*, pp. 132–33.

his forties who greeted him in Japanese, and whom he later found had been fervently studying Japanese on his own. The reasoning for such an act is left unclear, although Japan's recent victory against Russia and her prominence in the world theater was probably a factor, even though Roka later says categorically that Turkey was not galvanized by Japan's victory the way that other Asian countries were. In any event, either the man's Japanese was still quite poor or Roka had no interest in him, for we never hear of or about him again.

In his section of miscellaneous observations, Roka mentions the odd Turkish postal system (just as Kamata Eikichi had a few years earlier), the shape of a Turkish fez, the difficulty of purchasing tickets for various forms of transportation, Turkish greetings, bribery among government officials, the Turkish writing system, Islam in education, the Turkish navy, the architecture of homes, the role of women, and the Turkish view of Japan. The section is notable for its lack of historicity, its refusal to see in Istanbul the depth that was revealed in Jerusalem and Nazareth. Roka's agenda was set before he departed from Japan, the points of interest already indelibly chosen; this left no room for the excitement of discovery. He was relatively certain, even before he began the journey, what he would find in Palestine and Russia. What came in between was incidental or of little or no interest. I say this not as a criticism of Roka but to illustrate a parallel between his work and his predecessors: in reading Bashō's *Narrow Road to the Deep North*, for example, one notices that some legs of his journey receive much attention, while others are given no mention whatsoever. The common reasoning behind this is that some places, being neither *meisho* or having any special *uta makura* associated with them, were beneath mention, and thus Bashō does not mention them. Inhabitants of those locales may have been sources of regional lore, but Bashō was intent upon following a certain path and seeing certain sights, and so he does not plumb the possible depths. Roka was similarly intent. Certainly Turkey could have provided volumes of reflection on the past, if Roka had taken the time to learn from it. But such was not his agenda.

After Constantinople, Roka headed across the Balkan peninsula, then passed through Romania (the port of Galati), and on to Russia. Nothing struck a cord with him until he crossed the border to Reni, but then he writes:

The train left Reni behind, swaying gently as it moved. Entering the Russia that I knew—the Russia of Gogol, Turgenev, Tolstoy, Goncharov, and my contemporaries Gorkii and Chekhov—rather gave me the feeling of entering my own home town. Although it was an obscure corner of Russia, it was Russia all the same, and one step into it I felt relaxed.[40]

Although he cannot speak Russian—he is armed only with a pocket-sized version of a primer on conversational Russian—he enjoys himself on the train, exchanging food and vodka with the other passengers whom he finds rustic but pleasant. The stations along the way generally offered some dining facility, of which Roka availed himself, enjoying inexpensive tea and sweets. The rail route went through Odessa, Kiev, Kursk, and Tula. Of the scenery outside the train window, Roka writes:

Traveling in Russia is like a sea voyage across the ocean. Yesterday and today we travel through the same landscape. There are no mountains, but the earth rolls like big waves. In five miles there is a church and the clear thatch rooftops of a village; in twenty miles a town of smoke stacks. The wheat is ripe, but has not been harvested yet. The grass is cut, and piled in fragrant mounds here and there. There are occasional groves of white birch. There are groves of red pines. There is an old man carrying large sickle on his shoulder, following a horse cart with a large yoke. There are children in red shirts who raised both arms in the air to wave to the train. One forgets one's country, one forgets one's differences, and simply becomes a young child in the bosom of a vast Nature.[41]

But even Nature could be too much for him; after another day of riding across the plains, he begins to chafe at the monotony:

The sun rises, the sun sets; we go and go further. There hasn't been a single tunnel for three days. Clearly these are the vast Russian plains. I wrote a comical poem:

40. Tokutomi, *Junrei kikō*, pp. 151–52.
41. Tokutomi, *Junrei kikō*, p. 154.

> If one measured by inches
> The plain of Musashi
> And sprinkled it all about
> Then there would be the Russian plain
> Of which there is quite too much[42]

The plains of Musashi, on which present-day Tokyo stands, comprise the largest flat area of land in Japan, but they paled in comparison. Roka was at a loss how to find beauty in this sight. Russia at first seemed special because of his familiarity with Russian literature, but the endless horizon as seen from the train was not what he remembered from Tolstoy's novels. He writes very little more, until he arrives at Yasnaya Polyana, 130 miles south of Moscow, on June 30.

By this time, Tolstoy was an old man who had retired to his country estate to live out the last years of his life. His wife and assorted family and guests were also in attendance, and despite the fact that Roka arrived unexpectedly, he was lodged on the grounds in guest quarters. Roka says in his travelogue that he did not really have a particular objective in this visit; he simply wanted to "see [Tolstoy's] face."[43] Roka had read a Japanese translation of *War and Peace* sixteen years previously, and he had written an abbreviated biography of Tolstoy nine years previously in which he expressed great admiration and respect for the man. But of course, Tolstoy was unaware of this, nor could he have ever read the biography, which only appeared in Japanese. All he knew of Roka was that he had written *The Cuckoo*, and that he was the brother of Sohō.

Roka took the train to the stop nearest Yasnaya Polyana, then headed further on foot. Eventually he found a ride on a peasant's horse cart. He approached Yasnaya Polyana during the early hours of the morning, which could only enhance the special aura that he had already attached to the place in his mind. He writes:

> The horse cart headed northwest, alongside ripe fields of wheat. Cornflowers and larkspurs where blooming amongst the wheat. Oh, quiet Russian summer morn! The sun had

42. Tokutomi, *Junrei kikō*, pp. 154–55.
43. Tokutomi, *Junrei kikō*, p. 157.

already risen, and it glimmered sleepily; a mist obscured the distant forest, and the fields were a solid white sea of dew. Somewhere a bird cried out. There was not a soul to be seen. My body, half in a dream state, swayed in the horse cart. I could see a pale chapel in the crests of the wheat, and just an hour from the station I came upon a small village. This was the village of Yasnaya Polyana.[44]

He goes on to describe everything that he sees—cedars, birches, and lindens; houses with blue rooftops and white walls—with a tone of wonderment. Although he does not say so explicitly, Roka conveys that this was exactly what he had been expecting after having read about the place. Despite the wonderment of his arrival, his first interview with Tolstoy is awkward at best; the latter discovered the former loitering about the garden, by his own admission in a "dreamlike state." Despite the language barrier, much of Roka's visit with Tolstoy was spent in conversations on Tolstoy's political, social, and religious views. The two did not always agree, but it would seem they enjoyed the banter well enough. But when Tolstoy was too busy to entertain Roka—which was often, as Roka was not the only other person at the

Yasnaya Polyana

44. Tokutomi, *Junrei kikō*, p. 163.

estate—Roka was left to reflect on Yasnaya Polyana, and it is in these passages that he comes closest to the sort of lyricism he had expressed in the Middle East. For example, on his first evening, he writes:

> After dinner we each went our separate ways . . . I took a stroll in the garden. The lindens, birches, oaks, and cedars were left to grow wildly; the beautiful flowers, some blooming, others not, were also left to grow in the untamed grass. In one corner near the house there was a cultivated patch of cherries, raspberries, and the like. There was a crude

Lev Tolstoy in garden

hothouse, in which a few tropical plants were placed, and a warm bed in which cucumbers and eggplants grew in disarray. Eventually the sun set. The bell for tea rang, and I could hear raucous laughing voices coming from the main house. I thought that they were probably having a most interesting conversation, but I was too tired, and so retired to my room, blew out the candle, and fell into the dreams of my first night at Yasnaya Polyana.[45]

The estate was as conducive to Roka's work as it was to Tolstoy's. At times, one feels that Roka feels a greater affinity with the house and grounds than he does with the inhabitants—he appropriates and assimilates them in his mind, as he had appropriated the characters and events in Tolstoy's novels. It was truly a case of Tolstoy's works transcending their author, for Roka is loath to discuss Tolstoy's novels with their creator, perhaps for fear of defiling his own vision of them. Instead, Roka imagines Anna Karenina working in the fields and romanticizes the labor of the peasants. When he is introduced to various Russians on the estate and in the village, he is often reminded of characters from Tolstoy novels, and remarks on how accurate Tolstoy's portrayal of the time and place was.

Running through the estate was the Varonka River, where Tolstoy and his family often bathed. Roka joins them on occasion, recording the pleasures afforded by the warm water and the verdant scenery surrounding the river. On his last day at Yasnaya Polyana, he goes for a walk down toward the Varonka, waxing poetic on his already forming memories of his stay. Upon reaching the river banks, he discovers that Tolstoy is already there. He takes one last bath in the Varonka, then, in a moment when Tolstoy is not in the bathing hut, scribbles a poem in English on a pillar therein with a pencil. He appends in the travelogue a Japanese version of the poem, which is much more expressive than the "original" (a translation of the Japanese version follows it):

> Fare thee well, Varonka!
> Forever shall I remember thee.
> Thou hast been my Jordan
> O thou blessed Varonka!

45. Tokutomi, *Junrei kikō*, p. 175.

[A Jordan born for my purposes,
I take my first bath in this Varonka River
I came looking for the elixir of eternal life
Shall I discover it within my own soul?]

Great poetry it is not, but still worthy of note, if we remember Roka's lukewarm and disappointed response to the real Jordan River, the source of "eternal life." Throughout his journey, Roka is looking for the "elixir of (eternal) life" but fails to find it where he expected it in the Holy Land. Instead, he finds it unexpectedly in the Russian countryside—or so he wants the reader to believe. The imagery of Roka swimming (being baptized) in the Varonka and finding his elixir in such an unpretentious place is, admittedly, rather heavy handed. Still, it provides the unique element to the journey that Japanese readers may have expected; despite the conventions of using *uta makura* to describe *meisho*, and the tradition of traveling the beaten path, travel writers (premodern and modern) were still obligated to add some fresh element to their work. Bashō is famous for this, and his medium of *haiku* poetry lends itself to it because of the inclusion therein of an "eternal" (known and experienced) and "momentary" (unique and new) element. Here Roka accomplishes the same end by finding the eternal elixir in a new place.

By July 5, Roka and Tolstoy had discussed all they could discuss in their limited English and Tolstoy's son's wedding was imminent, making it impossible for Roka to continue imposing on the family. Although the two men had had their differences in political discussions on the role of Japan in the world, and Roka had taken offense at some of the things Tolstoy had said, the former still admired the latter. The final entry from Yasnaya Polyana is a poem expressing reverence for Tolstoy:

I gaze at the light from the master's study
We all know that this is the light that illuminates the world
The shadow cast from the lamp in the master's window.[46]

46. Tokutomi, *Junrei kikō*, p. 213.

Tolstoy in his study

Before Roka left Japan, he tells us that his plan had been to visit the
Holy Land, see Tolstoy, climb the Swiss Alps, view the beautiful Italian landscape, play in Paris, taste the fog of London, then cross the
Atlantic ocean and see the United States, then finally cross the Pacific,
thus circumnavigating the globe. But, he confesses, after visiting Yasnaya Polyana, he decides to return to Japan by the newly opened
Trans-Siberian Railway. This change of heart may have been brought
about by exhaustion, or perhaps a lack of purpose in these other destinations; in any event, Roka does not elaborate. Before his repatria-

tion, however, he decides to spend two weeks visiting the famous cities of St. Petersburg and Moscow.

In St. Petersburg, he draws parallels between that city and Tokyo: the Neva River reminds him of the Sumida River, and the city's origins—it was built on swampy land three hundred years earlier—are like those of *bakufu*-era Edo. The analogy can only be taken so far, as the Russian landscape and climate is so different from central Japan's; he later mentions that although there is an area for swimming in the Neva, a cold drizzle makes it a gloomy proposition. The brown water of the river is "desolate and horrible," making him think of death.[47]

Guided about by two members of the Japanese legation, Roka visits a number of tourist sites, such as the Winter Palace ("The Hermitage"), the central park, St. Isaac's Cathedral, and the popular theater. His reflections, though, remain focused on the present. He anticipates a revolution after seeing the theatrical district and the unrest therein. Mention of the past is not absent, but it is done in a cursory fashion and without the emotion seen in the Holy Land.

In Moscow, Roka stays with three students who show him around the city. Once again, he makes an analogy between Russia and Japan by saying that the distance between St. Petersburg and Moscow is about that between Tokyo and Kyoto, and that there are "many similarities" between the old Russian capital and the old Japanese capital, none of which are clearly described. He is surprised by the number of churches, beggars, prostitutes, and cabs in Moscow, and he notes that the "cursed vodka" is everywhere. He goes to the Kremlin and recounts some historical facts associated with the building in a dispassionate manner. In short, nothing in Moscow or St. Petersburg moves Roka; he is merely a tourist there, no longer a pilgrim. The closest he comes to an emotional response to his environment comes in the last entry before he boards the train home. He writes:

> While in Moscow, one day I went with Mr. K to Sparrow Hills. They are to the southwest of Moscow, more than a mile from the Kremlin. With a commanding view of the Moscow River, they are, so to speak, as Kōnodai is to the Edo River.[48]

47. Tokutomi, *Junrei kikō*, p. 218.
48. Kōnodai is located in the northwestern part of Ichikawa city in Chiba Prefecture.

On top of the hill there is a tea house. I drank some tea, and commanded a view of Moscow. The flowing river and city of churches lay before my eyes like a painting, the edges of the fields blending into the distant summer sky. An afternoon sprinkle had just ended, and there was a lingering threat of rain. Sunshine leaked through the clouds, now coming now going. The clear golden roof of the Saviour's Cathedral would shine, then be obscured by clouds, Moscow itself appearing and disappearing like a dream. Napoleon stood here one hundred years ago. This is what remains of his ambitious undertaking! Those who chase after the states of this world are all like that, they are just grasping at the heavens. I recalled Vereshchagin's painting, and sadly I lingered as a woman nearby the tea house played a terribly melancholy, gut-wrenching Gypsy song on a mandolin.[49]

He was Truly the Hero of the World, But Where is He Now?

Sparrows, their spirits soaring, on the hills

A night of dreams filled me with chills!

A body thrown into the sea, like the shells

Of clams, make endless mirages

The clouds over Moscow flounder in the sky

An old, sad Gypsy song

The Saviour's Cathedral shines gold beams

Rain shall come to the Moscovian sky.

Shall it be rain, or shall it be fire? Only God knows the future. My prayer is that he takes pity on Russia.[50]

Here Roka alludes to the fires set by Russian arsonists upon Napoleon's invasion of Moscow in 1812. Most of the city was destroyed, and Roka

---

49. The reference here is to Vasily Vasilyevich Vereshchagin (1842–1904), a Russian painter. Vereshchagin made the scenes he saw on his many journeys overseas the subjects of his paintings. Among the places he painted were the Caucasus, the Danube River, Turkistan, the Balkans, Syria, Palestine, and Japan. He also painted scenes of Napoleon's invasion of Russia; these paintings were very popular and widely reproduced, and it is undoubtedly to these that Roka refers.
50. Tokutomi, *Junrei kikō*, pp. 233–34.

anticipates a repeat of history. He finds the scene foreboding of political turmoil to come—the rain and fire metaphors for an uprising, the unsettled sky a metaphor for the unsettled state of the country. Clearly influenced by Tolstoy's ideas of nonresistance and nonparticipation, he implies that all rebellious actions are simply acts of vainglory—after all, even the efforts of the great Napoleon resulted in nothing—and instead promotes a withdrawal from the political realm and a return to a traditional lifestyle, such as that Tolstoy was living on Yasnaya Polyana. At the same time, Roka echoes a centuries-old sentiment from Japanese literature: the Buddhist concept of impermanence. Kamo no Chōmei opens *An Account of My Hut* with lines that embody this idea; the beginning lines of the *Tale of Heike* also express an all-pervading impermanence. Regardless of his Christian sympathies, it would have been hard for Roka to grow up in Japan and not internalize this concept. Thus, Tolstoy's ideas appealed on both a conscious and subconscious level.

Roka's return trip to Japan took him across land via the Trans Siberian Railway, the construction of which had begun in 1891 and was completed only two years before Roka's trip in 1904. Previously travelers had returned to Japan by sea and, as we have seen, wrote little of the unremarkable ocean voyage. But Roka's journey took him across new territory, and if his travelogue is any reflection on his state of mind, it was territory that impressed and moved him. The train departed Moscow on July 19 and arrived in Vladivostok on August 1; stops in between included Tula, Samara (Kuibyshev), Chelyabinsk, Ufa, Irkutsk, and Lake Baikal. Whereas he found the landscape in southwestern Russia monotonous, the landscape across northern Russia inspired him to write poem after poem. Perhaps he was grateful to leave the frenetic urban landscape behind, or perhaps the variety of the mountains and plains provided some visual relief; in any event, nature looms large in his journal. He chooses the same objects he focused on before: birch trees, wheat, various grasses, the moon, etc. Unfortunately, the monotony of the landscape lends itself to monotony in the poetry—in one case, the word "Siberia" appears six times in twelve lines. Nonetheless, that Roka chose to pay attention to his homeward-bound leg and wrote more than a cursory journal entry is notable in itself, and not all of the poetry is poor. Near Irkutsk, he writes:

On a fir branch
Withered stiff
Sits a sliver of the moon
Over the mountains
Where bears live[51]

And on the shores of Lake Baikal, he writes:

A lone star
Floats in the sky
Of black clouds,
The deep night roils
Over Baikal[52]

Other poems mention the people he sees along the way, their figures always appearing solitary and poignant. But if Roka made friends with his fellow passengers, they were of little importance to him. He cursorily mentions a few of the others on the train but gives them little heed. He preferred to focus on the pastoral side of Russia in a romantic vein, one that idealized a simple life, free from political intrigues. Traveling through the countryside, separated from its inhabitants by the speed of the train, it was easy for Roka to impose his ideas on that world regardless of its realities.

As a kind of postscript to *Record of a Pilgrimage*, Roka's includes a final entry entitled "My Beloved Country":

August 2, 3 P.M. The Russian ship *SS Mongolia* left Vladivostok and cut through the waves of the Sea of Japan which bathe the shores of Japan and Russia. On the 4th we entered the verdant bay at Tsuruga in a light morning rain.

I left Yokohama on April 4, and pulled into Tsuruga on August 4. Those one hundred and twenty days were both long and short.

Ah, the flavor of the first spring water at the inn upon my landing! Ah, the flavor of cold rice packed with Nara pickles! Ah, the waving of the green fields that I gaze at from the train window!

51. Tokutomi, *Junrei kikō*, p. 244.
52. Tokutomi, *Junrei kikō*, p. 245.

The train headed eastward through the rice fields. As we reached windy Kiyomigata the summer evening fell and the moon was full.

The pine fields at Miho turn tranquilly toward

The new moon over Siberia's Ob River

August 5. At dawn rpain fell in drizzles, but then stopped. At 6 A.M. I removed my pilgrim's shoes at the Oitatsu hermitage in Zushi.

A catalpa bow drawn by the hand of God

Lets loose the arrow

To return home

The beautiful sea, the beautiful mountains; my prayer is to offer Japan to the gods.[53]

NAGAI KAFŪ

Nagai Kafū, one of the most prominent names in modern Japanese literature, spent more time abroad than most of his peers. As a young man, Kafū dreamed of going overseas, particularly to France, home of the literature of Maupassant and Zolà. He was, however, a bit of a dilettante, and his father disapproved of his plans, preferring that he stay in Japan. In the end, he finagled passage to the United States, where he lived and worked for four years between 1903 and 1907. He went through a number of temporary jobs in a number of cities; most of his time was spent between Tacoma, Kalamazoo, Washington, D.C., and New York City. He had had hopes of studying in Louisiana, where he had heard French was used as often as English, but the climate in the south proved unfavorable to his health, and he opted for the cool dry weather of Michigan instead. Finally, in 1907, he was able to make it to his beloved France, where he visited Lyons and Paris. After ten short months in Europe, he returned to Japan.

The most famous literary products of Kafū's time overseas are his collections *Tales of America* and *Tales of France*, both of which remain

53. Tokutomi, *Junrei kikō*, pp. 251–52. The term Roka uses here for Japan is *Akitsushima*, an old name for the country that dates back to the Heian period. In the first line, the word for "God" is *Ōkami*; in the last line the word for "gods" is *kami*.

in publication today. Although Kafū based much of what he wrote in the works on his observations and experiences, the works are, ultimately, fiction, enough so to be excluded from the category of *kikōbun-gaku*. However, Kafū also kept a diary during his travels that was published serially in the magazine *Civilization* under the title *Excerpts from a Diary of a Journey to the West*.[54] He also wrote many small topical pieces on his experiences for publication.

Kafū was a very keen observer of things foreign. But of course, one could say this of Nomura Fumio, too. What makes Kafū's observation noteworthy is his absolute comfort in his surroundings. Kafū knew about American and European civilization and culture in great detail, so almost nothing surprises or astonishes him. This is not to say that his travelogues are dull or blasé; on the contrary, they are rich in description and appreciation. In short, Kafū is one of the least "Japanese" of the Japanese travel writers. In translation, his writing could easily be mistaken for that of an Englishman or Frenchman visiting the United States, or an American visiting France.

Kafū's trip to the U.S. was a literary and aesthetic pilgrimage, not the hedonistic lark his family feared it to be. Before leaving Japan, Kafū had studied Chinese literature, but his true interest lay in Western literature, and he wanted to pursue a career in writing works that incorporated the Western style. But in 1903, Kafū was still a young man who needed to experience more of life before he could be a successful writer—he knew that, and he also knew that the experiences he required could not be had in Japan, or China, for that matter. He needed to live in the West, to integrate Western culture and society so firmly in his mind that it all but pushed Japan out. As a result, we see in his travel writing a disregard for the "sights," or *meisho*, and in its place an interest in the underbelly of America—destitute Chinese immigrants in New York City, prostitutes, etc.—that was usually ignored by shorter-term travelers led by professional guides.

Of course, Kafū had time and anonymity on his side in his travels, which gave him the leisure to make friends and the privacy necessary to earn their trust. Moreover, Kafū found a consolation in the

54. *Civilization* was published by some of Kafū's friends, most notably Inoue Aa (1878–1923). *Excerpts from a Diary of a Journey to the West* appeared in 1917 many years after Kafū's repatriation. In his introduction, he says the he originally did not intend the work for publication but upon later thought, decided that it might be of interest to others.

desolation of the working classes, with whom he felt an affinity. During his time in New York City, he would often head for Chinatown after work to bathe in the pathos he saw there:

> While I find it frightful to see the unsightly and wretched lives led by the prostitutes who live in the back alleys of Chinatown, eating birds' nests, I also experience a kind of bitter consolation in it. They are basically human. They are someone's children. They have mothers. They have lovers. Nevertheless, they have ended up corrupt to the extreme. I, who have lost all my hopes, feel an intimate empathetic connection when I have contact with these corrupt people. When I see them dead drunk, shouting wildly, tears of humanity well from the depths of my soul.[55]

These are not the words of a starry-eyed traveler, impressed by the glory and grandeur of the industrialized world. Nor are they those of a traveler who wants only to visit historically significant sites. They come from someone who saw the complexities of Western society, one who was strongly influenced by French Naturalist ideas and who felt drawn to the lowest echelon of that society.

As far as the nonhuman landscape was concerned, Kafū was equally uninterested in the famous scenes. One day, on a boat off New York after a trip to see the Statue of Liberty, of which he speaks well, if not tersely, he writes:

> The steamship we had boarded at one point went so far offshore that we couldn't make out the distant coastline, but eventually it ran alongside the quiet shore. The bright summer sun in the clear blue sky shone down on the peaks of snow-white clouds floating above the horizon, the calm sea, and the trees on the shore, with their thickly entwined branches. The whiteness of the clouds, the blueness of the water, and the greenness of the trees gave off an unspeakably felicitous sparkle. When I looked over I saw that the shoreline had given way to a low strip of pasture, and here and there on the water's surface tall, thick reeds sprouted forth, the pure white sails of the ship reflected in their

---

55. Nagai Kafū, *Seiyū nisshi shō*, in *Sekai kikō bungaku zenshū* (Tokyo: Horupu shuppan, 1979), p. 47.

New York skyline, 1908

shadows. A flock of wild geese flew scattered like flower
petals. I was happy to have seen this sort of wet landscape,
like a painting, unexpectedly in this nameless place. It was
unlike being in any of the sights in the world's famous
places.[56]

The final line uses the term *meisho* for "famous places," undoubtedly
on Kafū's mind after seeing the statue. That was a fine sight, he says,
but the unexpected and otherwise unremarkable shore was certainly
superior. Previous Japanese travelers had seen these sights, but they
had not remarked on them. Why did it take decades for someone to
write about them? In the earlier writers' minds, natural aesthetics were
confined to Japan, and, in some cases, China. Digesting all the "new"
nature outside of their realm of knowledge was a daunting task.
Choosing to ignore it was probably not a conscious decision, but if
we imagine the frustration of trying to incorporate so much that was
new into a literary tradition that was so highly codified for centuries,
the reticence of the earlier writers seems justified. Kafū was bold
enough to record the "new," although it would take much longer for
his work to become a base on which others would build.

Like the journeys of many of the Heian, Kamakura, and Muromachi domestic travelers, Kafū's trip was not an exciting adventure but
rather an arduous undertaking. To be sure, he had many advances in
transportation at his disposal—it was certainly easier to board a train
and travel hundreds of miles without much effort than to walk or ride
in a stuffy palanquin across rough terrain exposed to the elements—

56. Nagai Kafū, *Natsu no umi*, in *Sekai kikō bungaku zenshū* (Tokyo: Horupu shuppan, 1979),
    p. 28.

but this did not alleviate the overwhelming sense of melancholy that seemed to chase him to every destination, particularly in the United States, brought on by his insistence on fraternizing with the lowest class. He was rarely happy in America; he complained in his diary that life there, "did not please [his] poetic interests," and he pleaded to go to France to study her literature.[57] One might think it a recipe for a bitter and angry journal, but it proved the perfect setting for the quintessentially Japanese travelogue, one that encompasses the sort of ryojō and ryoshū so integral to traditional kikōbungaku.

Kafū's travelogues can be divided into two categories: biographical and auto-biographical. The former group includes *Two Days in Chicago* (1905), *The Summer Sea* (1905), *Midnight in a Bar* (1906), *Fallen Leaves* (1906), and *A Record of Chinatown* (1906). The latter group comprises entries from Kafū's diary *Excerpts from a Diary of a Journey to the West*. The biographical works are not about famous people, historical or contemporary; rather, they are about common folk in common circumstances. Kafū knew Western history, he knew the import of people and places, but he rarely mentioned them. They had their place, but that place was not in the line of Kafū's focus. This is because for Kafū, the *hon'i* of the West was its ambience, not a certain place or event, and that ambiance comprised the mundane happenings of everyday life. Indeed, Emile Zolà, one of Kafū's favorite authors, specialized in depicting this sort of ambiance of the lower classes, and it was that which Kafū sought. And so, Kafū did go in search of *meisho*, but he attached his own significance of place. For this reason, it would be easy for a literary critic to dismiss Kafū's travelogue as one colored by Western literature and distant from its Japanese roots, but such a criticism fails to recognize the character of Kafū's fascination and its ultimately deeper connection with locale.

In the autobiographical section, Kafū wrote sporadically. Many of the entries are on his feelings and concerns vis-à-vis his interest in literature, particularly that of France. Other entries comment solely on the weather; however, these entries are not the terse record of "rain" or "cloudy" found in other diaries. Rather, they invariably invoke a mood, and usually a melancholy one. About halfway through the work, Kafū began to frequent the theater and opera often, and he dutifully

57. Nagai, *Seiyū nisshi shō*, p. 41.

recorded what he saw. One other common topic is his relationship with
an American prostitute, Edyth, whom he met in Washington and who
followed him to New York City. We almost never hear of his work,
except that he went to it or came home from it. His duties in the Japanese legation in Washington, D.C., and working for the Yokohama
Specie Bank in New York were of no import to him beyond the salary
he brought in as a result of his labors. Indeed, he says that being forced
to socialize with his coworkers after hours was unbearable.[58]

Kafū's sensitivity to the natural physical landscape dominates the
entire work. Typical of a daily entry is the following, written in Kalamazoo, in which we learn nothing of his activities that day but much
of his surroundings:

> May 3. I know not how to describe the sight I saw yester-
> day evening—as the last of dusk faded the light seemed to
> return above the surrounding hills, resting itself upon the
> roots of the ancient oak trees. The distant thick line of trees,
> separated from me by a broad expanse of meadow, appeared
> dimly in yesterday's evening light. Countless lantern lights
> shone in this early evening, and from the distance the voices
> of women singing to a piano accompaniment wafted to me
> as if from a dream. Silently, almost reticently, I gazed out at
> this captivating early summer evening. I lost track of time,
> buried in the thought that in the future, if I should desire
> to compose a picture of the American countryside, such a
> want would surely come from the light of this evening.[59]

A month later, he stopped in Kingston, New York, on his way to New
York City:

> June 21. Windy; no break in the heat. At dusk [my friend]
> Imamura and I went for a walk in the neighborhood where
> there were many fireflies fluttering about in the grove and
> tall grasses. Their light is not as pretty as that of fireflies in
> Japan, but in some way they bring on a feeling akin to the
> cool summer evenings of the far east, and thus insistently
> bring on feelings of *ryoshū*.[60]

58. Nagai, *Seiyū nisshi shō*, p. 47.
59. Nagai, *Seiyū nisshi shō*, p. 40.
60. Nagai, *Seiyū nisshi shō*, p. 41.

In July he began his job in Washington, D.C. Of the city, he wrote:

> July 30. It is extremely hot. Everyday when the scent of the honeysuckle growing on the wall of the legation wafts towards us on our lunch break, two or three hummingbirds fly by, their wings buzzing. It is said that this bird is not seen but during the summer in the southern climes of America.
>
> August 3. Everyday the heat is tremendous, but in the city of Washington old maples cast their shade everywhere so the carriage roads are tolerable, and pretty flower beds are planted in every intersection. When I went [to one of those carriage roads] to a bench in the evening, I was able to read quietly by the light of the street lamp. I'm reading Maupassant's travelogue, *Sur l'eau*.[61]

Kafū is often in places brimming with famous sights, such as the countless monuments and memorials in Washington, D.C., but they are not part of his journey. In New York, the only famous sights he mentions by name are the Statue of Liberty and the Brooklyn Bridge, and in the former's case he does so in reference to France, not the U.S.: the sight of the statue gazing out over the ocean makes him think of Paris and the passion of her arts. He is filled with sorrow at the thought that he had never savored that passion in person. And in Washington, D.C., it would seem nothing is worth note, save the hummingbirds and the honeysuckle. He never tells us what the legation itself was like, for that had little bearing on his state of mind.

At first, America is a large disappointment for Kafū, who relentlessly extols the superior qualities of France and French literature. He goes to an oil painting exhibition at the New York School of the Arts, only to comment that not one painting moved him. He sighs and wonders, "Perhaps America is no good."[62] After much time and many theater trips, however, he occasionally finds pleasure in the United States, albeit pleasure associated with France. On a December evening, after seeing a performance of Sardou's play *Sorcière* starring the French actress Sarah Bernhardt, he claims that his first thought in going abroad was to attend the theater in the West, for reading a play

61. Nagai, *Seiyū nisshi shō*, p. 41.
62. Nagai, *Seiyū nisshi shō*, p. 45.

Brooklyn Bridge

simply does not compare to seeing it performed. Now that he has seen the "world's best *tragédienne*," he exclaims, he has fulfilled his objective in going abroad.[63] Three months later he writes:

> March 24. The bank closed early today because it is Saturday. It was a little late, but I went to go see the comic play *The Squaw Man*, which had recently received good reviews. The protagonist has a chance meeting with an old lover in the wilds of Utah, which made me cry a bit. I can no longer look at plays with the cold critical eye I used to have when I lived in Japan. America has made me a grateful poet![64]

By this point, Kafū has begun to take pleasure in his effective "exile" in America; distant from France though he may be, he is still closer than he had been in Japan. Exposure to the French arts comes in small bits, which he enjoys vicariously. In October 1906, he writes that he often goes to small eatery run by a Frenchman. There, on his way home from working at the bank, he enjoys a glass of wine with his

63. Nagai, *Seiyū nisshi shō*, p. 44.
64. Nagai, *Seiyū nisshi shō*, p. 45. *The Squaw Man* is a play by Edwin Milton Royle.

evening meal. He uses French to order his food from the *garçon*, and peruses the Paris newspaper. He admits, "I cannot help but love this lonely, solitary life I have here overseas."[65]

There are times that Kafū's diary reads overly melodramatically, as if he were looking for loneliness instead of suffering unhappily from it. He disdained his relatively comfortable living, and purposely sought out the impecuniousness and destitution found in urban areas, mostly in immigrant communities such as Chinatown. I find this not a reason to criticize Kafū but rather evidence of his aesthetic leanings, which are a curious pastiche of French Naturalism and traditional Japanese pathos (*aware*). Pathos and longing are found in travelogues across the ages; however, the longing is usually for one's home, such as the longing expressed by the narrator in *Tosa Diary* for the capital, from which he/she has been separated for so long. In Kafū's case the longing is for France, not Japan.

This difference aside, the parallels are striking: both authors have been sent far away from their beloved locale (the capital/France) against their desires; both feel that their present location (Tosa/America) is undistinguished and lacking in the cultural refinements; both refuse to see the beauty of their present surroundings without reference to the desired locale. That Kafū was drawing on that tradition is implicit in the text. And so, although Kafū spent enough time to make him an ineffectual travel writer by Guido Verbeck's reckoning (see chapter 1), we see that he maintained the mindset of the temporary resident, one who could not sever his connection to another place where he would rather be.

ANEZAKI CHŌFŪ

Anezaki Chōfū, also widely known in the West as Anesaki Masaharu, was a scholar of philosophy and religion who traveled in the West for extended periods beginning in 1900. In the course of his career, he was a professor at Tokyo University, chaired Japanese Literature and Life for two years at Harvard University, and also authored numerous influential books in English on Japanese religion, particularly Buddhism. His

65. Nagai, *Seiyū nisshi shō*, p. 50.

books, although published nearly a century ago, are still widely respected by scholars, and he is credited with having largely introduced Japanese culture to the Western world. Anezaki was also, of the writers discussed here, perhaps the most fluent and knowledgeable about the world outside of Japan; thus, it is of particular interest to see how much the Japanese literary tradition informed his writing.

Anezaki's purpose in journeying abroad was to study world religions. Thus, he went to India to examine the origins of Buddhism, and Europe to visit places of historical significance for Christianity. He visited India, Switzerland, Italy, Germany, and England, but it was upon Italy that he focused in his travelogue, *A Diary of Gathering Flowers* (1909), a work that perfectly blends the Japanese and Western traditions of travel writing.

Anezaki was well versed in the history and historical role of the Italian sites he visited, but he did not assume that his readers shared in this knowledge. As he moved from locale to locale, he introduced each with a brief summary of its significance, usually associated with Christianity, art history, or a combination of the two. Perhaps owing to his extensive knowledge of Western religion, he clearly felt at home abroad; there is none of the offended air of the early travelers in his voice. He was fluent in English and had picked up some Italian and French, thus preventing him from ever having trouble with a language barrier.

European customs were not foreign to him, either; rather, they were so common that they rarely call for attention. In the first pages, he says that he "wanted to express that although Eastern and Western civilizations are different, human emotions are the same."[66] A simplistic idea to be sure, but thankfully Anezaki does not belabor it. Instead, he demonstrates it by discussing and describing his experiences without pointing to the obvious cultural departures; when he writes poetry, and he does so often, he appeals to universal human sensibilities, not exclusively Japanese references. In other words, although the poems are in traditional *waka* meter, they are rarely in the highly allusive style of the premodern era.[67] They do, however,

---

66. Anezaki Chōfū, *Hanatsumi nikki* (Tokyo: Hakubunkan, 1909), p. 2.
67. The exception to the rule is the title, which is a mild twist on both Enomoto Kikaku's (1661–1707) *Hanatsumi* and Yosa Buson's (1716–83) *Shin hanatsumi* (1777). The latter is a memorial for Buson's mother, as this work is a memorial for Anezaki's friend.

focus on the natural landscape and the emotions evoked by it, a traditional aspect of *waka* that easily appeals even to the uninitiated (Western) reader.

Anezaki tells us in his preface that a friend had asked him to "bring home a diary with something of interest in it," and upon that friends' death (after Anezaki's return to Japan), he decided to complete the work as a dedication. But a reading of the text quickly shows that this is more than a simple lyrical memorial. The beginning section opens with a dramatic description of the mountains in Switzerland, passages in which Nature figures prominently, the lush winter images virtually dripping off the page. This is a departure from the standard beginning of *kikōbun*, in which the author bids farewell to family and friends, but Anezaki does it for a reason: he is *not* sorry to be away from Japan, he does not miss home. His journey is a chance for him to learn more about religion and explore the beauty therein. The resulting travelogue is an interesting mix of academic thesis and emotive observations; it is a blend of Tayama Katai's second and third types of travelogue: those that give locational information and those that focus on the author's emotions (see chapter 1). In this sense, it owes most of its style to premodern domestic travelogues and very little to the spirit of adventure or exploration of the early Meiji period.

A Diary of Gathering Flowers begins its narrative in the town of Göschenen on April 5, 1908. In the Alps a, heavy snowfall still lies on the ground. The first sentence reads, "I had thought to spend this day gazing at the spring moon on the shores of Lake Lugano, but instead I am passing this evening in the mountains of Göschenen, surrounded by snow." This opening showcases the landscape but not the aspects of it that are particularly foreign—the beauty that Anezaki sees is in natural phenomena and structures common in Japan as well as Europe. These are the sights that a Japanese writer can easily incorporate in his poetry: snow, rain, mountains, the moon, the four seasons, cliffs, peaks, the sky overhead. Unlike Muragaki in Hawai'i (who could not find the right idiom for his poetry) and Narushima Ryūhoku (who substituted the deeds of Napoleon for a natural motif), Anezaki discovers that nature as he knows it exists in the West, too, and although some concessions must be made for different flora and fauna, the traditional *waka* form is suitable for describing the Swiss landscape. In retrospect it is a little surprising that earlier travel writers did not recognize this fact, but perhaps the experience of being abroad was so distracting that it prevented the quiet gaze necessary to compose from the soul.

Anezaki often notes similarities between what he sees in Europe and scenes from either the Chinese or Japanese tradition. He says that a scene near Lugano is "like something described in a poem by a Tang poet," and that a field he passes has a lake at one end, like the battlefield at Nikkō.[68] In San Mammette, he sees a bridge over a stream called the Val Solda that looks to him "like [that in] a Chinese landscape painting."[69] In Rome, the sight of brightly attired pedestrians and carriages under a brilliantly sunny sky reminds him of Tokyo during flower-viewing season.[70] In Florence, the beautiful new leaves on the birch trees remind him of the young leaves on the Zelkova trees on the Musashino plain. He muses whether the Zelkova tree in his own garden in Japan is budding, too, and is moved to compose a poem:

> The light green leaves
> of the birch tree
> in Tuscany
> I liken
> to the spring in Musashino[71]

These comparisons do not mean that Anezaki was incapable of seeing the true beauty around him without the simile of the familiar scenes of home. Rather, the comparison to East Asian landscapes enhances the description, much as *uta makura* enhance the imagery in a poem by alluding to a greater whole. It was too late, or perhaps too difficult, to begin a new catalogue of codified *uta makura* for the *meisho* of the West, but Anezaki does the next best thing—he draws on the rich imagery of the East Asian landscape to bolster his descriptions of the Western landscape.

Even when Japan is not being evoked, Nature looms large in the poetry of *A Diary of Gathering Flowers*. The poetry from the Alps is typical:

---

68. Anezaki, *Hanatsumi nikki*, pp. 10–11.
69. Anezaki, *Hanatsumi nikki*, p. 26.
70. Anezaki, *Hanatsumi nikki*, p. 269.
71. Anezaki, *Hanatsumi nikki*, p. 81.

Spring has arrived
The white Alpine snow
has begun to melt
into waterfalls of white threads
amongst the rocks[72]

Looking up
above the peaks
that seem to open to the sky
lie more peaks
visible amidst the clouds[73]

Rain or snow
it endures a thousand years
in a precarious state
it stands beside
the barren, stern cliff[74]

A sled runs through
the snow drifts,
tossing and scattering it
the swirling snow surges
in the void ahead[75]

In a mountain village
amongst the quietly
falling snow
even the birds are silent
the sun has set[76]

This treatment of winter is not site specific—substitute "the mountains of Koshi" (located in northwest Japan, where annual snowfall is heavy) in place of "Alps" and the imagery would be just as fitting. The sled, the mountain village, and the snow are all subjects in Saigyō's poems on winter in his collection *Poems of a Mountain Home*, written

72. Anezaki, *Hanatsumi nikki*, p. 5.
73. Anezaki, *Hanatsumi nikki*, p. 6.
74. Anezaki, *Hanatsumi nikki*, p. 8. This particular poem is about a pillar of ice that has formed next to a boulder.
75. Anezaki, *Hanatsumi nikki*, pp. 12–13.
76. Anezaki, *Hanatsumi nikki*, p. 14.

in the twelfth century. Indeed, given the imagery in most of Anezaki's poems, they would not be out of place among the poems of the imperial anthologies, such as the *Kokin wakashū* (ca. 920) and the *Shin kokin wakashū* (ca. 1201). Anezaki is able to ignore that the houses of the village are of a different architecture, that the people in the houses are of a different race, and that the birds are undoubtedly of a different species than in his homeland. His focus is instead on a moment in time that strikes the eye with uncommon beauty, as was Saigyō's focus centuries before. Thus, with these uncomplicated poems, he indirectly reinforces his statement that "although Eastern and Western civilizations are different, human emotions are the same," and it is those human emotions that occupy the heart of verse.

One may ask, are the poems then less than they should be? Is Anezaki missing an opportunity to focus on the *hon'i* of Switzerland and Italy? If we apply the same standards to Anezaki's poems as we do to domestic poems, the answer must be no: although domestic *waka* do celebrate certain aspects of *meisho*, those aspects are often phenomena ubiquitous in the Japanese archipelago. What connects the *meisho* with the phenomenon is that the latter is particularly stunning in the former, not that it exists only in the former and in no other locale. There are cherry blossoms throughout Japan, but in Yoshino they are exceptional. The harvest moon appears everywhere in the archipelago, but viewed at the Kashima Shrine, it is striking. And although it snows throughout Europe, the snow is especially remarkable deep in the mountains. Indeed, if Anezaki were to focus on the singular sights in the Alps, such as the architecture or the people, his poems would hold less appeal because his audience could not begin to imagine the subject. By focusing on the familiar yet somehow exceptional, he creates poems that draw on the readers' imagination and helps them create in their mind's eye the vision before the poet.

Also of note is that Anezaki interacts with nature in an unprecedented way. He not only stops to *see* the landscape, he *enters* it, experiencing it with all his senses. One day in Carceri, a remote area he visits in tracing the life of Saint Francis of Assisi (1181–1226), he spends as much time admiring nature as he does the connections with the famed saint. He tours the area, being led by an old monk:

I headed across a bridge to a mountain path that led through a thick grove. The old monk opened the gate ahead of us and told me to go into the garden, leaving me to my own devices. I went along in the shade of the trees and opened a gate to find a path that, although it was on the same mountain, went through a verdant garden. Therein, flanked by rows of cypress, lay a shrine of the Virgin. Amongst the grasses were red and white marguerite blossoms, and violets grew in the shade of the rocks; it was a whole different world than that of the stone rooms of the monastery. I entered the shrine and lay down in a sunny spot on the grass, bathing in the sunlight of the quiet valley. Flowers bloomed in profusion by my head, and small insects flitted about the blossoms.

> Compared to
>
> the mendicant's bed
>
> laid upon a stone
>
> this mat of grass
>
> is a brocade

I could hear the songs of birds, somewhat like the nightingale, in the grove. Occasionally I could also hear the song of the cuckoo and the sound of the bells around the goats' necks as they grazed in the mountains.[77]

When Roka went out to Tolstoy's gardens, he must have seen similar sights, but he did not write of them. Anezaki notes the colors of the flowers, the peaceful aura of the garden, the joy of the soft ground; his interests lie exclusively in the familiar simplicity exemplified by the natural landscape. In comparison to the *bakumatsu* travelers, his focus is notably turned away from the technological advancements of the day and instead aimed at the aspects of Europe most like Japan.

Anezaki is struck by the natural beauty compared to the austere living arrangements in the monastery, but, more importantly, he lies down in the grass to appreciate the surroundings, making the grass his mat: the term "grass pillow" (*kusa makura*) is a *makura kotoba* in

77. Anezaki, *Hanatsumi nikki*, pp. 206–7.

traditional *waka*, and is connected to the term "travel" (*tabi*). Here Anezaki uses the words *kusa no shitone* ("mat of grass"), which also evoke the act of traveling. Similarly, traditional imagery appears throughout *A Diary of Gathering Flowers*: one day upon his return to Assisi after a day of sightseeing, he writes that the "sun, low in the west, shone on the town of Assisi. The setting sun dyed the various clouds, which appeared deep scarlet and deep purple in the sky." The image of purple clouds in the western sky, a symbol of Amida's Pure Land Paradise—was surely familiar to Anezaki, who was a scholar of Buddhism.

In a domestic travelogue these images may have been unremarkable, but in the context of a foreign travelogue they were unprecedented. Until this time, Japanese travel writers had segregated their imagery such that allusion to traditional forms was virtually absent in their works. It was as if nature as they knew it existed only in the Japanese archipelago, and the Western world could not produce the emotional response that constitutes the core of the *waka* tradition. Anezaki breaks through that barrier in his effort to show the similarity of "human emotions."

Outside of the poetry, however, Anezaki writes much about each locale's historical significance. Because of his extensive learning in philosophy and religion, he is at ease explaining, giving an even-handed balance of fact and related elaboration. Although Anezaki was a Buddhist, he maintained a deep appreciation for the Judeo-Christian tradition and often expressed admiration and awe at significant Christian sites. His praise never reaches the heights of Tokutomi Roka's encomia, but then again any disappointments he had were usually hidden away. Because of his objective in Italy—to see some of the greatest works of Italian art—he spends much of his time visiting cathedrals and monasteries. His hosts welcome him and guide him through galleries, where he focuses primarily on the works of Fra Angelico (ca. 1400–1455). His descriptions of Angelico's paintings are extensive, and they distract him from the lyrical trends established earlier in the travelogue. After the tour de force of the opening passages, the narrative suddenly becomes a dry, textbook study of Italian art. Half way through the work, Anezaki seems to remember his earlier muse and once again begins to reflect on and interact with his surroundings, only to return to dry description again at the end. If there is one criticism to make of *A Diary of Gathering Flowers*, it is that its pacing is awkward. However, the content of the reflective passages more than compensate for this failing.

In addition to using common imagery, Anezaki emphasizes the similarity between "human emotions" in one other significant way: he finds many similarities between Pure Land Buddhism and Christianity. In particular he focuses on the teachings of Hōnen (1133–1212), one of the founders of Pure Land Buddhism in Japan, and how they are paralleled by the teachings of Saint Francis, the founder of the Franciscan church. Hōnen is best known for bringing Buddhism to the commoner by promoting the recitation of the *nembutsu*, an invocation of the name of Amida Buddha. Saint Francis is best known for promoting and practicing frugality, and for his work with the indigent. The commonality between the two was their claim that salvation could be had through the compassion of another, Amida or Jesus Christ. The affinity was indisputable to Anezaki, who claimed, "People who say that the bases of human emotions in the East and West are different are people who do not understand human emotions. Those who see Christianity and Buddhism as two separate entities are no different than one who stands surrounded by the narrow walls of his own enclosure."[78]

In his discussion of Saint Francis and Hōnen, Anezaki writes in a form somewhere between the *uta monogatari* style, in which a prose narrative supplements a poem, as in *The Tales of Ise*, and the *kotoba gaki* style, which tells of the circumstances behind the composition of a poem, as in the *Collection of Myriad Leaves* poetry anthology. In these poems nature is virtually absent; instead, Anezaki expresses admiration for the holy men. This is not, however, a departure from traditional *waka* evocation: poems in the *Collection of Myriad Leaves* that celebrate the deeds and accomplishments of the imperial family read quite similarly. For example, when visiting a former residence of Saint Francis, Anezaki writes:

> In the wall of the hall there remains a hole. That is where Saint Francis would leave medicine for the lepers, and where today is kept the rope that he used as a belt. On that belt

78. Anezaki, *Hanatsumi nikki*, p. 230.

remains some blood from his chest wound (the wound that
appeared on Saint Francis' chest as it had appeared on
Christ's chest). I do not know whether the blood from his
chest wound was coughed up through his throat, but it was
probably the last blood to come from a body that had
endured the privations of life.

> The rope belt
> of he who gave himself
> to the Lord—
> Untie it, oh bodhisattva
> and welcome his spirit
> Even from a mouth of blood
> came praise
> for the Lord
> The remains of an era
> have come to rest here[79]

Compare this to poem 204 in *Myriad Collection of Leaves* written as
a tribute to Prince Yuge (d. 699) after his death:

> Our lord and prince, ruling in peace,
> Child of the Bright One above,
> God as he is, has taken
> His divine seat in the Heavenly Palace
> Far above. We, awe-stricken,
> Lie prostrate and weep
> Day after day, and night after night,
> And to our weeping there is no end.[80]

Although the religious doctrines that flavor the poems differ, the dedicated praise for the subject is the same. Both poets imagine the subject in the heavens, a place more appropriate than earth for them. St.
Francis, after living a pious life, should be welcomed by the spirits.

79. Anezaki, *Hanatsumi nikki*, pp. 235–36.
80. Translation from *The Man'yōshū: The Nippon Gakujutsu Shinkōkai Translation of One Thou-
      sand Poems* (New York: Columbia University Press, 1965).

Prince Yuge, descended from the gods, is naturally at home in the heavens. Both are missed by the mundane, and both achieved greatness while on earth. In Anezaki's poem, the use of the word *bodhisattva* (*shōju*) emphasizes his juxtaposition of Buddhism and Christianity, ultimately hinting at a reconciliation between the two religions in stating that Buddhist saints would welcome a Christian saint in one catholic heaven.

Despite the rich allusion to the past and its traditions, *A Diary of Gathering Flowers* has some modern aspects to it. First, the language that Anezaki chose to write in, except for that of his poetry, was colloquial Japanese. This was one of the earliest overseas travelogues to be written in what was then a new form, although writers and scholars had been experimenting with the style for over two decades, and it gives the work a distinctly modern flavor. Second, its objective scholarly approach in the passages describing art work and architecture is much more similar to Western travelogues of the time, such as Henry James' *English Hours* (1905) and *Italian Hours* (1909), than earlier Japanese works.[81] Although there is no record of Anezaki reading James or other travel writers, he certainly had the linguistic skills to do so, and the authorial voice in those scholarly sections of *A Diary of Gathering Flowers* intimates a familiarity with the Western travel writing tradition.

Third, Anezaki was aware that his travails—difficulty with transportation and housing, etc.—were minor modern inconveniences compared to earlier travelers. He says that although he experiences the emotions associated with being in a foreign land, far away from home, his loneliness cannot compare to the ascetic lifestyle of Saint Francis or of similarly austere Buddhist monks.[82] Anezaki admires these historical figures; the purpose of his journey is to capture the essence of their religious piety and the landscape that inspired it. He most certainly is *not* traveling to a new, modern place in order to see what may be; rather he is traveling to the romantic past, to recapture the glory of what was.

81. *Italian Hours* as a collection of essays was published in 1909, but it comprises two previous works, *Transatlantic Sketches* (1875) and *Portraits of Places* (1883), plus four new essays. Most of the essays in *Italian Hours* were originally published separately in various popular periodicals such as *Atlantic Monthly*, *Nation*, *Scribner's Magazine*, and *Century Magazine*.
82. Anezaki, *Hanatsumi nikki*, p. 264.

One may argue that this was what Tokutomi Roka did in the Holy
Land as well. However, the salient difference between what Anezaki
and Tokutomi Roka accomplish is that in Roka's case he expresses a
total disdain for the present while reveling in the glories of the past.
Anezaki, on the other hand, is able to admire the present landscape
in which the past dwells. He enjoys the comforts of the modern age
and avoids criticizing the cases of indigence and destitution that earlier travelers single out as representative of what is wrong with Western ways. He sees nature as preserving the continuity between the
past and the present. He also finds reason to pause in reflection on
the brutality as well as the glory of human history. Visiting ruins in
Rome, he writes:

> The spring of the Roman Empire may never come again, but
> the small flowering grasses bloom every spring, as they have
> since time immemorial.
>
>> It has lost its charm—
>
>> Thousands of flowers bloom
>
>>> as if to ridicule
>
>>> the acts of man
>
>>> amongst the ruins[83]

> There were various chapels in the small valley area, but there
> is no need to recount each one's history. Now there are only
> piles of rubble and half fallen walls left. Among them, there
> are the remains of a round wall, the inside of which is shaped
> like a shallow crypt. This is where the fire of the gods was
> kept and guarded carefully; there were also many people
> who were slaughtered here. It is a sacred yet frightening
> memorial.[84]

It is not just Roka's work that contrasts *Diary of Gathering Flowers* by
romanticizing the past; decades earlier in *Diary of a Journey Westward*
Narushima Ryūhoku sang the praises of the past with his paeans to
both the French nobility and Napoleon Bonaparte, selectively avoid-

83. The first character in the second line is missing from the original text, and so the transla-
    tion is surmised from context.
84. Anezaki, *Hanatsumi nikki*, p. 272.

ing any mention of the tragic human loss caused by the French Revolution and the Napoleonic wars. Anezaki continues in this vein with the following poem, written on seeing a profusion of flowers blooming near a spring in the ruins:

> All signs of the water-gatherers
> have vanished
> only the spring
> bubbles forth
> for many ages[85]

The only part of the modern world that bothers Anezaki are occasional scrapes with insensitive natives. For the most part his hosts, largely priests or monks who showed him about religiously significant sites, were kind and generous, and he praised them highly. It was not simply their generosity that pleased him, though; because they shared a common interest in religious history, they shared common values. The clergy rarely asked any questions of Anezaki, simply treating him as they would any outside visitor and focusing on the items of interest at hand. The priests and monks were not interested in becoming more worldly, nor was Anezaki interested in being a cultural critic like Yamashita Yūtarō or a cultural ambassador like Yano Ryūkei. However, one day after he has been sightseeing in Rome, contemporary Italian culture drags him from his historical reveries into an disagreeable present:

> While I was gazing around [at the sights] a number of peddlers came selling their wares. When I ignored them and tossed their wares aside, there was one young man among them who went over to them, conferred about something with them, then came up to me and said something incomprehensible. When I asked him what he was saying, it turned out that he was saying "*rao tse, rao tse.*" That is to say, the result of the young man's consult with the other peddlers was the resolution that I was Chinese, and he had decided to try to say something to me in Chinese. Somehow he had come to know the name of Laozi, and I discerned that that was what he was saying. It is doubtful that the youth knew

85. Anezaki, *Hanatsumi nikki*, p. 274.

anything about Laozi, and it was quite strange to hear
Laozi's name coming from the mouth of an Italian youth
while I was gazing at Rome's Seven Hills. In Germany, there
were often people who would call out Li Hongzhang's name,
"*li han chan, li han chan*," and throw rocks at me, but here
they called me "Laozi."[86]

Anezaki takes this unpleasantness in stride. This is all we hear of it,
and it is a rarity in his otherwise glowingly positive travelogue. He is
an erudite traveler, comfortable in unfamiliar surroundings and unwill-
ing to dwell on the mundane or banal.

The route he follows take him from the north to the south, then
loops back to the eastern coast. After Rome he goes to Naples and
Pompeii, then back through Assisi, Rimini, Ravenna, Ferrara, Padova,
Venice, and Triest. *Diary of Gathering Flowers* ends when he departs
Venice. The final entry is firmly placed in the present, but fittingly
rich in natural imagery:

> I went to the station by gondola in the rain. From behind
> the hanging blinds I could only see the stone platforms and
> steps of the houses; the water dashed against the stones,
> making a gurgling noise. The charm of the city in the gen-
> tle rainwater was entirely different from other towns dirtied
> with mud.
>
> The train departed at seven o'clock, and I turned to see
> the city on the water in the rain. Once back on the main-
> land, the green of the trees, wet with the rain, were truly
> exquisite. More than the palace on the water, the natural ver-
> dancy was fresh, and made me feel like I had just awakened
> from a warm dream. There are many ruins in Venice, but
> the fresh climate is perfect for the leaves wet with rain in
> the open fields.[87]

Thus, in a terse but sensible fashion, Anezaki captures the beauty of
Venice. It is distinct, in that it is a city built on the water, but the thing
that makes that characteristic stand out is an element of nature—rain.

---

86. Anezaki, *Hanatsumi nikki*, pp. 281–82. Li Hongzhang (1823–1901) was a general and polit-
    ical leader during the late Qing Dynasty. He was known for helping China adopt West-
    ern industrial technology.
87. Anezaki, *Hanatsumi nikki*, p. 437.

In *Diary of Gathering Flowers*, the natural beauty of Italy is given a particular Japanese expression.

After Italy, Anezaki traveled to England, France, and Switzerland and back to Italy. He wrote a short travelogue of his experiences titled *Journal of Where I've Been*, which opens on October 19, 1902, six months after the final entry in *Diary of Gathering Flowers*. *Journal of Where I've Been* is barely one-tenth the size of *Diary of Gathering Flowers*, but is not a lesser work for it. Each entry overflows with nostalgia and lyricism; nowhere are there the extended examinations of art or religion seen in *Diary of Gathering Flowers*. Most notable in this piece are the literary and artistic allusions; in Rome, for example, Anezaki quotes from Lord Byron (1788–1824) and Arthur H. Clough (1819–61), and he mentions Percy Shelley (1792–1822), Jean Jacques Rousseau (1712–78), Edward Gibbon (1737–94), and Johann Goethe (1749–1832). Byron's poems on Italy, particularly "Childe Harold's Pilgrimage" and Clough's poem "Amours De Voyage" provide ample reflections on the continental landscape, and often Anezaki finds himself reliving the poets' verses on the road.

He is struck by the beauty and historical significance of place, but his connection to these things is based solely in the Western tradition. The text is not annotated (implying an assumption of readerly familiarity with various Western works and history), but it could easily have as many footnotes as an annotated edition of any premodern Japanese literary work. There are volumes of information and minutiae behind the main text. Also, unlike *Diary of Gathering Flowers*, *Journal of Where I've Been* is written in literary Japanese, which lends an air of antiquity to the work.

Running though the work is the theme of modern dilapidation and ruin. Modernity, as distinct from Westernization, is seen as destructive and harmful. The Romanticist poets of the eighteenth and nineteenth centuries echo Anezaki's sentiments, and their attention to nature as an eternal element appeals to him. In Italy, Anezaki writes:

> On this poignant day, the sun sinks again behind St. Peter's cathedral in the Vatican, and shall rise again over the rustic fields of the Italian countryside. Oh, how many times has it shown upon these hills and fields since the beginning of time? Everyday, while the sun shines the same rays, the stones on the Seven Hills are stationary, and the thousands

of stars drip their dew below, countless men are born and
die, countless countries rise and fall, only to rise again.[88]

He goes on to note the transitory nature of life, equating it to the
evanescent bubble, an image quite familiar to the Japanese reader. In
Geneva, he says that although he was pleased to sleep once again in
a clean Swiss inn, he knew that it was "but a temporary lodging," echoing Chōmei's comments on man's temporary dwellings.[89] Nature,
and by extension, the eternal, is often kept from Anezaki's grasp, as
when he laments the swiftness of the train, for it prevents him get-
ting a clearer view of the "peace of the mountains and the valleys."[90]
The hustle and bustle of the modern world also interrupts his reveries, as when he visits a church in Milan:

> I entered the church, wherein services for the day's saint
> were underway. The wondrous sound of the choir, along
> with the smoke from the incense, swirled around the pillars
> and resounded in the hall, and I too felt the urge to sing the
> praises of the saints.
>   I left the church, pulled by the mysterious heavenly
> music; the screech of the train whistle and the street hawk-
> ers was horrid. Crossing over the threshold, I had once again
> returned to the evil world of the twentieth century.[91]

The thrill and excitement of seeing a modernized world that so dominated the early Meiji travelogues is utterly absent here. Anezaki
wants no part of the new technology, no part of that which makes the
West distinct from Japan. His search is for the familiar and thus comforting; he eschews the strange.

Anezaki is one of the first Japanese travel writers to appropriate
the Western canon as a base of reference. In the early chapters of this
book, we saw writers at a loss for literary allusion amid a world so
wholly unfamiliar. What little they could create in the way of new *uta
makura*—gas lights, steam engines, and central heating—were awkward and necessarily modern, and had little in common with tradi-

88. Anezaki Chōfū, *Ware ya izuko no ki*, in *Hanatsumi nikki* (Tokyo: Hakubunkan, 1909), p. 468.
89. Anezaki, *Ware ya izuko no ki*, p. 446.
90. Anezaki, *Ware ya izuko no ki*, p. 449.
91. Anezaki, *Ware ya izuko no ki*, p. 458.

tional Japanese poetics. With a growing acquaintance with Western literary tradition, however, Japanese writers such as Anezaki recognized that a rich world of allusion waited them. Like his predecessors centuries before, Anezaki makes liberal use of earlier works, only occasionally providing the reader with any reference to his sources. The beauty in this landscape, he tells us, cannot be expressed in a Japanese poetic idiom, but it can be expressed with sublime beauty in a Western idiom.

On some occasions, however, he admits that he is not up to the task, as when in Rome he writes, "I have not the genius of Gibbon, nor the pen of Goethe, and am but a tourist from an oriental heathen country. I am simply sunk in my own fathomless deep emotion, wondering about the nature of my own existence." The self-deprecation here is partly tongue-in-cheek, but the inability to express himself as clearly as he would like is genuine. The significance of all he sees around him is overwhelming, and he continues, "Although I have seen historical sites and artistic relics, they are inexhaustible; there is no way for my pen to write of them all."[92]

Lest the reader interpret this as a weak excuse for a lesser text, let me point out that what Anezaki does here is none too different from what Matsuo Bashō does at Matsushima in *Narrow Road to the Deep North*; faced with an obligation to express his feelings on an awesome sight, he simply states that it cannot be done any better than it already has. Bashō concedes to Saigyō, and Anezaki concedes to Gibbon and Goethe. It is important to note that Anezaki's use of Western allusions is not merely a case of name-dropping. His focus is carefully chosen, and his diction, unfortunately, almost impossible to recreate in translation, retains a poetic antiquity that is fitting to its company. He has thoroughly enveloped himself in the world of the Romanticists while retaining a distinctly Japanese voice. Often in his references to Western figures he prefaces their names with the word "my" (*waga*), such as "my Wagner" and "my Master" (in reference to Rousseau), expressing his internalization of their worthy stature.[93]

At the end of *Journal of Where I've Been*, Anezaki quotes a letter he writes to a friend:

92. Anezaki, *Ware ya izuko no ki*, pp. 476–77.
93. Anezaki, *Ware ya izuko no ki*, p. 450 and p. 447, respectively.

Now I am to leave European soil, where I have made my
home for the past two and half years. Once I have set foot
on the ship, I shall cease to be a European anymore. When
I passed through the Straits of Messina two and a half years
ago I knew nothing yet of European civilization—indeed, I
knew nothing of myself. What shall I speak of in the face of
the ancient mountains and rivers as my ship passes through
these same Straits of Messina tonight? Although the knowledge that recent European civilization is a vacant vessel may
make my two and a half years' effort seem in vain, perhaps
I shall be comforted slightly by the single thought that the
"truth is in the past."[94]

If his feelings about contemporary Europe were in doubt, this letter
dispels it. Modern Europe is "vacant" (*kūkyo*), there is nothing of interest to be had there. Indeed, for most of his travelogue, it deserves no
mention at all. The reason why the present is empty is implicit: one
cannot be nostalgic about it. In other words, Anezaki is not a Lud-
dite. He does not desire to *return* to the past. Rather, he wants to *recall*
the past, to experience the *ryoshū* of the traditional Japanese traveler.

In addition to *Journal of Where I've Been*, there are two other aux-
iliary travelogues written on this trip to Europe. The first, *From Paris
to London*, opens with a poem by William Wordsworth (1770–1850)
on the Westminster Bridge that reads in part:

Earth has not anything to show more fair:
Dull would he be of souls who could pass by
A sight so touching in its majesty
This city now doth like a garment wear

The beauty of the morning: silent, bare,
Ships, towers, domes, theatres, and temples lie
Open unto the fields and to the sky—
All bright and glittering in the smokeless air.[95]

Anezaki's opening lines echo the sentiments of this poem; he finds
the city gleaming and bright in the morning—quite a change from

94. Anezaki, *Ware ya izuko no ki*, p. 492.
95. As quoted in Anezaki Chōfū, *Pari kara Rondon e*, in *Hanatsumi nikki* (Tokyo: Hakubunkan,
    1909), p. 496.

Journal of Where I've Been. This trip from Paris to London was a light-hearted one, on which the author visits numerous friends he had made on his previous travels through these cities. He is still in search of nostalgia, but this time it is primarily for his own rather recent experiences. He enjoys meeting familiar faces, and although he and his acquaintances occasionally go out to enjoy a museum or other cultural site, the focus is on his own emotional journey through his recent past. We also see much more of Anezaki the person in his accounts of everyday happenings, happenings that it would seem were too mundane or recent to merit mention in *Journal of Where I've Been*. For example, on July 13, he writes that he received a letter from the secretary of the Asia Society that informed him that a dissertation he had submitted the previous autumn on the *Four Āgamas* had regrettably been lost in a fire at the printer's shop in Yokohama.[96] This dissertation, he tells us, took him ten years of hard work to write, and now it had been lost in an instant. It is a compelling passage, but one strongly rooted in the present and divorced from geographical place.

The second work, *Diary of Field Grass*, opens with a verse by the Scottish poet Robert Burns (1759–96) that celebrates the natural landscape of Scotland. It is perhaps a misleading beginning, however, for most of this short essay describes the everyday activities of the author and not the scenery he views. Save for a short passage in which Anezaki quotes poetry by Sir Walter Scott (1771–1832) as he gazes at the landscape that inspired it, the travelogue is a prosaic account of his tour of Scotland. On three occasions, he composes *waka* on the Scottish landscape, but it is uninspired poetry. The one aspect that makes this work stand out among Anezaki's travelogues is his willingness to describe and warmhearted attitude toward his contemporary hosts. Reading only *Journal of Where I've Been* would lead one to picture a sort of modern malcontent, one who could never find joy in the present. But *Diary of Field Grass* reveals a cheerful and friendly man who takes pleasure in common activities. It would seem that the intended audience for *Diary of Field Grass* may have been different

96. The *Four Āgamas* are a collection of Hīnayāna scriptures. They include the Dīrghāma ("Long" treatises on cosmogony), the Madhyamāgama ("middle" treatises on metaphysics), the Samyuktāgama ("miscellaneous" treatises on abstract contemplation), and the Ekottarāgama ("numerical" treatises, subjects treated numerically). Source: William Edward Soothill and Lewis Hodous, *A Dictionary of Chinese Buddhist Terms* (Gaoxiong: Buddhist Culture Service, 1971).

from Anezaki's other essays, despite the fact that all were sold together in one volume.

In *Diary of Field Grass*, he describes his visits to various museums and exhibits in an informative fashion, providing the necessary background information for the uninformed reader. For example, of the main museum in Glasgow he writes:

> Within the hall are collected items of natural history, industry, and the arts, but paintings are especially numerous. However, items of particular distinction are few. I have seen Whistler's portrait of Carlisle in a photograph before, and I feel I know it well. There is no disputing that this painter came to Japan and that he admired Japanese painting. Like his picture of the London Bridge, much of his painting is a copy of *ukiyo* paintings. The colors in his portrait of Carlisle, too, are in the old style of Japanese paintings filled with deep blues; it is well suited to the slightly gloomy and depressed arrangement of the painting. Moreover, the economy of the brush and the simplicity of the decoration are at once both Japanesque and revealing of Carlisle's nature—they are quite fitting for the portrait of a man deep in thought. However, as far as this painting having a Japanese air about it is concerned, it is only in the matching of the colors and the use of the brush; the deep gloom is certainly a product of a northern spirit, and is a profound quality that is never seen in Japanese paintings.[97]

Even without having seen the painting, one can easily imagine the aspects of its appearance that Anezaki focuses on here, especially assuming a passing familiarity with *ukiyo* ("floating world") paintings. The description is clear and absent the emotive lyricism one might expect from the same author in *Journal of Where I've Been*.

In sum, Anezaki shows himself capable of writing in a number of styles, some applying more traditional *kikōbungaku* style than others, that recurringly express a nostalgia for or appreciation of the past. The past he recalls is a European past, not a Japanese past. Indeed, in some cases, his travelogues in translation could, like Nagai Kafū's, be mistaken for those of a Westerner. This is not to say, however, that he has abandoned his national literary tradition. His economy of lan-

---

97. Anezaki Chōfū, *Haragusa nikki*, in *Hanatsumi nikki* (Tokyo: Hakubunkan, 1909), p. 578.

guage and thick literary allusion, especially in *Journal of Where I've Been*, is distinctly Japanese. Western travelogues from the same period invariably provide more information and detail for the reader—some might say to the detriment of the text, for an allusion explained in great detail loses some of its beauty in the same way that an explained punchline loses its punch.

The introspection and reflection of late Meiji travelogues greatly exceeds that of the previous decades. Far from departing from the *kikōbun* tradition, the late Meiji overseas travel writers were, in a way, *returning* to an established style by evoking nostalgia and focusing on nature. The criticism that later travelogues paled in comparison to premodern works is leveled at style, not content. For if one reads these works carefully, one quickly sees that, even though codified *uta makura* had been abandoned, the need to identify and focus on the established *hon'i* of a locale was just as strong as it had ever been. That historical allusion was central to most of these works, and not that it was allusion appropriated from the Other, is evidence that even new travelers employed old techniques. The exception, Nagai Kafū's case, makes up for its lack of historical focus by exuding the sort of pathos and nostalgia also so integral to *kikōbungaku*.

Conclusion

The very first travelers, such as the shipwrecked Hamada Hikozō, wrote flat and objective accounts of what they had seen overseas, which had little in common with the poetical domestic *kikōbungaku*. These travelers express unabashedly the fascination they held for the technological advancements of the Industrial Revolution, and they are rarely able to attend to or comment on anything but their immediate experiences. Also, these early travelers were rarely men of letters, and consequently it never occurred to them to apply the *kikōbungaku* conceit in their writing. I mention them if only to establish at what point in the modern time line precedent(s) were or were not set: in the *bakumatsu* era, overseas travel writing was relegated to an observational, dispassionate voice. Nomura Fumio tells us how many head of cattle he saw in the smallest of English villages, but he does not tell us of their pastoral surroundings.

Among those who followed in the second wave were many scholars, such as Narushima Ryūhoku, trained in both the Japanese and Chinese classics, for whom it was natural to write in an elliptical and allusive manner. These writers' works are indisputably artistic accomplishments, but they still lacked the attention to nature and the natural landscape that is such an integral part of traditional *kikōbungaku*. Instead, they focused on the human significance of place. Moreover, their focus was on the past and not the present. Contemporary life, if mentioned, was always placed in the realm of the prosaic and hence little beyond a curiosity, if not distasteful. Unlike that of the first travelers, these writers' admiration for the West was focused on her past and not her present.

The third wave begins to show a sensitivity to nature, albeit limited. Kurihara Ryōichi sees the beauty of the Seine River, Mori Ōgai responds favorably to the natural aspects of the cityscapes he sees, and Arisugawa no Miya Taruhito describes a rich and full spectrum of colors in the area surrounding St. Petersburg. However, most of these mid-Meiji writers are occupied with describing contemporary life. Unlike those in the first wave, these writers have the background knowledge necessary to assess what they see with some reason; misunderstandings are rare, whereas they are rampant in the earliest travelogues. At the end of the nineteenth century, most educated Japanese were excited by the prospect of their own country joining the ranks of the advanced colonizing Western powers. Westerners were no longer suspect "barbarians" but rather potential comrades in the world theater. This period of naïve optimism and amity—for few, if any, Western countries saw Japan as a potential equal—colored the attitudes of the overseas Japanese. Yano Ryūkei constantly compares Japan with the West, and usually on Western standards. Mori Ōgai describes much of what he sees in fantastical terms; Europe is a veritable paradise because of her tremendous infrastructure. Likewise, Kamata Eikichi was constantly amazed at the conveniences that life in the modern West afforded.

The last wave, represented here by Shimamura Hōgetsu, Tokutomi Roka, Nagai Kafū, and Anezaki Chōfū, appropriated Western cultural history and applied Japanese literary technique to it. They focus on nature, but when they did so, they did it not in their own context but rather in reference to Western precedents. Critics may argue that this was an abandonment of traditional *kikōbungaku* methods, but I would disagree. These men, particularly Anezaki Chōfū, retain much of the domestic travelers' poetics: they are not interested in the contemporary, they celebrate historical events, and they envelope themselves in nostalgia. The one thing they do not do is pine for home (Japan), but it should be pointed out that neither Saigyō nor Bashō did much either.

Like many other facets of Japanese history, the story of overseas *kikōbungaku* is one of waxing and waning cycles. Through the *bakumatsu* and Meiji periods, writers expressed their impressions of the West and her people. Rapid political changes influenced these writers in ways to be expected: national pride notably increases with the Japanese victories in the Sino-Japanese (1894–95) and Russo-Japanese (1904–5) wars. But in addition to the political elements, there are also clear indications of the authors' shift in aesthetic response to the West. At first, Japanese travelers had no point of reference from which to evaluate the art or natural beauty of the West. It would take decades before any traveler could knowledgeably comment on the quality of a building or painting, on the sublimity of a vista, or the grace of a musical movement. And once they did reach that point, many of them had left traditional *kikōbungaku* sensibilities behind in favor of Western ones. For if they tried to employ *uta makura* imagery, they would be faced with the choice of creating an entirely new *uta makura* (something that would take centuries, if precedent was an indicator), or using modified versions of domestic or Chinese imagery. The latter choice, although taken by some of the earliest travelers, was largely abandoned by the mid-Meiji period, apparently because to use it was to concede that feudal Japan had more to offer than modern Japan. The default mode was to appropriate Western imagery for Western places, albeit while writing in Japanese.

Moreover, if a travel writer were to evoke *ryojō* or some nostalgia for his homeland, he could be accused of longing for the old-fashioned and familiar. The aspects for which travelers over the ages pine are seasonal changes, festivals, local foods, and family members. None of these is representative of modernization, and the first three are strongly rooted in history and times past. To long for these things yet ignore the industrial modernization one saw in the West would surely be an admission of feudalism, something most Meiji thinkers avoided at all costs. In order to experience *ryojō*, and express it, travel writers were thus obligated to focus on Western history and imagery, for although it was equally anchored in the past, it was still an integral part of those civilizations that had modernized ahead of Japan.

Despite his apparent consideration of travel writing and the use of *uta makura* therein, Ueda Bin writes as if he were a pioneer in "western *kikōbungaku*," when actually he had many predecessors. In his 1908 essay "A Discussion of My Impression of the West," he observes that Japanese who travel to the West "these days" are either scholars going to research a particular specialty or government employees going in some official capacity. He, on the other hand, wishes to record his impressions of the West in a poetic light.[1] By sheer numbers, his observation is true—more Japanese travelers were on academic, government, or commercial business than not, but we have seen that the accumulated product of their writing is clearly not poetically impoverished. Indeed, if he were truly to pursue the objective of establishing modern, Western *uta makura*, he could have accomplished much more by building on the poetic imagery of Narushima Ryūhoku or Nakai Ōshū instead of creating his own new, unique list. His essay on *utamakura* came too late for overseas travel literature. Ueda's idea of combining *kikōbungaku* with Western-based imagery was a noble one, but it faced too great a challenge.

The skillful blending of Japanese and Western travel literature is almost wholly abandoned at the beginning of the Taishō Period (1912–26). Certainly the number of Japanese travelers to the West did not slacken at this time—indeed, it increased steadily. It was not until the Pacific War was underway that Japanese travel to the West began to decrease. And until that time, particularly due to formation of the League of Nations in 1920 and Japan's position as a permanent seat on the council, the Japanese who traveled abroad and who wrote of their experiences often discussed political issues, mainly the possibility of world peace. Their travelogues, such as that of Inoue Hideko's (1875–1963) *World Trends as Seen Through a Housewife's Eyes* (1923), tend to be naïve missives about foreign friends and brotherly love. With the advantage of hindsight, their advocacy of a unified world a few years before World War II is ironic, and helps emphasize how subjective even an apparently objective travelogue can be. More importantly, the style and imagery they use is heavily flavored by Western writing of the time. *Waka* virtually disappears from these travelogues, and with it the meter that goes hand in hand with *uta makura*.

My purpose here was not to identify trends and then insist that all works follow them. Rather, it was to examine tendencies and to follow the elements of *kikōbungaku* that survived modernization. As a result, there are many threads left unfollowed: travel guides,

1. Ueda Bin, "Seiyū inshō dan," in *Ueda Bin zenshū* (hokan) (Tokyo: Kaizōsha, 1931), p. 193.

reportage, diaries of emigrants, and general commentaries on the West, such as Fukuzawa Yukichi's *Conditions in the West* that were based on authors' experiences overseas. Certainly by the turn of the century, the literature being produced on the West was voluminous and defies any neat categorization or analysis. But in the selection of works examined here, we see that the traditions of *kikōbungaku* were not left behind on Japanese shores in the modern era. The nostalgia felt for "home" was the same whether the contrast object for home was in the next (Japanese) prefecture or half way around the globe.

Glossary

angya	行脚. A religious pilgrimage, mostly carried out during the medieval period. Many pilgrims wrote travelogues of their experiences.
aware	哀れ. Pathos, a traditional aesthetic in Japanese literature from the earliest eras to the present day.
bakufu	幕府. The Tokugawa period government, also called a SHOGUNATE because it was headed by a SHŌGUN (see below).
bakumatsu	幕末. The period marking the decline and fall of the BAKUFU; generally identified as the period 1853–68.
bunkenroku	聞見録. See KENBUNROKU below.
chōka	長歌. "Long poem," a poem in which lines consist of five and seven syllables alternately, ending with two lines of seven syllables.
dōchūki	道中記. "On-the-road records," primarily Tokugawa-period records of road conditions, travelers' costs, available lodging, etc. Similar to MEISHOKI and MEISHO ANNAI but not necessarily about a "famous place."
han	藩. Feudal domain during the Tokugawa period. Some han rebelled against the BAKUFU, bringing about the Meiji Restoration.
hitsudan	筆談. "Written conversation," referring to the written exchange between Japanese and Chinese who shared

no common language. Although syntax and grammar suffered, communication was often achieved.

hon'i　本意. "Essential character," the special characteristic of a certain locale.

honji suijaku　本地垂迹. "Original Ground-Manifest Trace," the religious doctrine in which Shintō deities are seen as manifestations of Buddhist deities.

hyōryū　漂流. "Drifting," referring in travel literature primarily to shipwrecks. During the Tokugawa period, the few travelogues written about the world outside of Japan were by rescued shipwrecked sailors.

kakarimusubi　係り結び. "Bound Ending," a classical grammatical form used largely in the Nara and Heian periods (712–1185), although it appears occasionally in later texts.

kana　仮名. Refers to the phonetic systems of hiragana and KATAKANA, both used in writing Japanese.

kanbun　漢文. Classical prose Chinese as composed by Japanese, sometimes with diacritical marks that indicate syntax in Japanese.

kanshi　漢詩. Classical Chinese poetry as composed by Japanese.

katakana　片仮名. One of the KANA phonetic systems used to write Japanese.

kenbunroku　見聞録. "Records of things seen and heard," the predominant term used for travelogues of abroad from the Meiji period. Alternately written BUNKENROKU.

kikō bungaku　紀行文学. "Travel literature," referring to all travel literature in a broad sense, from all periods of Japanese literary history. Alternately written *kikōbun* 紀行文.

kotobagaki　詞書. "Headnote," an introductory note that explains the circumstances surrounding the composition of a poem.

makura kotoba　枕詞. "Pillow word," a fixed word or expression associated with another word or expression, used chiefly in poetry as a form of allusion.

meisho　名所. "Famous place," any place widely recognized as notable and celebrated in Japanese art and literature. Traditional *meisho* are all within Japanese borders, although some locales in China qualify as secondary *meisho*. *Meisho* are usually associated with some particular characteristic, such as a certain flower, tree, bird, etc., which are referred to in that place's UTA MAKURA.

meisho annai 名所案内. "Guide to famous places," this genre of travel literature gave the traveler practical information about famous places but without a fictional framework, as sometimes found in MEISHOKI.

meisho zue 名所図会. "Picture guidebooks," a Tokugawa period genre. These works were gazetteers that recorded the famous sights, landmarks, shrines, temples, etc., of specific localities, and had accompanying landscape paintings. A subgenre of MEISHOKI.

meishoki 名所記. "Famous place records," a travelogue style from the Tokugawa period. These works were guidebooks of famous places. Some were fictional, others not.

metsuke 目付. "Inspectors," those Japanese on the early missions to the West whose responsibility it was to make sure other mission members followed protocol.

michiyuki 道行. The portion of a UTA NIKKI that describes going on a journey. Works such as *Sarashina Diary* contain significant *michiyuki* sections but are not wholly travelogues.

mono no aware 物の哀れ. An aesthetic concept that denotes an awareness of the world, particularly the pathos therein.

nembutsu 念仏. The invocation of the name of Amida Buddha, practiced by some followers of Pure Land Buddhism. It was generally held that recitation of the *nembutsu* would gain the compassion of Amida and entrance into the Pure Land.

nihommachi 日本町. Japanese communities in Southeast Asia in the sixteenth and seventeenth centuries, the citizens of which were primarily involved in business, some of which related to the SHUINSEN trade.

nikki bungaku　日記文学. "Diary literature," a genre that includes many travelogues.

ryojō　旅情. "Feeling of being on a journey," a term defined by Japanese dictionaries as the poignancy one feels on a journey. It encompasses many emotions, including melancholy, tedium, and nostalgia.

ryoshū　旅愁. "Loneliness on a journey," a term used to describe loneliness caused by separation from one's home.

sakkoku seisaku　鎖国政策. "Closed country policy," a governmental policy of the Tokugawa period that banned foreign travel to and from Japan, except in a small number of exceptional circumstances.

shingeki　新劇. "New theater," as opposed to the traditional dramatic arts such as *kabuki, noh,* and *jōruri.*

shōgun　将軍. "General," the military and political leader of the Tokugawa government.

shogunate　Refers to the Tokugawa government. See also BAKUFU.

shuinsen　朱印船. "Vermilion seal ship," the licensed foreign trade during the late sixteenth and early seventeenth centuries, primarily in the Philippines and Southeast Asia. NIHOMMACHI were established as a result of this trade. The system was established by Toyotomi Hideyoshi in an attempt to legitimize Japanese traders and distinguish them from WAKŌ. Ships were given a nontransferable license by the shogunate, issued on a per-trip basis, authorizing them to carry a certain cargo and land at a certain port. The license bore the vermilion seal of the SHŌGUN, hence the name.

sōan bungaku　草庵文学. "Grass hut literature," a genre that consists of travelogues and miscellany by aesthetes who chose to abandon life in the cities for a simplified life in a remote area. They often lived in small dwellings, hence the name "grass hut."

tanka　短歌. "Short poem," a poem consisting of five lines in a 5–7–5–7–7 syllabic structure.

tōkaidō　　　　東海道. "Eastern sea road," a heavily traveled highway that ran along the eastern Japanese seaboard. Along the highway were established stations, where travelers often rested, ate, and were entertained. This road became particularly important in the Tokugawa period, when it was the subject of numerous travelogues and some visual art.

ukiyo　　　　　浮世. "Floating World," a euphemism for the urban demi monde, particularly during the Tokugawa period (1600–1868).

uta makura　　歌枕. "Poetic pillow," a codified allusion to a place or thing (in later usage).

uta monogatari　歌物語. "Poetic tale," poetry with accompanying prose. The prose provides the setting and background information for the poem. The early Heian *Tales of Ise* 伊勢物語 is perhaps the most famous example.

uta nikki　　　歌日記. "Poetic diary," a diary that contains a mixture of poetry and prose. It may also contain a MICHIYUKI section, as does *Sarashina Diary*.

waka　　　　　和歌 "Japanese poetry," a loose term that encompasses CHŌKA and TANKA, as distinguished from Chinese poetry.

wakō　　　　　倭寇 "Japanese pirate," referring to the Japanese pirate-traders of the late sixteenth and early seventeenth centuries. These pirate-traders, not always Japanese, despite the name, were notorious in the Southeast Asian seas, and brought about the BAKUFU's establishment of the SHUINSEN trade system.

yūkō　　　　　遊行 "Pilgrimage," referring to travel literature written by religious pilgrims, mostly in the medieval period.

yūmei　　　　　有名. "Famous," in travel literature resonating with reference to MEISHO.

zuikō　　　　　随行. "Accompaniment," referring to travelogues written by poets who attended officials or high ranking travelers. In the Heian period, accompaniment writers composed in Chinese. In later eras, they wrote in Japanese, often including poems along with prose.

Character List for Proper Nouns

Abutsu	阿仏
Aeba Kōson	饗庭篁村
Akiyama Tokusaburō	秋山徳三郎
Akizato Ritō	秋里籬島
Andō Hiroshige	安藤広重
Anezaki Chōfū	姉崎嘲風
Arai Hakuseki	新井白石
Arakawa Hidetoshi	荒川秀俊
Arisugawa no Miya Taruhito	有栖川宮熾仁
Asai Ryōi	浅井了意
Ashiya Nobukazu	芦谷信和
Asō Tadakichi	麻生弥吉
Asukai Masayasu	飛鳥井雅康
Atsu Sukeyuki	阿津祐之
Bei Yue Heng Shan	北岳恒山
Bo Zhuyi	白居易
Chizuka Reisui	遅塚麗水
Chōshū	長州
Daikokuya Kōdayū	大黒屋光太夫
Date Munenari	伊達宗城
Doi Kōchi	土井光知
Dong Yue Tai Shan	東岳泰山
Emi Suiin	江見水蔭
Enchin	円珍
Ennin	円仁

256

Enomoto Kikaku	榎本其角
Fuchibe Tokuzō	淵辺徳蔵
Fujiwara	藤原
Fukuda Sakutarō	福田作太郎
Fukuzawa Yukichi	福沢諭吉
Geijutsuza	芸術座
Gennyo	現如
Gotō Shōjirō	後藤象治郎
Gotō Tatsuzō	後藤達三
Gyōe	尭恵
Hamada Hikozō	浜田彦蔵
Hasekura Tsunenaga	支倉常長
Hashimoto Tsunatsune	橋本綱常
Hashizume Kan'ichi	橋爪貫一
Hatakeyama Yoshinari	畠山義成
Hayashi Ki	林紀
Hayashi Razan	林羅山
Hizen	肥前
Hong Shiwei	洪士偉
Hora Tomio	洞富雄
Hosokawa Junjirō	細瀬潤次郎
Ibuse Masuji	井伏鱒二
Ikeda Akira	池田晧
Ikeda Nagaoki	池田長発
Imagawa Ryōshun	今川了俊
Imamura Seinosuke	今村清之助
Inō Tadataka	伊能忠敬
Inoue Aa	井上唖々
Inoue Hideko	井上秀子
Inoue Tsutomu	井上勤
Ishii Kendō	石井研堂
Ishikawa Shuntai	石川舜台
Ishizuki Minoru	石附実
Itagaki Taisuke	板垣退助
Itsukushima	伊藤博文
Iwakura Tomomi	岩倉具視
Iwamatsu Tarō	岩松太郎
Jippensha Ikku	十辺舎一九

Jōjin	成尋
Kaibara Ekiken	貝原益軒
Kakinomoto no Hitomaro	柿本人麻呂
Kamata Eikichi	鎌田栄吉
Kamei Takayoshi	亀井高孝
Kanagaki Robun	仮名垣魯文
Kanda Takahira	神田孝平
Kasuga Shrine	春日神社
Katsuragawa Hoshū	桂川甫周
Kawaguchi Hisao	川口久雄
Kawakami Bizan	川上眉山
Kawashima Chūnosuke	川島忠之助
Kawazu Magoshirō	河津孫四郎
Ki no Tsurayuki	紀貫之
Kimura Kazuaki	木村一信
Kirino Toshiaki	桐野利秋
Kobayashi Kaoru	小林馨
Koide Hidezane	小出秀実
Kubo Tenzui	久保天随
Kume Kunitake	久米邦武
Kurihara Ryōichi	栗原亮一
Kurimoto Jōun	栗本鋤雲
Kuroda Kiyotaka	黒田清隆
Kōda Rohan	幸田露伴
Lin Cexu	林則徐
Mamiya Rinzō	間宮林蔵
Mashizu Shunjirō	益頭駿次郎
Matsui Sumako	松井須磨子
Matsumoto Byakuka	松本白華
Matsuo Bashō	松尾芭蕉
Matsuzawa Hiroaki	松沢弘陽
Minamoto	源
Mishima Saiji	三島才二
Mizukuri Shūhei	箕作秋坪
Mogami Tokunai	最上徳内
Mori Rintarō	森林太郎
Mori Ōgai	森鴎外
Moriyama Takichirō	森山多吉郎

Muragaki Awaji-no-Kami	村垣淡路守
Muragaki Norimasa	村垣範正
Murakami Teisuke	村上貞助
Muramatsu Tsuyoshi	村松剛
Murata Fumio	村田文夫
Nagai Kafū	永井荷風
Nagamine Hideki	永峰秀樹
Nakagawa Kiun	仲川喜雲
Nakahama Manjirō	中浜万次郎
Nakai Hiroshi	中井弘
Nakai Ōshū	中井桜洲
Nakamura Keitarō	中村敬太郎
Nakamura Masanao	中村正直
Nakamura Naokichi	中村直吉
Nan Yue Heng Shan	南岳衡山
Narugami Katsumi	鳴神克巳
Narushima Ryūhoku	成島柳北
Natsume Sōseki	夏目漱石
Niijima Jō	新島襄
Nishihonganji Temple	西本願寺
Nishikawa Joken	西川如見
Nomura Fumio	野村文夫
Nozu Michitsura	野津道貫
Numata Jirō	沼田次郎
Oda Jun'ichirō	織田純一郎
Ōhashi Otowa	大橋乙羽
Ōkubo Toshimichi	大久保利通
Ōmachi Keigetsu	大町桂月
Ōsone Shōsuke	王曾根章介
Ōtomo no Yakamochi	大伴家持
Peng Lai	蓬莱
Saigyō	西行
Saigō Takamori	西郷隆盛
Sakamoto Ryūma	坂本龍馬
Sakurai Ōson	桜井鴎村
Satō Tasuku	佐藤佐
Satsuma	薩摩
Sawa Tadashi	佐和正

Seki Shinzō	関信三
Shibata Takenaka	柴田剛中
Shibusawa Eiichi	渋礢栄一
Shimamura Hōgetsu	島村抱月
Shimizu Masujirō	清水益次郎
Shinshō	信生
Shinshō maru	神昌丸
Shirase Nobu	白瀬矗
Shiroko	白子
Shizuishi Nagase	静石長瀬
Sōkyū	宗久
Suehiro Tetchō	末広鉄腸
Sugawara Takasue no Musume	管原孝標女
Sugimura Sojinkan	杉村楚人冠
Sugita Genpaku	杉田玄白
Sugiura Aizō	杉浦愛蔵
Sugiura Kōzō	杉浦弘蔵
Sumidagawa Matsugorō	墨田川松五郎
Sumidagawa Namigorō	墨田川浪五郎
Sumiyoshi maru	住吉丸
Sutoku	崇徳
Suzuka	鈴鹿
Suzuki Tōzō	鈴木棠三
Tada Keiichi	多田恵一
Taira	平
Takahashi Jirō	高橋二郎
Takasu Yoshijirō	高須芳次郎
Takatsuki	高槻
Takayama Ukon	高山右近
Takechi no Kurohito	高市黒人
Takenouchi Yasunori	竹内保徳
Takimoto Kazunari	瀧本和成
Tanizawa Shōichi	谷澤尚一
Tayama Katai	田山花袋
Tezuka Hikaru	手塚晃
Togawa Shūkotsu	戸川秋骨
Tokugawa Akitake	徳川昭武
Tokugawa Iemochi	徳川家茂

Tokugawa Ieyasu	徳川家康
Tokugawa Yoshinobu	徳川慶喜
Tokutomi Roka	徳富蘆花
Tokutomi Sohō	徳富蘇峰
Tomita Hitoshi	富田仁
Tomiyama Dōya	富山道治
Toyotomi Hideyoshi	豊臣秀吉
Tsubouchi Shōyō	坪内逍遥
Ueda Bin	上田敏
Ueda Hiroshi	上田博
Ueda Toshirō	植田敏郎
Wan Zhang	万丈
Xi Yue Hua Shan	西岳華山
Yamada Nagamasa	山田長政
Yamashita Yūtarō	山下雄太郎
Yanagawa Shunsan	柳河春三
Yano Ryūkei	矢野龍渓
Yawata Shrine	八幡神宮
Ying Zhou	瀛洲
Yoda Gakkai	依田学海
Yosa Buson	与謝蕪村
Yosano Akiko	与謝野晶子
Yoshida Genkichi	吉田元吉
Yoshino Sakuzō	吉野作造
Zhong Yue Gao Shan	中岳嵩山
Zōki	僧基

Character List for Titles

23,000 Miles Through America and Europe　　欧米記遊二萬三千哩

A Captain's Diary　　船長日記

A Collection of Myriad Leaves　　万葉集

A Comforting Pillow of Grass　　なぐさめ草

A Diary of Gathering Flowers　　花つみ日記

A Diary of Itagaki's Tour of Europe and America　　板垣君欧米漫遊日記

A Diary of Viewing Mt. Fuji　　富士御覧日記

A Discussion of Exploring South America's Amazon　　南米アマゾン探検談

"A Discussion of My Impression of the West"　　西遊印象談

A Journey to Ise　　伊勢紀行

A Journey West: A New Discourse on a Voyage　　西洋紀行・航海新説

"A London Inn"　　倫敦の宿

A Personal Record of the South Pole Expedition　　南極探検私録

A Pumpkin's Account　　南瓢記

A Record of a Pilgrimage to Mt. Tendai and Mt. Wudai	参天台五台山記
A Record of Chinatown	ちやいなたうん記
A Record of Exploring the Amazon	アマゾン探検記
A Record of Famous Places on the Tōkaidō	東海道名所記
A Record of Fujikawa	藤河の記
A Record of Joseph Heco's Shipwreck	ジョセフ彦蔵漂流記
A Record of Manjirō's Shipwreck	満次郎漂流記
A Record of My Wife's Travels	吾妻路之記
A Record of the Mission to America	遣米使日記
A Record of the South Seas	南海紀聞
A Record of Things Seen and Heard in the West	西洋見聞録
A Record of Things Seen and Heard on a Journey to the West	目見耳聞・西洋紀行
A Record of Travel on the Coast Road	海道記
A Record of Viewing Mt. Fuji	覧富士記
A Record of Wandering in the Southern Seas	南海流浪記
A Sketch of Things Heard on a Raft in the North	北槎聞略
A Souvenir from the Capital	都のつと
A Souvenir from the South Pole	南極土産
"A Survey of the Northern English Landscape"	北英水山の概観

A Tune from Ojima	小島の口ずさみ
Account of the Imperial Pilgrimage to Mt. Kōya	高野御幸の記
An Unsolicited Tale	とはずがたり
Around Sano	さののわたり
Bakumatsu Meiji kaigai taiken shishū	幕末明治海外体験詩集
Bakumatsu Meiji kaigai tokōsha sōran	幕末明治海外渡航者総覧
Bankoku shinwa	万国新話
Bungaku josetsu	文学序説
Chikusai's Progress East	竹斎東過
Child of the Capital	京童
Chūsei nikki kikō shū	中世日記紀行集
Circle of Knowledge	智環啓蒙
Civilization	文明
Dai Nippon enkai yochi zenzu	大日本沿海輿地全図
Diary of a Journey Westward	航西日乗
Diary of a Pilgrimage	巡礼紀行
Dairy of a Pilgrimage to Mt. Kōya	高野参詣日記
Diary of a Tour	環遊日記
Diary of a Tour of Europe and America	欧米巡回日誌
Diary of a Trip to Europe	欧行日記
Diary of a Voyage Around the World	世界周遊旅日記
Diary of a Westward Voyage	航西日記
Diary of Field Grass	原ぐさ日記
Diary of the Imperial Residence in Paris	巴里御在館日記
Diary of the Waning Moon	十六日記
Dīrghāma	長阿含
Eikoku tansaku	英国探索
Ekottarāgama	増阿含
English History	英国史略

Enpitsu kibun	鉛筆紀聞
Excerpts from a Diary of a Journey to the West	西遊日誌抄
Exploration on Site: The Whaling Ship	実地探検 捕鯨船
Exploring the World: 150,000 Miles	世界探検十五万哩
Fallen Leaves	落葉
"First Impressions of Paris"	巴里に於ける第一印象
Footprints in the Snow	思出の記
From Japan to Japan	日本から日本へ
"From London"	倫敦より
From Paris to London	パリからロンドンへ
Futsu-Ei kō	仏英行
"Gendai no kikōbun"	現代の紀行文
General history of civilization in Europe	欧羅巴文明史
German Diary	ドイツ日記
Glories and Graces	文華秀麗集
Grand Record of Travels in England	大英游記
Greater Learning for Women	女大学
Gyōsō tsuiroku	暁窓追録
Halfway Around the Globe	半球周遊
Hanatsumi	花つみ
Histoire de France	法蘭西志
Histoire de la Révolution Française	仏国革命史
History of Germany	日耳曼史略
Hizakurige of the West	西洋道中膝栗毛
Hōan jisshu	匏菴十種
Hyōryū kidan zenshū	漂流奇談全集
Hyōryūki	漂流記
Ikoku hyōryū kidanshū	異国漂流奇談集
Ikoku hyōryūki shū	異国漂流記集
Ikoku hyōryūki zoku shū	異国漂流続集
"In Paris"	巴里にて
Ionushi	庵主

Itagaki-kun Ōbei man'yū nikki	板垣君欧米漫遊日記
Itagaki-kun Ōbei man'yū roku	板垣君欧米漫遊録
Izumi	和泉
Jibun sagashi no tabi : jidō bungaku o yomu	自分捜しの旅・児童文学を読む
Jon Manjirō hyōryūki	ジョン万次郎漂流記
Journal of a Westward Voyage	航西日乗
Journal of Where I've Been	我れやいづこの記
Journey in the Year 1616	丙辰紀行
Journey of a Deaf Mute	唖之旅行
Journey to Mt. Fuji	富士紀行
Journey to Shirakawa	白河紀行
Journey to the East Country	東国紀行
Journey to the Eastern Barrier	東関紀行
Journey to the North Country	北国紀行
Journey to Zenkōji	善光寺紀行
Jōyaku jūichi kokki	条約十一国記
Kaei tsūgo	華英通語
Kaichi shinhen	開知新編
Kaijō nikki	海上日記
Kankai ibun	環海異聞
Kawakatsu ke monjo	川勝家文書
Kawauchi	河内
Kengai shisetsu nikki sanshū 3	遣外使珀日記纂輯三
Kiki shinwa	奇機新話
Kindai Nihon no kaigai ryūgaku shi	近代日本の海外留学史
Kindai Nihon no nikki	近代日本の日記
Kinsei hyōryūki shū	近世漂流記集
Kinsei kikō bungei nōto	近世紀行文芸ノート
Kisoji meisho zue	木曾路名所図会

Kōkai nikki	航海日記
Kokin wakashū	古今和歌集
Kokugun chūya jikoku taisūhyō	国郡昼夜時刻数表
Letter from London	龍動通信
Madhyamāgama	中阿含
Man'yū kitei	漫遊記程
Meiji bunka zenshū	明治文化全集
"Meiji no kikōbun"	明治の紀行文
Meiji Ōbei kenbunroku shūsei	明治欧米見聞録集成
Meiji Six Society	明六社
Meiroku zasshi	明六雑誌
Michiyukiburi	道行きぶり
Midnight in a Bar	夜半の酒場
Miscellany from a Tour of Europe and America	欧米漫遊雑記
Miscellany from Abroad	外遊漫録
Miscellany of a Tour	周遊雑記
Miyako rinsen meisho zue	都林泉名所図会
Mori Ōgai no "Doitsu nikki": Ōgai bungaku no fuchi	森鴎外の「ドイツ日記」・鴎外文学の縁
Nagasaki yowasō	長崎夜話草
Nanban kibunsen	南蛮紀文選
Narrow Road to the Deep North	奥の細道
Narushima Ryūhoku, Hattori Bushō, Kurimoto Jōun shū	成島柳北・服部撫松・鋤雲集
Natsu no umi	夏の海
Nature and Man	自然と人生
New Novels	新小説
New Poems of Willow Bridge	柳橋新詩
Nihon hyōronsha	日本評論社
Nihon hyōryū hyōchaku shiryō	日本漂流漂着史料

Nihon kikō bungeishi	日本紀行文芸史
Nihon koten bungaku zenshū (new edition)	日本古典文学全集・新編
Nihon shiseki kyōkai sōsho	日本史籍協会叢書
Nihon shisō taikei	日本思想大系
Nikki, kikōbungaku	日記、紀行文学
Nittō guhō junrei kōki	入唐求法巡礼行記
Notes of Travel	行歴抄
Ōbei jun'yū nikki	欧米巡遊日記
Ōbei kikō	欧穂紀行
Ōbei man'yū zakki	欧米漫遊雑記
Ōkōki	欧行記
Oku no hosomichi	奥の細道
Ōmi	近江
On the Road in Tsukushi	筑紫道記
Ōshū kenbutsu	欧洲見物
"Paris from a Traveler's Window"	巴里の旅窓より
Poems of a Mountain Home	山家集
Postal Dispatch News	郵便報知新聞
Raijū sōhō	雷銃操法
Reconstruction	改造
Record of a Journey from the Great Tang to the Western Regions	大唐西城記
Record of a Journey to Arima	有馬道の記
Record of a Journey to Kyūshū	九州道の記
Record of a Pilgrimage	巡礼紀行
Record of a Pilgrimage to Itsukushima	鹿苑院殿厳島詣記
Record of a Pilgrimage to the Great Shrine	太神宮参詣記
Record of a Pilgrimage to Yoshino	吉野詣記
Record of An Excursion to All Provinces	諸州巡覧記

Record of An Excursion to Japanese Provinces	和州巡覧記
Record of Ancient Matters	古事記
Record of Jōha's Journey to View Mt. Fuji	紹巴富士見道記
Record of the Imperial Tour	御巡国日録
Record of the Kaidō	海東記
Record of the Road to Azuma	あづまの道の記
Record of Viewing Historical Mt. Fuji	富士歴覧記
Report from Yano Fumio	矢野文雄通報
Ryochū ryokō	旅中旅行
Saga Journal	嵯峨記
Saharin bungaku no tabi	サハリン文学の旅
Sakka no sekai taiken: Kindai Nihon bungaku no dōkei to mosaku	作家の世界体験・近代日本文学の憧憬と模索
Sakka ronshū kuina no tabi : Sorujenitsuin, Yasuda Yojūrō, Shimao Toshio, hoka	作家論集クイナの旅・ソルジェニツィン, 安田与重郎, 島尾敏雄, 他
Samyuktāgama	雑阿含
Sarashina Diary	更級日記
Seiyō jijō	西洋事情
Seiyō kenbun shū	西洋見聞集
Seiyō kenbunroku	西洋見聞録
Seiyō kibun	西洋紀聞
Seiyō kikō: Kōkai shinsetsu	西洋紀行・航海新説
"*Seiyō kikō: Kōkai shinsetsu kaidai*"	西洋紀行・航海新説解題
Seiyō tabi annai	西洋旅案内
Sekai kikō bungaku zenshū	世界紀行文学全集
Settsu	摂津
Shank's Mare	膝栗毛
Shin hanatsumi	新花摘
Shin kokin wakashū	新古今和歌集
Shōchū bankoku ichiran	掌中万国一覧

Stories of Barbaric Places	蛮談
Strange Tales from Overseas	海外異聞
Sui-Tang jiahua	隋唐嘉話 (隋唐佳話)
Taifutsu nikki	滞佛日記
Tales of America	あめりか物語
Tales of France	ふらんす物語
Tales of Ise	伊勢物語
The 53 Stages of the Tōkaidō	東海道五十三次
The Cuckoo	不如帰
The Diary of Asuka Imasa'ari	飛鳥井雅有の日記
The Diary of Shinshō	信生法師日記
The Great Events of History	西洋易知録
The Hermit	廬主
The New Journal of the Poetic Arts	花月新誌
The Record of Ise	伊勢記
The Records of a Travel-worn Satchel	笈の小文
The Sakhalin Region	北蝦夷地部
The South Pole Expedition	南極探検
The Summer Sea	夏の海
Things Seen and Heard Overseas	海外見聞録
Tōkaidō meisho zue	東海道名所図会
Tokugawa Akitake tai-Ō kiroku	徳川昭武滞欧記録
Tomeisho zue	都名所図会
Tosa Diary	土佐日記
Traveling on the Road	道行きぶり
Travels in New Countries	新国紀行
Travels in Sumatra	閼珍紀行
Travels in Tartary	東韃地方紀行
True Account of a Tour of America and Europe	米欧回覧実記
True Record of the Tokugawa	徳川実紀

Twelve Selected Poems from Paris	買黎十二詠節録
Two Days in Chicago	市俄古の二日
Ueda Bin zenshū (hokan)	上田敏全集・補巻
Umi o koeta Nihon jinmei jiten	海を越えた日本人名事典
Universal History	パアリー万国歴史
"Uta makura"	歌枕
Ware ya izuko no ki	我れやいづこの記
World Trends as Seen Through a Housewife's Eyes	婦人の眼に映じたる・世界の新潮流
Yamato meisho zukai	大和名所図会
Yano Fumio tsūhō	矢野文雄通報
Yasō dokugo	野叟独語
Yochi jissoku roku	輿地実測録)
Zasshin	雑信
Zōki hōshi shū	僧基法師集

Bibliography

TRAVELOGUES

Anezaki Chōfū. *Hanatsumi nikki*. Tokyo: Hakubunkan, 1909.

Arisugawa no Miya Taruhito. *Ōbei jun'yū nikki*. Kyōto: Tokudaiji ku'naikyō, 1883; reprint, *Meiji Ōbei kenbunroku shūsei*, vol. 2. Tokyo: Yumani shobō, 1987.

Chūsei nikki kikōshū. Nihon koten bungaku zenshū, vol. 48, Nagasaki Ken, ed. Tokyo: Shōgakukan, 1994.

Fuchibe Tokuzō. *Ōkō nikki*, in *Kengai shisetsu nikki sanshū 3. Nihon shiseki kyōkai sōsho*, vol. 98. Tokyo: Tōkyʊ daigaku shuppankai, 1930.

Fukuda Sakutarō. *Eikoku tansaku*, in *Seiyō kenbun shū*, Numata Jirō and Matsuzawa Hiroaki, eds. *Nihon shisō taikei*, vol. 66. Tokyo: Iwanami shoten, 1974.

Furukawa Masao. *Furukawa Masao no yōkō manpitsu. Meiji bunka zenshū*, vol. 16. Yoshino Sakuzō, ed. Tokyo: Nihon hyōronsha, 1928.

Futabatei Shimei. *Tabi nikki, Nyūroki*, in *Futabatei Shimei zenshū*, vol. 6. Tokyo: Chikuma shobō, 1989.

———. *Yūgai kikō*, in *Futabatei Shimei zenshū*, vol. 7. Tokyo: Chikuma shobō, 1989.

Hamada Hikozō (aka Joseph Heco). *Floating on the Pacific Ocean*. Los Angeles: Glen Dawson, 1955.

Ichikawa Sanki and Ichikawa Haruko. *Ōbei no sumizumi*. Tokyo: Kenkyūsha, 1933.

Ichikawa Wataru. *Bakumatsu kengai shisetsu kōkai nichiroku*, in *Kengai shisetsu nikki sanshū 2. Nihon shiseki kyōkai sōsho*, vol. 97. Tokyo: Tōkyō daigaku shuppankai, 1929.

————. *Biyō Ōkō manroku*, in *Kengai shisetsu nikki sanshū 2. Nihon shiseki kyōkai sōsho*, vol. 97. Tokyo: Tōkyō daigaku shuppankai, 1929.

Ikeda Akira. *Kankai ibun. Kaigai tokōki sōsho*, vol. 2. Tokyo: Yūshōdō shuppan, 1989.

Imagawa Ryōshun. *Michiyukiburi*, in *Chūsei nikki kikō shū. Nihon koten bungaku zenshū (new ed.)*, vol. 48. Tokyo: Shōgakukan, 1994.

Inoue Hideko. *Fujin no me ni eijitaru: Sekai no shinchōryū*. Tokyo: Jitsugyō no Nihonsha, 1923.

Iwamatsu Tarō. *Kōkai nikki*, in *Kengai shisetsu nikki sanshū 3. Nihon shiseki kyōkai sōsho*, vol. 98. Tokyo: Tōkyō daigaku shuppankai, 1930.

Iwaya Sazanami. *Sazanami shinyōkō miyage*, in *Meiji Ōbei kenbunroku shūsei*, vols. 31 and 32. Tokyo: Yumani shobō, 1910, 1987.

Kamata Eikichi. *Ōbei man'yū zakki*. Tokyo: Hakubunkan, 1899; reprint, *Meiji Ōbei kenbunroku shūsei*, vol. 20. Tokyo: Yumani shobō, 1987.

Kamei Takayoshi, ed. *Hokusa bunryaku*. Tokyo: Iwanami shoten, 1990.

Katsu Yasuyoshi. *Kōkai nikki*, in *Kengai shisetsu nikki sanshū 2. Nihon shiseki kyōkai sōsho*, vol. 97. Tokyo: Tōkyō daigaku shuppankai, 1929.

Kawaguchi Hisao, comp. *Bakumatsu Meiji kaigai taiken shishū*. Tokyo: Daitō bunka daigaku tōyō kenkyūjo, 1984.

Kimura Yoshitake. *Hōshi Meriken kikō*, in *Kengai shisetsu nikki sanshū 2. Nihon shiseki kyōkai sōsho*, vol. 97. Tokyo: Tōkyō daigaku shuppankai, 1929.

Kobayashi Kaoru. "Kōsei nichijō; Meiji go nen Ryū okina yōkō kaikei roku kaidai." In *Meiji bunka zenshū*, vol. 16, Yoshino Sakuzō, ed. Tokyo: Nihon hyōronsha, 1928.

————. "Seiyō kikō: Kōkai shinsetsu kaidai." In *Meiji bunka zenshū*, vol. 16, Yoshino Sakuzō, ed., 15–18. Tokyo: Nihon hyōronsha, 1928.

Kume Kunitake. *Bei Ō kairan jikki*. Tokyo: Shūkō shobō, 1878, 1975.

————. *The Iwakura Embassy, 1871–1873: A True Account of the Ambassador Extraordinary and Plenipotentiary's Journey of Observation Through the United States of America and Europe*. Graham Healey and Chushichi Tsuzuki, trans. Richmond: Curzon Press, 2002.

Kurihara Ryōichi. *Itagaki-kun Ōbei man'yū nikki*. Morooka Kuni, ed. *Meiji Ōbei kenbunroku shūsei*, vol. 2. Tokyo: Yumani shobō, 1883, 1987.

Kurimoto Jōun. *Hōan jusshu*, in *Narushima Ryūhoku, Hattori Bushō, Kurimoto Jōun shū. Meiji bungaku zenshū*, vol. 4. Tokyo: Chikuma shobō, 1969.

Kuriyagawa Hakuson. *Inshōki*. Tokyo: Sekizenkan, 1922.

Kuroda Kiyotaka. *Kan'yū nikki*, in *Meiji Ōbei kenbunroku shūsei*, vols. 5–7. Tokyo: Yumani shobō, 1887, 1987.

Mamiya Rinzō. *Todatsu chihō kikō*, Hora Tomio and Tanizawa Shōichi, eds. Tokyo: Heibonsha, 1988.

Mashizu Shunjirō. *Ōkōki*, in *Kengai shisetsu nikki sanshū 3. Nihon shiseki kyōkai sōsho*, vol. 98. Tokyo: Tōkyō daigaku shuppankai, 1930.

Matsuo Bashō. *The Narrow Road to the Deep North and Other Travel Sketches.* Nobuyuki Yuasa, trans. London: Penguin Books, 1966.

———. *Oku no hosomichi.* Tokyo: Iwanami shoten, 1979.

Minakami Takitarō. "Berufasuto no ichinichi." In *Minakami Takitarō zenshū*, vol. 2. Tokyo: Iwanami shoten, 1984.

———. "Dōsō." In *Minakami Takitarō zenshū*, vol. 2. Tokyo: Iwanami shoten, 1984.

———. "Kaji." In *Minakami Takitarō zenshū*, vol. 2. Tokyo: Iwanami shoten, 1984.

———. "Kiri no miyako." In *Minakami Takitarō zenshū*, vol. 2. Tokyo: Iwanami shoten, 1984.

———. "Kisha no tabi." In *Minakami Takitarō zenshū*, vol. 2. Tokyo: Iwanami shoten, 1984.

———. "Kurabu." In *Minakami Takitarō zenshū*, vol. 2. Tokyo: Iwanami shoten, 1984.

———. "Nichiyō." In *Minakami Takitarō zenshū*, vol. 2. Tokyo: Iwanami shoten, 1984.

———. "Nire no kokage." In *Minakami Takitarō zenshū*, vol. 2. Tokyo: Iwanami shoten, 1984.

———. "Rondon jidai no Kōri Torahiko kun." In *Kōri Torahiko zenshū*, vol. 1. Tokyo: Iizuka shobō, 1981.

———. "Shingapōru no hitoya." In *Minakami Takitarō zenshū*, vol. 2. Tokyo: Iwanami shoten, 1984.

———. "Taito no hitosumi." In *Minakami Takitarō zenshū*, vol. 2. Tokyo: Iwanami shoten, 1984.

Mori Ōgai. *Doitsu nikki*, in *Mori Ōgai zenshū*, vol. 20. Tokyo: Iwanami shoten, 1937.

———. *Kantō nichijō.* In Kawaguchi Hisao, *Bakumatsu Meiji kaigai taiken shish.* Tokyo: Daitō bunka daigaku tōyō kenkyūjo, 1984.

———. *Kōsai nikki*, in *Mori Ōgai zenshū*, vol. 20. Tokyo: Iwanami shoten, 1937.

Mori Tsugitarō. *Ōbei shosei ryokō*, in *Meiji Ōbei kenbunroku shūsei*, vol. 27. Tokyo: Yumani shobō, 1906, 1989.

Muragaki Norimasa. *Kenbeishi nikki*, in *Kengai shisetsu nikki sanshū 1. Nihon shiseki kyōkai sōsho*, vol. 96. Tokyo: Tōkyō daigaku shuppankai, 1928.

———. *The First Japanese Embassy to the United States of America*. Shibama Chikakichi, ed.; Miyoshi Shigehiko, trans. Tokyo: Nichibei kyōkai (The America-Japan Society), 1920.

———. *Kōkai Nikki: The Diary of the First Japanese Embassy to the United States of America*. Tokyo: The Foreign Affairs Association of Japan, 1958.

Murata Fumio, *Seiyō kenbunroku*, in *Meiji Ōbei kenbunroku shūsei*, vol. 1. Tokyo: Yumani shobō, 1869, 1987.

Nagai Kafū. *Chainataun no ki*, in *Sekai kikō bungaku zenshū*. Tokyo: Horupu shuppan, 1979.

———. *Natsu no umi*, in *Sekai kikō bungaku zenshū*. Tokyo: Horupu shuppan, 1979.

———. *Ochiba*, in *Sekai kikō bungaku zenshū*. Tokyo: Horupu shuppan, 1979.

———. *Seiyū nisshi shō*, in *Sekai kikō bungaku zenshū*. Tokyo: Horupu shuppan, 1979.

———. *Shikago no futsuka*, in *Sekai kikō bungaku zenshū*. Tokyo: Horupu shuppan, 1979.

———. *Yahan no sakaba*, in *Sekai kikō bungaku zenshū*. Tokyo: Horupu shuppan, 1979.

Nakai Hiroshi. *Man'yū kitei*, in *Meiji bunka zenshū*, vol. 16, Yoshino Sakuzō, ed. Tokyo: Nihon hyōronsha, 1928.

———. *Seiyō kikō: Kōkai shinsetsu*, in *Meiji bunka zenshū*, vol. 16, Yoshino Sakuzō, ed. Tokyo: Nihon hyōronsha, 1928.

Nakamura Kichizō. *Ōbei inshōki*, in *Meiji Ōbei kenbunroku shūsei*, vol. 33. Tokyo: Yumani shobō, 1910, 1989.

Nakashōji Ren, *Ōbei jun'yū zakki*, in *Meiji Ōbei kenbunroku shūsei*, vol. 23. Tokyo: Yumani shobō, 1900, 1989.

Narushima Ryūhoku. *Kōsai nichijō*, in *Meiji bunka zenshū*, vol. 16, Yoshino Sakuzō, ed. Tokyo: Nihon hyōronsha, 1928.

Natsume Sōseki. "Rondon." In *Natsume Sōseki zenshū*, vol. 15. Tokyo: Iwanami, 1995.

———. "Rondon no jūmin." In *Natsume Sōseki zenshū*, vol. 15. Tokyo: Iwanami, 1995.

———. *Rondon shōsoku*, in *Bunchō, Yume jūya, Eijitsu shōhin*. Tokyo: Kadokawa shoten, 1956.

Nozu Michitsura. *Ōbei junkai nisshi*, in *Meiji Ōbei kenbunroku shūsei*, vol. 4. Tokyo: Yumani shobō, 1886, 1987.

Ogino Mannosuke. *Gaiyū sannen*, in *Meiji Ōbei kenbunroku shūsei*, vol. 27. Tokyo: Yumani shobō, 1906, 1989.

Ōhashi Otowa. *Ōbeishōkan*, in *Meiji Ōbei kenbunroku shūsei*, vol. 23. Tokyo: Yumani shobō, 1900, 1989.

Okada Seizō. *Kōsei shōki*, in *Kengai shisetsu nikki sanshū 3. Nihon shiseki kyōkai sōsho*, vol. 98. Tokyo: Tōkyō daigaku shuppankai, 1930.

Ōtani Kahyoe. *Ōbei man'yū nisshi*, in *Meiji Ōbei kenbunroku shūsei*, vol. 21. Tokyo: Yumani shobō, 1900, 1987.

Saionji Kinmochi. "Akorasu okina no seijika." In *Tōan zuihitsu*, Kunikida Doppo, ed. Tokyo: Chūō kōronsha, 1990.

———. "Futsu no daitōryō Bisumaruku-kō no wairo o uku." In *Tōan zuihitsu*, Kunikida Doppo, ed. Tokyo: Chūō kōronsha, 1990.

———. "Gamubetta no risōkoku." In *Tōan zuihitsu*, Kunikida Doppo, ed. Tokyo: Chūō kōronsha, 1990.

———. "Hōjin nanigashi Pari ni kyōheki o kizuku." In *Tōan zuihitsu*, Kunikida Doppo, ed. Tokyo: Chūō kōronsha, 1990.

———. "Ikanaru kore fūryū." In *Tōan zuihitsu*, Kunikida Doppo, ed. Tokyo: Chūō kōronsha, 1990.

———. "Nihon ryōri." In *Tōan zuihitsu*, Kunikida Doppo, ed. Tokyo: Chūō kōronsha, 1990.

Sakurai Ōson. *Ōshū kenbutsu*. Tokyo: Teibi shuppansha, 1909.

Satō Hidenaga. *Beikō nikki*, in *Kengai shisetsu nikki sanshū 1. Nihon shiseki kyōkai sōsho*, vol. 96. Tokyo: Tōkyō daigaku shuppankai, 1928.

Sekai kikō bungaku zenshū. Shiga Naoya, Satō Haruo, Kawabata Yasunari, eds. Tokyo: Shūdōsha, 1959; reprint, Shiga Naoya, Satō Haruo, Kawabata Yasunari, Kobayashi Hideo, and Inoue Yasushi, eds. Tokyo: Horupu shuppan, 1979.

Shibata Takenaka. *Futsu-Ei kō*, in *Seiyō kenbun shū*, Numata Jirō and Matsuzawa Hiroaki, eds. *Nihon shisō taikei*, vol. 66. Tokyo: Iwanami shoten, 1974.

Shibusawa Eiichi. *The Autobiography of Shibusawa Eiichi*, Teruko Craig, trans. Tokyo: Tōkyō University Press, 1994.

———. *Ōbei kikō*, in *Meiji Ōbei kenbunroku shūsei*, vol. 26. Tokyo: Yumani shobō, 1903, 1989.

———. *Taifutsu nikki*, in *Nihon shiseki kyōkai sōsho*, vol. 126. Tokyo: Tōkyō daigaku shuppankai, 1928.

Shimamura Hōgetsu. *Kaijō nikki. Shin shōsetsu*, vol. 8 (August 1902): 137–45.

————. *Hokuei sansui no gaikan*. *Shin shōsetsu*, vol. 3 (March 1903):137–45.

————. *Ryochū ryokō*. *Shin shōsetsu*, vol. 12 (December 1902): 174–84.

————. *Shingapō yori*. *Shin shōsetsu*, vol. 6 (June 1902): 174–75.

————. *Zasshin*. *Shin shōsetsu*, vol. 11 (November 1902): 180–83.

Shimizu Masujirō. *Itagaki-kun Ōbei manyūroku*, in *Meiji Ōbei kenbunroku shūsei*, vol. 2. Tokyo: Yumani shobō, 1883, 1987.

Suehiro Tetchō. *Oshi no ryokō*, in *Meiji Ybei kenbunroku shūsei*, vol. 19. Tokyo: Yumani shobō, 1891, 1987.

Sugimura Sojinkan. *Daiei yūki*, in *Sojinkan zenshū*, vol. 2. Tokyo: Nihon hyōronsha, 1937.

————. *England Through Japanese Eyes*, in *Sojinkan zenshū*, vol. 7. Tokyo: Nihon hyōronsha, 1937.

————. *Hankyū shūyu*, in *Sojinkan zenshū*, vol. 2. Tokyo: Nihon hyōronsha, 1937.

Takebe Tongo. *Seiyū manpitsu*, in *Meiji Ōbei kenbunroku shūsei*, vol. 25. Tokyo: Yumani shobō, 1902, 1989.

Tamamushi Sadayū. *Kōbei nichiroku*, in *Seiyō kenbun shū*, Numata Jirō and Matsuzawa Hiroaki, eds. *Nihon shisō taikei*, vol. 66. Tokyo: Iwanami shoten, 1974.

Togawa Shūkotsu. *Ōbei kiyū niman-sanzenri*, in *Meiji Ōbei kenbunroku shūsei*, vol. 29. Tokyo: Yumani shobō, 1908, 1989.

Tokugawa Akitake. *Tokugawa Akitake tai-Ō kiroku*. Tokyo: Nihon shiseki kyōkai, 1932.

Tokutomi Roka. *Junrei kikō*. Tokyo: Chūō kōronsha, 1989.

Tokutomi Roka and Tokutomi Ai. *Nihon kara Nihon e*, vols. 1 and 2. Tokyo: Kanaobun'endō, 1921.

Yamashita Yūtarō. *Kaigai kenbunroku*, in *Meiji Ōbei kenbunroku shūsei*, vol. 2. Tokyo: Yumani shobō, 1886, 1987.

Yanagawa Masakiyo. *Kōkai nikki*, in *Kengai shisetsu nikki sanshū 1. Nihon shiseki kyōkai sōsho*, vol. 96. Tokyo: Tōkyō daigaku shuppankai, 1928.

Yano Ryūkei. *Rondon tsūshin*, in *Yano Ryūkei shū. Meiji bungaku zenshū*, vol. 15. Tokyo: Chikuma shobō, 1969.

————. *Shūyū zakki*, in *Meiji Ōbei kenbunroku shūsei*, vol. 3. Tokyo: Yumani shobō, 1886, 1987.

————. *Yano Fumio tsūhō* in *Yano Ryūkei shū. Meiji bungaku zenshū*, vol. 15. Tokyo: Chikuma shobō, 1969.

SECONDARY SOURCES

Adams, Percy G. *Travel Literature and the Evolution of the Novel*. Lexington, Kent.: The University Press of Kentucky, 1983.

Agawa Hiroyuki, ed. *Tabi. Nihon no meizuihitsu*, vol. 15. Tokyo: Sakuhinsha, 1983.

Alcock, Rutherford. *The Capital of the Tycoon: A Narrative of a Three Years' Residence in Japan*. New York: Bradley, 1863.

Arakawa Hidetoshi, comp. *Kinsei hyōryū kishū*. Tokyo: Hōsei daigaku shuppan, 1969.

Ashiya Nobukazu, Ueda Hiroshi, and Kimura Kazuaki. *Sakka no sekai taiken: Kindai Nihon bungaku no dōkei to mosaku*. Tokyo: Sekai shisōsha, 1994.

Ayuzawa Shintarō. *Hyōryū: Sakoku jidai no kaigai hatten*. Tokyo: Shibundō, 1956.

Beasley, W. G. *Japan Encounters the Barbarian: Japanese Travelers in America and Europe*. New Haven: Yale University Press, 1995.

Berkeley, Hastings. *Japanese Letters: Eastern Impressions of Western Men and Manners*. London: John Murray, 1891.

Bernard, Donald R. *The Life and Times of John Manjiro*. New York: McGraw-Hill, Inc., 1992.

Bird, Isabella. *Unbeaten Tracks in Japan*. New York: G.P. Putnam's Sons, 1880; reprint, Rutland, Vt.: Charles E. Tuttle Co., 1973.

Black, Jeremy. *The British and the Grand Tour*. London: Croom Helm, 1985.

Bowring, Richard John. *Mori Ōgai and the Modernization of Japanese Culture*. Cambridge: Cambridge University Press, 1979.

Braisted, William R., trans. *Meiroku Zasshi: Journal of the Japanese Enlightenment*. Cambridge, Mass.: Harvard University Press, 1976.

Brazell, Karen. "Mori Ōgai in Germany: A Translation of *Fumizukai* and Excerpts from *Doitsu Nikki*." *Monumenta Nipponica*, vol. 26, nos. 1–2 (1971).

Bresler, Laurence. "The Origins of Popular Travel and Travel Literature in Japan." Ph.D. diss., Columbia University, 1975.

Burks, Ardath W., ed. *The Modernizers: Overseas Students, Foreign Employees, and Meiji Japan*. Boulder and London: Westview Press, 1985.

Christian, R. F., ed. and trans. *Tolstoy's Diaries*, vol. 2 (1895–1910). New York: The Scribner Press, 1985.

Classic Travel Stories. Introduction by Fiona Pitt-Kethley. London: Braken Books, 1994.

Cranston, Edwin A. *A Waka Anthology*, vol. One: *The Gem-Glistening Cup*. Stanford: Stanford University Press, 1993.

Dodd, Philip, ed., *The Art of Travel: Essays on Travel Writing*. London: Frank Cass & Co. Ltd., 1982.

Duus, Peter. *The Japanese Discovery of America: A Brief History with Documents*. Boston: Bedford Books, 1997.

Ericson, Mark D. "The Bakufu Looks Abroad: The 1865 Mission to France." *Monumenta Nipponica*, vol. 34, no. 4 (1979).

Fogel, Joshua A. *The Literature of Travel in the Japanese Rediscovery of China: 1862–1945*. Stanford: Stanford University Press, 1996.

Fukuda Hideichi and Herbert E. Plutschow. *Nihon kikōbungaku benran: kikōbungaku kara mita Nihonjin no tabi no ashiato* [A Handbook for the Study of Classical Japanese Travel Diaries]. Tokyo: Musashino shoin, 1975.

Fukuzawa Yukichi. *Seiyō jijō. Fukuzawa Yukichi zenshū*, vol. 1. Tokyo: Iwanami shoten, 1958.

———. *Autobiography*. Eiichi Kiyooka, trans. New York: Columbia University Press, 1966.

Furuhashi Nobuyoshi, Miura Sukeyuki, and Mori Asao. *Tabi to ikyō*. Tokyo: Benseisha, 1994.

Fussell, Paul. *The Norton Book of Travel*. New York: W. W. Norton & Co., 1987.

Haga Tōru. *Ōgimi no shisetsu*. Tokyo: Chūō kōronsha, 1968.

———. "Western Cities as Observed by the Iwakura Mission." Takechi Manabu, trans. *The Japan Foundation Newsletter*, vol. XVIII, no. 1 (August 1990): 1–9.

Hanne, Michael, ed. *Literature and Travel*. Atlanta, Ga.: Rodopi, 1993.

Igarashi Tomio. *Nihon kikō bungaku no kenkyū: seikatsu, kōtsū, minzokuteki kōsatsu*. Tokyo: Kashiwa shobō, 1986.

Ishizuki Minoru. *Kindai Nihon no kaigai ryūgaku shi*. Tokyo: Chūō kōronsha, 1992.

James, J. M. "A Short Narrative of Foreign Travel of Modern Japanese Adventurers." *Transactions of the Asiatic Society of Japan*, vol. 8 (1879): 191–204.

Jippensha Ikku. *Shank's Mare*, Thomas Satchell, trans. Rutland, Vt.: Tuttle Books, 1960.

Kanagaki Robun. *Seiyū dōchū hizakurige*. Tokyo: Iwanami shoten, 1958.

Kaneko Kinjirō. *Renga-shi to kikō*. Tokyo: Ōfusha, 1990.

Katō, Hidetoshi. "America as Seen by Japanese Travelers." In *Mutual Images: Essays in American-Japanese Relations*, Akira Iriye, ed. Cambridge, Mass.: Harvard University Press, 1975.

Katō Kyūzō. *Hajimete sekai isshō shita Nihonjin.* Tokyo: Shinchōsha, 1993.

Kawakami Tetsutarō. "Kaisetsu." In *Ryoshū* in *Yokomitsu Riichi zenshū*, vol. 8. Tokyo: Kawade shobō, 1955.

Keene, Donald, ed. *Anthology of Japanese Literature from the Earliest Times to the Mid-Nineteenth Century.* New York: Grove Press, 1960.

————. *Modern Japanese Diaries: The Japanese at Home and Abroad as Revealed through Their Diaries.* New York: Henry Holt & Co., 1995.

————. *Seeds in the Heart: Japanese Literature from Earliest Times to the late Sixteenth Century.* Henry Holt and Co.: New York, 1993.

————. *Travelers of a Hundred Ages.* New York: Henry Holt & Co.,1989.

————. *World Within Walls: Japanese Literature of the Pre-Modern Era, 1600–1867.* New York: Holt, Rinehart and Winston, 1976.

Kindai Nihon no nikki. Odagiri Susumu, ed. Tokyo: Kōdansha, 1984.

Kitakami Jirō. *Umi o watatta Nihonjin.* Tokyo: The Japan P.E.N. Club, 1993.

Kominz, Laurence. "Pilgrimage to Tolstoy: Tokutomi Roka's *Junrei Kikō.*" *Monumenta Nipponica*, vol. 41, no. 1 (1986).

Kowalewski, Michael, ed. *Temperamental Journeys: Essays on the Modern Literature of Travel.* Athens and London: The University of Georgia Press, 1992.

Kushida Magoichi. "Reimei o omowaseru koro." In *Meiji kikō bungaku shū furoku. Meiji bungaku zenshū*, vol. 94. Tokyo: Chikuma shobō, 1974, addendum.

Leed, Eric J. *The Mind of the Traveler: from Gilgamesh to Global Tourism.* New York: Basic Books (HarperCollins), 1991.

Lickorish, L.J., and A.G. Kershaw, *The Travel Trade.* London: Practical Press, Ltd., 1958.

Man'yōshū. Kojima Noriyuki, Kinoshita Masatoshi and Satake Akihiro, eds. *Nihon koten bungaku zenshū*, vols. 2–5, Tokyo: Shōgakukan, 1972.

McCullough, Helen Craig, comp. and ed. *Classical Japanese Prose: An Anthology.* Stanford: Stanford University Press, 1990.

Michael, Maurice Albert, comp. *Traveller's Quest: Original Contributions towards a Philosophy of Travel.* Freeport, N. Y.: Books for Libraries Press, 1950.

Miner, Earl. *Japanese Poetic Diaries.* Berkeley: University of California Press, 1969.

Miyoshi, Masao. *As We Saw Them: The First Japanese Embassy to the United States*. New York: Kodansha International, 1979.

Nagai Kafū. *American Stories*. Mitsuko Iriye, trans. Modern Asian Literature Series. New York: Columbia University Press, 2000.

———. *Amerika monogatari*. Tokyo: Fukutake shoten, 1983.

———. *Furansu monogatari*. Tokyo: Shinchōsha, 1951.

Narugami Katsumi. *Nihon kikō bungeishi*. Tokyo: Tsukuda shobō, 1943.

Nikki, kikōbungaku. Kenkyū shiryō Nihon koten bungaku, vol. 9, Ōsone Shōsuke et al., ed. Tokyo: Meiji shoin, 1984.

Nippon Gakujutsu Shinkōkai. *The Man'yōshū*. New York: Columbia Unversity Press, 1965.

Nishikawa Nagao and Matsumiya Hideji, eds. *"Bei-Ō kairan jikki" o yomu: 1870 nendai no sekai to Nihon*. Tokyo: Hōritsu bunkasha, 1995.

Noda Utarō. *Fūkei to bungaku*. Tokyo: Bun'ichi sōgō shuppan, 1979.

———. *"Meiji no kikō bungaku."* In *Meiji kikō bungaku shū furoku. Meiji bungaku zenshū*, vol. 94. Tokyo: Chikuma shobō, 1974.

Norwich, John Julius. *A Taste for Travel*. New York: Alfred A. Knopf, 1987.

Numata Jirō. *"Bakumatsu no kengai shisetsu ni tsuite: man'en gannen no kenbei shisetsu yori keiō gannen no kenfutsu shisetsu made."* In *Seiyō kenbun shū*. Numata Jirō and Matsuzawa Hiroaki, eds. *Nihon shisō taikei*, vol. 66. Tokyo: Iwanami shoten, 1974.

Numata Jirō and Matsuzawa Hiroaki, eds. *Seiyū kenbun shū. Nihon shisō taikei*, vol. 66. Tokyo: Iwanami shoten, 1974.

Odagiri Susumu. *Kindai Nihon no nikki*. Tokyo: Kōdansha, 1984.

Ōtani Ryōkichi. *Tadataka Inō: The Japanese Land Surveyor*. Sugimura Kazue, trans. Tokyo: Iwanami, 1932.

Plummer, Katherine. *The Shogun's Reluctant Ambassadors*. Portland, Ore.: The Oregon Historical Society, 1991.

Plutschow, Herbert. *Four Japanese Travel Diaries of the Middle Ages*. Ithaca, N.Y.: Cornell University, 1981.

———. *"Japanese Travel Diaries of the Middle Ages."* Ph.D. diss., Columbia University, 1973.

Princeton Companion to Classical Japanese Literature. Earl Miner, Hiroko Odagiri, and Robert E. Morrell, eds. Princeton: Princeton University Press, 1985.

Reischauer, Edwin O., trans. *Ennin's Diary: The Record of a Pilgrimage to China in Search of the Law*. New York: Ronald Press Co., 1955.

————. *Translations from Early Japanese Literature*. Cambridge, Mass.: Harvard University Press, 1951.

Seidensticker, Edward. *Low City, High City: Tokyo from Edo to the Earthquake*. New York: A.A. Knopf, 1983; reprint, Cambridge, Mass.: Harvard University Press, 1991.

Shimauchi Keiji. *Nihonjin no tabi: Koten bungaku ni miru genkei*. Tokyo: Nihon hōsō shuppan kyōkai, 1989.

Shirai Chūkō. *Chūsei kikō bungaku ronkō*. Tokyo: Bunka shobō hakubunsha, 1994.

So, Kwan-wai. *Japanese Piracy in Ming China During the Sixteenth Century*. East Lansing, Mich.: Michigan State University Press, 1975.

Strassberg, Richard E., trans. and ed. *Inscribed Landscapes: Travel Writing from Imperial China*. Berkeley: University of California Press, 1994.

Suzuki Tōzō. *Kinsei kikō bungei nōto*. Tokyo: Tōkyōdō shuppan, 1974.

Tabi no jikō: tokushū. *Nihon no bungaku*, vol. 3. Tokyo: Yūseidō, 1988.

Takasu Yoshijirō. "Meiji no kikōbun." In *Meiji kikō bungaku shū*. In *Meiji bungaku zenshū*, vol. 94. Tokyo: Chikuma shobō, 1974.

Tanaka Akira and Takada Seiji, eds. *"Bei-Ō kairan jikki" no gakusaiteki kenkyū*. Hokkaidō: Hokkaidō daigaku tosho kankōkai, 1993.

Tayama Katai. "Gendai no kikōbun." In *Meiji kikō bungaku shū*. *Meiji bungaku zenshū*, vol. 94. Tokyo: Chikuma shobō, 1974.

Terada Torahiko. "Tabi nikki kara." In *Terada Torahiko zuihitsu shū*, vol. 1. Tokyo: Iwanami shoten, 1947.

Tezuka Hikaru, ed. *Bakumatsu Meiji kaigai tokōsha sōran*. Tokyo: Kashiwa shobō, 1992.

Tokeshi, David Patrick. *The Personal Cycle: to the West and Back*. M.A. thesis, University of Southern California, 1979.

Tomita Hitoshi, ed. *Umi o koeta Nihonjinmei jiten*. Tokyo: Nichigai asoshieetsu, 1985.

Trollope, Anthony. *North America*, vols. I and II. New York: Hippocrene Books, 1987 (first published in 1862).

Tsurumi Yōsuke. *Hokubei yūzeiki*. Tokyo: Dai Nihon yūbenkai, 1927.

Ueda Bin. "Uta makura." In *Ueda Bin zenshū* (hokan). Tokyo: Kaizōsha, 1931.

Umi o watatta Nihonjin. In *Nihonshi tanbō*, vol. 18. Tokyo: Kadokawa shoten, 1985.

Vaporis, Constantine Nomikos. *Breaking Barriers: Travel and the State in Early Modern Japan*. Cambridge, Mass.: Harvard University Press, 1994.

Index

About the Author

Susanna Fessler is Associate Professor of East Asian Studies and Chair of the Department of East Asian Studies at the State University of New York at Albany. Her publications include *Wandering Heart: The Work and Method of Hayashi Fumiko* (SUNY Press, 1998) and "Five Fables by Hayashi Fumiko" in *Studies in Modern Japanese Literature: Essays and Translations in Honor of Edwin McClellan* (Center for Japanese Studies, The University of Michigan, 1997).

Printed and bound by CPI Group (UK) Ltd, Croydon, CR0 4YY

13/04/2025

14656505-0003